LANGUAGE, THOUGHT, AND CULTURE

edited by paul henle

language
thought +
culture

by   roger w. brown
irving m. copi
don e. dulaney
william k. frankena
paul henle
charles l. stevenson

ann arbor paperbacks
the university of michigan press

Second printing 1966
First edition as an Ann Arbor Paperback 1965
Copyright © by The University of Michigan 1958
All rights reserved
Published in the United States of America by
The University of Michigan Press and simultaneously
in Toronto, Canada, by Ambassador Books Limited
Manufactured in the United States of America

PREFACE

Language has become an increasingly important field of study during this century. There has been a growing concern with it on the part of anthropologists, literary critics, philosophers, psychologists, and sociologists, to say nothing of linguists proper. Unfortunately, many of the developments have proceeded in isolation and with little regard for what was being done in other fields. This collection of essays attempts to begin a rapprochement of these various fields and to work toward an integrated study of language.

This study was made possible by a grant from the Rockefeller Foundation which brought together the following at the University of Michigan during the academic year 1951–52: Joe Kennedy Adams, William E. Bittle, Roger W. Brown, Irving M. Copi, William K. Frankena, Eliot Freidson, Charles C. Fries, Paul Henle, Harry Hoijer, Abraham Kaplan, Alexander Sesonski, Charles L. Stevenson, Paul Ziff. A supplementary grant from the Ford Foundation enabled James B. Chandler, Don E. Dulaney, and James L. Rogers to join the project. The work was carried on under the general direction of Mr. Stevenson. In weekly symposia and other meetings, the problems discussed in these essays were threshed out, and students of one discipline gradually came to see the interests and approaches of the others. On many points visits from other scholars were of great help. In the course of the year the members heard lectures by and discussed the study with Campbell Crockett, Else Frenkel-Brunswik, Eric A. Havelock, Helmuth Hungerland, Susanne K. Langer, Dorothy Demetracopou-

lou Lee, Theodore M. Newcomb, and I. A. Richards. While
the project was in its final stages, Douglas N. Morgan was kind
enough to join the discussions.

Within the year which the project ran, there was, of course,
not enough time to make any comprehensive survey of all the
work and problems relating to language and symbolism. Since
this was realized from the start, only those problems in which
the group felt particularly interested were taken up. Though
unsystematic, this procedure was thought preferable to trying
to cover everything superficially.

The topics of these essays were the subject of long continued
general discussion, and the book bears the imprint of the work
of all members of the group. This is not to say that there is
unanimous agreement on any of the topics—this would be too
much to expect in a group of this size and diversity of background—or that anyone except the author of an essay is responsible for the opinions in it. To make this point clear, it
may be well to state that, while relying on the work of others
and with great indebtedness to group discussion, the following
people wrote the following chapters: Messrs. Brown and
Dulaney, Chapter 3; Mr. Copi, Chapters 2 and 4; Mr. Frankena, Chapters 5 and 6; Mr. Henle, Chapters 1 and 7; Mr.
Stevenson, Chapters 8 and 9.

Grateful acknowledgment is made of a grant from the
Horace H. Rackham School of Graduate Studies for the publication of this book.

Mrs. Madge C. Byrne gave valuable assistance in the editing
of this work, and the final typing of the manuscript was done
by Mrs. Ione Irish.

CONTENTS

ACKNOWLEDGMENTS

We should like to take this opportunity to thank the following publishers for permission to quote from the following works:

Appleton-Century Crofts (*The Use of Language* by H. F. Pommer and W. M. Sale, Jr.), Harcourt Brace and Company (*Between the Acts* by Virginia Woolf, *The Conditions of Knowing* by A. Sinclair, *Interpretation in Teaching* by I. A. Richards, *Psychology of Intelligence* by Jean Piaget, *The Structure of English* by Charles Fries, *The Well Wrought Urn* by Cleanth Brooks), Henry Holt and Company (*Language* by Leonard Bloomfield, *A Preface to Logic* by Maurice Cohen), Charles Scribner's Sons (*Axel's Castle* by Edmund Wilson), Simon and Schuster, Inc. (*The History of Western Philosophy* by Bertrand Russell), Chatto and Windus (*Transformation* by Roger Fry), D. C. Heath and Company (*How We Think* by John Dewey), Prentice-Hall, Inc. (*A Grammar of Motives* by Kenneth Burke), New American Library of World Literature, Inc. (*Philosophy in a New Key* by Susanne Langer).

Chapter 1

LANGUAGE, THOUGHT, AND CULTURE

I.

Ordinarily, language is taken for granted. Its fluent and easy use leads to the assumption that it is a transparent medium for the transmission of thought. Because it offers no apparent obstacle to our customary flow of ideas, one assumes that it is a vehicle equally fitted to convey any beliefs. Scientifically, it is assumed to be of interest to linguists and perhaps to psychologists interested in child development or aphasia, but that is all. Such a conception of language has been challenged by a number of linguists and anthropologists. Edward Sapir, more than twenty years ago, maintained that:

The relation between language and experience is often misunderstood. Language is not merely a more or less systematic inventory of the various items of experience which seem relevant to the individual, as is so often naively assumed, but is also a self-contained, creative symbolic organization, which not only refers to experience largely acquired without its help but actually defines experience for us by reason of its formal completeness and because of our unconscious projection of its implicit expectations into the field of experience.[1]

Sapir added that the force of this claim could be realized only when the relatively similar Indo-European languages were compared with widely differing languages such as those indigenous to Africa and America.

Benjamin Lee Whorf in a series of papers [2] has developed Sapir's claim, maintaining that a language constitutes a sort of logic, a general frame of reference, and so molds the thought of its habitual users. He claimed also that, where a culture and a language have developed together, there are significant relationships between the general aspects of the grammar and the characteristics of the culture taken as a whole. To substantiate these theses, Whorf made a comparison of American Indian languages, notably Hopi, with European languages. Among the latter, he found the differences so insignificant in comparison to the differences from Hopi that he grouped them all together under the general title of SAE (Standard Average European).

If Whorf and his followers are right, the study of language takes on a new importance in the social sciences. Its place in psychology is greatly expanded, and it becomes of primary significance in all studies of culture. It may even provide the focal point about which the social sciences can best be integrated. For this reason we shall devote the present chapter to an examination of the thesis, beginning with a consideration of terms and then proceeding to discussions first of the relation of language to thought and then of the connection between language and culture.

II.

Since the connections which can be established between language, thought, and culture depend in part, of course, on the definitions of the terms involved, it is to this problem that we first turn. Such an analysis is particularly necessary before trying to establish relationships between thought and language. Ordinarily, language is the chief evidence for the existence and character of thought and, if Whorf's claim is to be anything more than a truism, the relevant aspects of the two must be clearly distinguished and kept separate.

We may begin by looking for aspects of language which are clearly separable from thought and which may be compared to it. Vocabulary, meaning by this simply the list of words to be found in the language, would clearly be one such item. Comparing this with the vocabulary of another language one might obtain some idea of the peculiarities of the language in question, or, at least, of the difference in the two vocabularies.

These differences might be compared with differences in ideas and opinions commonly expressed in the two languages. Another even more striking characteristic of languages is the mode of inflection, and diverse languages may be compared to see if differences here are connected with differences in what is expressed in the language. Again, the manner of sentence formation is a linguistic element, isolable from the content of a language and comparable with it. In some cases, also, terms in different languages, designating the same phenomena, belong to different word classes, so that, for example, what is represented by a noun in one language may be represented by a verb in another. This again is a concrete difference capable of being compared with the content of the two languages.

In the category which we have generically referred to as thought, perception must be included, as well as what may be called the conceptual organization of experience. Thus Whorf reports that in Shawnee the cleaning of a gun with a ramrod is described by something close to directing "a hollow moving dry spot by means of a tool." [3] This certainly shows a difference in organization—the emphasis in English being on the things, the physical objects, and the emphasis in Shawnee being elsewhere. According to some theories, differences in organization of this sort, if carried far enough, result in differences in philosophies. In any case they would show a difference in thought to be related to differences of language.

This enumeration of elements of language and thought would hardly be controversial. On bringing culture into the problem, however, one is faced with an anthropological controversy as to just what culture includes. We shall not attempt to settle the dispute, but shall merely outline the view which is most useful for comparison with language, without making any claims for this view in any other connection. A good statement of it makes culture "all those historically created designs for living, explicit and implicit, rational, irrational and nonrational, which exist at any given time as potential guides for the behavior of men." [4] From this standpoint, culture constitutes the set of modes of procedure or the guides to living which are dominant in a group. These are thought of not as isolated but as functionally interrelated, clustering together to form certain *themes,* a theme being a higher-level generalization. Generalizations of the lower level are simply those directly based on instances of conduct, constituting patterns of behavior. Generalizations of these patterns constitute themes, each theme containing notions exemplified in a number of patterns of behavior. Themes need not be consistent and as Opler has noticed such themes as "old age is desired and respected" and "all persons must continually validate their positions by participation in activities defined as peculiar to that position" may both be operative in the same culture.[5] Indeed the limitation of one theme by the operation of another conflicting one may be necessary to the survival of the society.

The problem, then, which Whorf poses may be restated a little more explicitly: What is the relationship between the mechanisms of language such as vocabulary, inflection, and sentence formation on the one hand and either perception and organization of experience or the broad patterns of behavior on the other? This question is reasonably specific, except for the sort of relation involved. Obviously, the most desirable and least controversial goal would be simply to set up correlations to show that certain linguistic elements vary, say, with certain aspects of culture. Given the correlations, it would not be necessary to assign causal priority, but there still could be inferences from one side to the other. In dealing with the relationship between vocabulary and the interests of a society there is enough direct evidence to indicate such a correlation, but hardly so with any of the other relationships. In these cases, collateral evidence must enter and, in part, must take the form of showing reason to believe that a correlation would be found if more evidence were available. This prediction of the correlation is made by claiming causal connections between various factors. Even in the case of the relationship between vocabulary and culture, this sort of evidence helps substantiate the evidence of direct correlation. We see every reason to believe, as part of our common-sense psychology, that a people should have words for objects with which they are concerned and that they should lack words for objects with which they have fewer dealings. We are therefore more ready to accept as adequate the evidence which exists for the connection between the two.

To claim a causal relation between language and culture is not, of course, to say which influences the other. Either may be the causal agent, both may be joint effects of a common cause, or there may be mutual causal action. Indeed this latter is to be expected with continuing factors such as language and culture. The connections which we shall investigate in the next section will be largely causal.

III.

With this brief discussion of the factors involved, we may turn to the evidence for relationships. It will be convenient to begin with the evidence for a connection between language and thought and to open the discussion with a consideration of the relationship between vocabulary and perception. Languages differ notoriously in vocabulary, and this difference is generally correlated with a difference in environment. Thus, Whorf notices that Eskimo languages have a variety of words for different kinds of snow where we have only one. Aztec is even poorer than we in this respect, using the same word stem for cold, ice, and snow.[6] Sapir gives detailed evidence over a broader field in claiming that the vocabulary of a language clearly reflects the physical and social environment of a people. Indeed, the complete vocabulary of a language would be "a complex inventory of all the ideas, interests, and occupations that take up the attention of the community. . . ."[7] He notices that among the Nootka of the northwest coast, marine animals are defined and symbolized with precise detail. Some desert people reserve the detailed lexicon for berries and other edible food plants. Similarly, the Paiute, a desert people, speak a language which permits the most detailed description of topographical features, a necessity in a country where complex directions may be required for the location of water holes. Sapir points out that what holds for the physical environment, holds even more clearly for the social. Status systems in various cultures, however complex, and differentiations due to occupations are all mirrored in languages.

So far, the argument merely shows that vocabulary reflects the environment of a people. Since the culture is largely dependent on this environment, especially where technology is relatively undeveloped, we have an argument suggesting at least that vocabulary and general ways of acting are effects of a common cause, so one may be an index to the other.

All this still says nothing concerning perception and would have little to do with it, if perception were merely a matter of recording what is presented. This is not the case, however, and there is abundant evidence to show that perception is influenced by mental set. Such effects of mental set have been summarized by Bruner and Goodman in a now classical paper. They say:

. . . subjects can be conditioned to see and hear things in much the same way as they can be conditioned to perform such overt acts as knee jerking, eye blinking, or salivating. Pair a sound and a faint image frequently enough, fail to present the image, and the subject sees it anyway when the sound is presented. Any student of suggestion, whether or not he has pursued Bird's exhaustive bibliography of the literature on the subject, knows thât. Not perception? Why not? The subject sees what he reports as vividly as he sees the phi-phenomenon.[8]

In addition, they point out, reward and punishment, experience, and social factors may all be of influence. Their own research goes on to show that children overestimate the size of coins, that the amount of overestimation is, in general, dependent upon the value of the coin, that the error is greater with coins than with cardboard discs of the same size, and that it is greater with poor than with rich children. Clearly, as they say, it will not do to consider a perceiver as a "passive recording instrument of rather complex design."

The question then becomes one of whether knowing an item of vocabulary—at least one which has application to sense experience—constitutes a set directed toward perceiving in terms of this word. The existence of such a set would mean noticing those aspects of the environment which pertained to the application of the term and tending to neglect others. Direct evidence on the point is not available, but it seems reasonable to conjecture that there is such a set. There is strong motivation to learn the language of a society on the part of children and newcomers, for only through knowing the language can wants be satisfied and communication be established. Ability to use the words of a language is thus prized, and this desire is reinforced by the discovery that the vocabulary is useful in dealing with the environment. Given the motivation to learn the language it is reasonable to infer a set favoring the application of it and so an influence on perception.

It would seem then to be consistent with what we know of mental set on other grounds to assume that the world appears different to a person using one vocabulary than it would to a person using another. The use of language would call attention to different aspects of the environment in the one case than it would in the other. Numerous illustrations of this sort may be given. The Navaho, for example, possess color terms corresponding roughly to our 'white,' 'red,' and 'yellow' but none which are equivalent to our 'black,' 'grey,' 'brown,' 'blue,' and 'green.' They have two terms corresponding to 'black,' one denoting the black of darkness, the other the black of such objects as coal. Our 'grey' and 'brown,' however, correspond to a single term in their language and likewise our 'blue' and 'green.' As far as vocabulary is concerned, they divide the spectrum into segments different from ours. It would seem probable that on many occasions of casual perception they would not bother to notice whether an object were brown or grey, and that they would not merely avoid discussions as to whether a shade of color in a trying light was blue or green, but they would not even make the distinction.

This example must not be taken as showing that the Navahos are incapable of making color distinctions which are familiar to us. They do not suffer from a peculiar form of color-blindness any more than we do since we lack words for the two sorts of black which they distinguish. The point is rather that their vocabulary tends to let them leave other distinctions unnoticed which we habitually make.

If we are right in claiming an influence of vocabulary on perception, it might be expected that vocabulary would influence other aspects of thought as well. The divisions we make in our experience depend on how we perceive and so would be subject to the same linguistic influence as perception. Once again, one would expect the influence to run in both directions. If, in thinking about the world, one has occasion to use certain ideas, one would expect them to be added to the vocabulary, either directly or through metaphor; this is probably the primary influence. Once the term is in the vocabulary, however, it would constitute an influence both on perception and conception.

Inflections also were listed among the linguistic items which might have an influence on thought. Since grammatical forms are less subject to change than vocabulary, such an influence, if it exists, would be far more pervasive than that of vocabulary. We shall contend that there is an influence and that it is similar to that of vocabulary, influencing perception by calling attention to certain aspects of experience rather than to others.

The way in which inflections most often operate may be illustrated by means of a hypothetical example. Suppose we have a verb-stem, say A, and suppose that, at some early stage of the language, A is used by itself. At a later stage, let us suppose that it seemed desirable to add tense indicators to the verb, representing, say, past, present, and future. These might be suffixed and might be schematized by Ax, Ay, and Az. Since every situation in which A was formerly used was one in which a suffix was applicable, a simplification would naturally suggest itself. The stem form was no longer needed by itself, since one of the suffixed forms would always be appropriate, yet it was easier to pronounce than any of them. It would naturally, therefore, be used in place of one of the suffixed forms with the meaning of that form. Thus, Ax might be abbreviated to A. Although this would be a convenience in conversation it would have the effect of depriving the language of any word having the old meaning of A. This might be no loss, but it would require an increase in thought in order to use the language. No longer could one simply notice that the conditions for the application of the stem word were present and proceed to use it. One would be required to notice in addition which of the suffixes applied. In order to speak of one aspect of experience, it would be necessary to notice—and speak of—another as well. This might be called a *forced observation* induced by inflection. Tense, discussed above, represents only one sort of forced observation, and it is apparent that the use of an English verb requires observations regarding number and person as well.

The use of the term 'forced observation' must not be construed to imply that a speaker of a language is conscious of being compelled to notice certain aspects of his environment. Most often he makes these observations naturally, almost unconsciously, and certainly with no feeling of constraint. Nor, of course, is the force actual or physical. A person can use the English vocabulary, disregarding distinctions of tense and person, and, under favorable circumstances, make himself understood. Under usual, and less favorable circumstances, however, he will not be understood and, in any case, he risks ridicule. This is the only external compulsion. Habitual use of the language provides an internal compulsion.

The observations which are forced differ in different languages. Thus Kluckhohn and Leighton comparing English with Navaho say:

English stops with what from the Navaho point of view is a very vague statement—"I drop it." The Navaho must specify four particulars which the English leaves either unsettled or to inference from context:

1. The form must make clear whether "it" is definite or just "something."
2. The verb stem used will vary depending upon whether the object is round, or long, or fluid, or animate, etc., etc.

3. Whether the act is in progress, or just about to start, or just about to stop, or habitually carried on, or repeatedly carried on, must be rigorously specified . . .

4. The extent to which the agent controls the fall must be indicated . . .[9]

Dorothy Lee has noticed that, in a similar fashion, Wintu requires the indication in suffixes of the evidence on which a statement is based thus forcing an observation. She says:

> He (the Wintu) cannot say simply *the salmon is good.* That part of *is good* which implies the tense (now) and the person (it) further has to contain one of the following implications: (the salmon is good) I see, I taste (or know through some sense other than sight), I infer, I judge, I am told.[10]

Just as is the case with vocabulary, one may claim that the forced observations imposed by inflections constitute a mental set. Because it must be mentioned in speaking, the time of an action is more likely to receive the attention of a user of English than of a user of Wintu. Again, it is easy to make a statement in English without considering the evidence for it. A Wintu might be expected to be more perceptive in this respect. The influence here is similar to that exerted by vocabulary except that it is concentrated on relatively fewer items—those which form the basis of inflection—and so is stronger with regard to these.

Finally, under the heading of language comes the factor of sentence structure. While again one would expect that the primary influence runs from thought and social needs to sentence structure, there may be a reciprocal influence as well.

To take the case of English and the SAE languages generally, there seem to be two dominant forms of sentence: first, what may be called the subject-predicate type of statement, of which "The book is red" may be taken as a paradigm; and second, what may be called the actor-action type, of which "John runs" or "John loves Mary" are typical. In the first type there is no action, merely a quality attributed to a subject, in the second the subject is thought of as taking an action. In either case, however, the subject typically is an enduring object—something recognizable through time. Even when the subject is not an object in this sense, the tendency is to speak of it as if it were. Thus, an automobile mechanic will talk of fixing the timing on a car in much the same terms that he speaks of fixing the tire, even though the timing is simply a relation of events while the tire is an object. One may claim that speaking of fixing the timing in this way is metaphorical, and this may be, but the point is that the metaphor proceeds via the conception of a stable physical object.

This tendency is pervasive in our language. In general, events are spoken of as if they were stable objects, and, in speech at least, much of the fluidity of passing experience seems to be lost. This tendency, as Whorf has noticed, extends even to time itself. We speak of it and even think of it as a substance of indefinite extent. We may isolate a segment of it in the same sense that we may cut a link of sausage, and we may save five minutes in something like the sense that we save a scrap of meat.

Such ways of looking at the world are of importance, not merely in the organization of the details of experience, but also for philosophy, in particular for logic and metaphysics. Classic logic took the subject-predicate form of statement as basic and insisted that any logical manipulations must be confined to this form. Sentences of the form "John loves Mary" had to be twisted until loving Mary was considered a predicate of John. Various arguments were classified and tested in terms of the relations between subject and predicate. While this conception of logic is almost completely rejected at present, there is no doubt that it was a major influence on thought up to the present century.

In metaphysics the notion of subject and predicate appears in a somewhat different form. One of the classic philosophic problems has been that of explaining the integration and organization of our sense-perception. It makes no difference whether one considers sensations given in isolation or presented in Gestalten, the problem still remains of relating the observations of one time with those of another. The classic answer to the problem, already fully developed in Aristotle, is that the universe is composed of *substances* and that everything perceived is an attribute of some substance. Substances or substance—whether there was only one substance in the universe, or many, depended on the philosopher—were thought of as continuing through time and, in some cases, even as lasting forever, and so connecting the perceptions of one time with those of another. Thus the broadest description of the universe according to most of the Western philosophic tradition would be to say that the world consists of substances and their attributes. The parallel between the metaphysical substance, which had, or was modified by, qualities, and the logical subject, which had, or was modified by, predicates, was apparent —so much so that substance was often defined as that which is always subject and never predicate. By the same parallel, attributes corresponded to predicates.

Much of the philosophy of this century has been a polemic against these conceptions. The older logic has been displaced by one which allows a predicate to connect several subjects and in which the whole notion of subject has nothing like its classical importance. In metaphysics, such otherwise divergent writers as Whitehead, Russell, and Bergson have agreed in rejecting the classical formulations of substance. Both the close parallel between substance and subject and the connection between classical logic and grammar have been deprecated. Thus Russell has insisted: " 'Substance,' in a word, is a metaphysical mistake, due to the transference to the world-structure of the structure of sentences composed of a subject and a predicate." [11] Having noticed this connection between SAE language and philosophy, we may turn to the contrast of both of them to the thought and language of the Hopi which Whorf has pointed out in considerable detail.[12] There are five principal points of divergence, and it will be seen that they represent differences either in grammar or in the conception of time. These major linguistic differences occur in the following points: (1) plurality and numeration, (2) nouns of physical quantity, (3) phases of cycles, (4) temporal forms of verbs, and (5) duration, intensity, and tendency. Each of these calls for some discussion.

1) SAE uses plurals and cardinal numbers, not merely for actual aggregates given all at once, but also for aggregates which Whorf calls 'imaginary' such as ten days, which cannot be given in one perception. Hopi does not use plurals in this latter case and where we would speak of ten days as an aggregate, the Hopi would say "until the eleventh day" or "after the tenth day."

There is a temptation to dismiss this difference between SAE and Hopi modes of speaking merely as a difference in idiom, having no significance for the underlying thought. If the preference for 'ten days' rather than 'after the tenth day' were considered alone, this would undoubtedly be the proper explanation. A difference in thought-pattern of the sort that Whorf is trying to show cannot rest on any single instance of linguistic usage, however striking it may be. Only the multiplication of instances makes it less probable that one is faced with a casual difference in manner of speaking and more probable that one is dealing with a difference in the mode of thought. Thus the total weight of evidence which Whorf presents is of importance rather than any single item.

2) Whorf distinguishes two sorts of SAE nouns, individual nouns, denoting bodies with definite outlines (e.g., a tree, a stick, a man) and mass nouns, denoting "homogeneous continua without implied boundaries" (p. 140—e.g., water, wood, meat, etc.). Where it is desirable to indicate boundaries for a mass noun, we do so by such phrases as 'pane of glass,' 'piece of soap,' 'cup of coffee,' 'bag of flour,' etc. The prevalence in such phrases of a combination of a term for a container with one for contents paves the way, Whorf thinks, for the philosophic notion of the world as a combination of form and matter. Such a theory he claims is instantly acceptable to common sense: "It is so through linguistic habit. Our language patterns often require us to name a physical thing by a binomial that splits the reference into a formless item plus a form" (p. 141).

Hopi nouns, in contrast, always have an individual sense,

even though the boundaries of some objects are vague or indefinite. There is no contrast between individual and mass nouns, hence no reference to container or body-type, and no analogy to provide the dichotomy of form and matter.

3) In SAE terms like 'summer,' 'morning,' and 'hour' which indicate phases of cycles are treated in much the same way as other nouns. They may serve as grammatical subjects and objects and may be pluralized and used with number-terms in the same way as nouns for physical objects. Even 'time' is treated as a mass-noun. Hopi is quite different in this respect. Terms denoting phases of cycles are linguistically distinct from nouns and constitute a separate form-class called temporals. Whorf says: "There is no objectification as a region, an extent, a quantity, of the subjective duration-feeling. Nothing is suggested about time except the perpetual 'getting later' of it. And so there is no basis here for a formless item answering to our 'time' " (p. 143).

4) Our system of tenses divides time into three distinct sections, past, present, and future and thereby aids in the objectification of time which is conceived by analogy to space. There are some difficulties with the scheme, notably in the variety of uses to which the present tense is put, and these, Whorf claims, are responsible for confusions of thought.

Hopi verbs have no tenses but only validity-forms, aspects and modal forms linking clauses. There are three validity-forms: one indicating simply that the speaker is reporting a past or present event, another indicating the speaker's expectation, and a third showing that he is making a statement generally recognized to be true. Aspect forms report differing degrees of duration in respect to the event, and the modal forms, employed only when an utterance includes two verbs or clauses, show relations, including temporal relations, between the two clauses. This grammatical structure, according to Whorf, avoids the objectification of time.

5) SAE languages express duration, intensity, and tendency through spatial metaphors. Thus:

We express duration by long, short, great, much, quick, slow, etc.; intensity by large, great, much, heavy, light, high, low, sharp, faint, etc.; tendency by more, increase, grow, turn, get, approach, go, come, rise, fall, stop, smooth, even, rapid, slow, and so on through an almost inexhaustible list of metaphors that we hardly recognize as such since they are virtually the only linguistic media available. The non-metaphorical terms in this field, like early, late, soon, lasting, intense, very, tending are a mere handful, quite inadequate to the needs. (p. 145)

Hopi on the contrary has no such metaphors, but expresses duration, intensity, and tendency literally, without any trace of the spatial figures found in SAE. There is even a special class of terms, the "tensors," constituting a separate part of speech, to express these factors, and it is a very large class of terms. Other linguistic devices are used as well.

Whorf sums up the influence of these linguistic differences on thought by saying that speakers of SAE tend to see the world in terms of things, the things themselves built up of a formless stuff given a determinate form. Non-spatial entities are conceived by spatial metaphor. The Hopi, on the other hand, seem

to have analyzed reality largely in terms of *events* (or better "eventing"), referred to in two ways, objective and subjective. Objectively, and only if perceptible physical experience, events are expressed mainly as outlines, colors, movements, and other perceptive reports. Subjectively, for both the physical and non-physical, events are considered the expression of invisible intensity-factors, on which depend their stability and persistence, or their fugitiveness and proclivities. It implies that existents do not "become later and later" all in the same way; but some do so by growing, like plants, some by diffusing and vanishing, some by a procession of metamorphoses, some by enduring in one shape till affected by violent forces. In the nature of each existent able to manifest as a definite whole is the power of its own mode of duration; its growth, decline, stability, cyclicity, or creativeness. (p. 147)

A similar connection between grammatical forms and prevalent modes of thought has been noticed in Wintu by Dorothy

Lee.[13] Each Wintu verb has two related forms to be used under different circumstances. The first category of stems, she finds, indicates among other things, that the subject participates as a free agent in the activity described by the verb. In contrast to this:

. . . to this stem of Category II is attached a suffix whose under-lying meaning seems to be that of natural necessity and which cor-responds to the modal suffixes of Category I. This suffix is used to express, all in one, futurity, causality, potentiality, probability, neces-sity; to refer to an inevitable future which might, can and must be, in the face of which the individual is helpless. Category II has reference to a state of being in which the individual is not a free agent.[14]

This difference in verb categories is significant as mirroring the prevalent conception of the universe. In part, the Wintu feels he can control his environment; for the rest, it is com-pletely beyond him. This underlying metaphysics is summed up as follows:

The Wintu has a small sphere wherein he can choose and do, can feel and think and make decisions. Cutting through this and circumscribing it is the world of natural necessity wherein all things that are potential and probable are also inevitable, wherein existence is unknowable and ineffable.[15]

Here again, then is a parallel between thought about the world in its broadest aspects and major grammatical categories. The aspect of grammar emphasized is different from the aspects prominent in Whorf's investigation, but the major conclusion is the same.

Before leaving this topic of the relation between language and thought, it may be well to notice what we have and have not sought to establish. We have looked for connections and causal relationships between language on the one hand and thought on the other. We have claimed an influence of vocab-ulary and inflection, acting primarily on preception, and an influence of methods of combination, affecting thought pri-marily at a more abstract level. In neither case have we claimed, nor would we want to claim, that language is the sole influence or even the primary influence. In neither case have we claimed that the causal relationship does not also run in the other direction as well. Because of the enduring character of language and the fact that a population changes in time, it well may be that language considered in the large is molded by environmental conditions, social organization, and prevalent modes of thought. This would not prevent language being an influence on thought in the development of the individual, and this is all we have claimed. Next, we have made no claim that a study of a language by itself would suffice to show the general character of thought of its users. Some general knowledge of the culture of the speakers would be required, and, indeed, it is doubtful that one could get the necessary intimacy with the language without this broader knowledge of the culture.

Neither, finally, have we argued that there is any compulsive influence of language upon thought, that language makes impossible all but certain modes of perception and organization of expression. Since perception and the organization of experience are ordinarily manifested only through language, the point being made here may be made in another way. In natural languages, the elements we have been considering—vocabulary, inflection and modes of sentence structure—do not make it impossible to express certain things, they merely make it more difficult to express them. In artificial languages of the sort with which a logician deals, and which are taken up in Chapter 4, the vocabulary is fixed. The rules for combination of symbols are explicit and the types of manipulation permissible are specified. In such model languages, one can often show that a given expression cannot be stated in the language. The situation is different in natural languages, however. Vocabulary may grow by the addition of new words or metaphorical extension of old ones, syntactical rules may sometimes be sacrificed without loss of intelligibility, and it would be difficult to show that any given expression cannot go into the language. At least it need be no part of the present argument that there are such impossibilities of expression. All we have contended is that certain linguistic features make certain modes of perception more prevalent or more probable, not that they completely rule out others. Similarly, in showing metaphysical implications of language, we have not meant to say that conflicting views would be inexpressible in the language. After all, Whorf, while arguing that the prevailing Hopi metaphysics is radically different from that inherent in the SAE languages, has given his account of the Hopi philosophy in an SAE language. Bergson, whose thought in retrospect appears to have greater affinities to typical Hopi modes of thought than to SAE, was highly successful in expressing himself in an SAE language.

It should be noted parenthetically, that in showing a connection between linguistic forms and metaphysics, we have not, of course, intended any implication concerning the truth of the rival systems. If Aristotle comes closer to the inherent SAE metaphysics than Bergson, it does not follow that he is more— or less—likely to be correct. The fact, which we have just seen, that a metaphysics may run counter to that typical of the language in which it is written shows, moreover, that metaphysical thought cannot be entirely linguistically conditioned.

The contention of this section, then, is that language is one of the factors influencing perception and the general organization of experience. This influence need not be primary or unique or compelling, but neither is it negligible.

IV.

In the discussion of the relations of language to culture there is at least the advantage of greater objectivity over the preceding section. There, in discussing the relation of language to thought, it was exceedingly difficult to determine the thought side of the comparison. In discussion of the influence of various linguistic elements on perception, the evidence was indirect and consisted in contending that, from what we know of mental set, we would expect these factors to constitute sets influencing perception. The only likely alternative to this procedure would be some sort of projective technique used to test whether speakers of different languages perceived ambiguous figures in radically different ways. Even here, the perception would be marked by its linguistic formulation, and it would probably be necessary to ask the subject to reproduce what was seen after an interval of time rather than to state what was seen. Even if users of different languages showed markedly different results, there would still be the problem of showing that the difference depends on language rather than on a set induced by other environmental factors. The extreme difficulty of administering such tests, as well as their inconclusive nature, leaves the kind of evidence we have cited as good as any which is likely to become available in the near future.

In discussing the relationship between language and the broader aspects of thought, the situation was somewhat, though not a great deal, better. There was at least direct evidence, a connection between grammatical forms and general characteristics of Western thought and philosophy. Here the grammatical forms could be described with relative assurance, but the evidence as to the dominant trends of Western philosophy, while a very widely held view, is merely an interpretation of an historical record. Similarly, when Whorf contrasted SAE and Hopi characteristic modes of thought, these represented interpretations, and interpretations based on a feeling for a social atmosphere rather than on anything so definite as a written record. While it represents the work of a sensitive observer based on long acquaintance with the people studied, and so constitutes valuable evidence, still, it is the sort of evidence characteristic of the beginning of a science rather than of an advanced stage.

In tracing the connection of language and culture, it is easier to give the evidence in a precise form. As in any scientific work there is, of course, an element of interpretation in generalizing from specific acts to patterns and from patterns to broader themes, but at least there are interpretations of individual acts which are public and verifiable. Though this line of investigation presents great difficulties and lacks the precision which it may later acquire, still it has a more hopeful outlook. Since, moreover, thought is concerned with, and so influenced by, general aspects of culture, this latter investigation of the relation of language to culture may be the key to the problem of the preceding section.

As before, we may consider vocabulary, inflections, and the building of compounds as the elements of language to be compared with patterns of culture. We have noticed before that there is a close relationship between vocabulary and environment, and, since the general patterns of behavior which we have taken as definitive of culture are equally a function of environment, one would expect a correlation with vocabulary. Certainly, one needs words for the objects involved in habitual action and, conversely, words which have no use in discourse are not likely to remain long in any active sort of vocabulary. Because of the very function of language, it may be taken for granted that language and culture are related in this way, and this conclusion would not generally be regarded as controversial.

With regard to the role played by inflections and modes of word-combination, there is, however, more room for dispute. In a discussion of the Hopi language which embraces both these points, Whorf has argued that differences between SAE and Hopi grammar correspond, not merely to differences in modes of thought, but to differences in the cultures as well. These differences center about differences in the conception of time.

In Hopi, we have noticed, days are not totaled by use of cardinal numbers, but are referred to by their order. It is as if, Whorf says, different days were thought of as successive reappearances of the same entity rather than as completely separate and distinct slices of time. Since time is viewed as having this sort of continuity, special importance attached to preparations for what is done at one time might be expected to leave its impress on reappearances of the same time. Preparation constitutes a relatively important part of Hopi life and involves such factors as prayer, practicing, rehearsing, as well as various magic rites and even mere good wishes to a project, to say nothing of the types of preparation considered relevant in SAE. Whorf says:

Hopi "preparing" activities again show a result of their linguistic thought background in an emphasis on persistence and constant insistent repetition. A sense of the cumulative value of innumerable small momenta is dulled by an objectified, spatialized view of time like ours, enhanced by a way of thinking close to the subjective awareness of duration, of the ceaseless "latering" of events. (p. 151)

And this difference in views of time, as we have seen, he holds to be a direct consequence of the structures of the languages.

In complete contrast to the Hopi treatment of time is the quantified, spatialized view involved in the SAE languages. Whorf finds correlated with this the prevalence of:

1) Records, diaries, book-keeping, accounting, mathematics stimulated by accounting;
2) Interest in exact sequence, dating, calendars, chronology, clocks, time wages, time graphs, time as used in physics;
3) Annals, histories, the historical attitude, interest in the past, archaeology, attitudes of introjection towards past periods, e.g., classicism, romanticism. (p. 153)

Whorf also attributes interest in speed and in saving time to this quantitative treatment of time. Some of the differences between Hopi and SAE cultures, therefore, seem explicable in terms of the differing treatments of time and this, as was argued in the preceding section, depends on differences in the grammatical structures of the languages.

Hoijer, in working with the Navaho, has reached a similar conclusion as to the relation of grammatical categories to culture.[16] He dealt, first of all, with Navaho verb forms and found in them a parallel to general traits of the society. Navaho verbs may be divided into two types, the neuter and the active. The neuter verbs represent states or conditions and show an absence of movement or action. Some represent qualities, such as being blue, or thin, or tall. Active verbs, on the other hand, represent events, actions, and movements. While at first sight the two kinds appear quite different, Hoijer finds in analysing the types of neuter verbs that each represents a withdrawal of motion of a certain sort. He summarizes his results as follows:

. . . it would appear that Navaho verb categories center very largely about the reporting of events, or better, 'eventings.' These eventings are divided into neuters, eventings solidified, as it were, into states of being by virtue of the withdrawal of motion, and actives, eventings in motion. . . .

But this is not all. A careful analysis of the meanings of Navaho verb bases, neuter and active, reveals that eventings themselves are conceived, not abstractly for the most part, but very concretely in terms of the movements of corporeal bodies, or of entities meta-phorically linked with corporeal bodies. Movement itself is reported in painstaking detail, even to the extent of classifying as semantically different the movements of one, two, or several bodies, and some-times distinguishing as well between movements of bodies dif-ferentiated by their shape and distribution in space.[17]

Extending the discussion to other aspects of the language, Hoijer finds a similar emphasis on motion and notices a strong cultural parallel. He says:

To summarize: in three broad speech patterns, illustrated by the conjugation of active verbs, the reporting of actions and events, and the framing of substantive concepts, Navaho emphasized movement and specifies the nature, direction, and status of such movement in considerable detail. Even the neuter category is relatable to the dominant conception of a universe in motion, for, just as some one is reported to have described architecture as frozen music, so the Navaho define position as a resultant of the withdrawal of motion.

Parallels to this semantic theme may be found in almost every aspect of Navaho culture taken as a whole. Even today the Navaho are fundamentally a wandering, nomadic folk, following their flocks from one pasturage to another. Myths and legends reflect this emphasis most markedly, for both Gods and culture heroes move restlessly from one holy place to the next, seeking by their motion to perfect and repair the dynamic flux which is the universe.[18]

Hoijer also finds an additional parallel between the Navaho language and culture, which this time involves a somewhat different aspect of the grammar, the sentence structure. He finds that the actor-action pattern of sentence so common in

SAE is foreign to Navaho. A person is associated with an action, rather than being the author or cause of it. Motion and position are treated as being inherent in an object, rather than as being induced by some agent. Hoijer notices how consonant this is with the general Navaho attitude toward nature as reported by Kluckhohn and Leighton.[19] They say that the Navaho does not seek to control nature or believe in doing so; rather, he attempts to influence it, often through songs and ritual. This lack of agency toward nature, as shown in practice, is mirrored in the grammatical construction which does not speak in terms of acting upon an object.

While this evidence adduced by Whorf and Hoijer is certainly striking, there is a question as to just how much it shows. Whorf himself was quite modest in his claims, maintaining that "there are connections but not correlations or diagnostic correspondences between cultural norms and linguistic patterns" (p. 159). Hoijer, however, wishes to go farther and claims that Whorf has understated his case, that more can be made of the correspondence. The attempt to establish correlations would certainly present a program for future investigations, though it is unlikely that more can be claimed for it at present as a general method. Hoijer, as we have just observed, found a striking parallel between the movement expressed in Navaho verb-forms and the general mobility of Navaho life, but it is doubtful that one would be even tempted to generalize and expect such correlations with mobility among all peoples. Certainly, many more studies like Hoijer's are required, extending over a wide range of languages, before much warrant could be given such a generalization. It is worth noticing also that Whorf's study of Hopi does not give verb-forms anything like the prominence that Hoijer gives them. The point would seem to be that every culture may, perhaps, be correlated with some aspect of the language accompanying it, but there is not yet enough evidence to suggest what this aspect may be without actual examination of the case. For the present it is necessary to study both the language and the culture to trace parallels, and so there can be no diagnostic employment of the correlations discovered. Only after many more studies of this sort would it be possible even to suggest which features of a grammar might in general be expected to correlate with a culture. This is not, of course, to condemn the investigations which have been made, but merely to point out that they stand at the beginning of a vast inquiry. More data are required before it is even possible to formulate specific hypotheses; but this is often the case at the start of a new science.

Chapter 2

THE GROWTH OF CONCEPTS

1. *The Nature of Concepts*

Before considering the ways in which concepts arise and develop in children and in societies, it will be fruitful to examine some of the different senses in which the word "concept" has been used. The widest divergence is that between the logician's and the psychologist's use. Frege has observed that the word is used in various ways: its sense is sometimes psychological, sometimes logical, and sometimes a confused mixture of both.[1] Carnap has distinguished between the psychological and logical meanings of "concept," characterizing the former as "a certain result or feature of a certain mental activity."[2] To give a more detailed explanation of the difference between the logical and psychological senses, it will be convenient to begin with a brief discussion of judgments and beliefs.

It is customary to distinguish between judgments and beliefs, although both are psychological. A judgment is an act which a mind or organism performs at a particular time. On the other hand, a belief is a state or disposition rather than an action. A person can have a belief, say that $2 + 2 = 4$, even at times when he is not engaged in making a judgment to that effect. Concepts, in the psychologist's sense, are ingredients in both judgments and beliefs, but are distinct from both. Thus, a person may at one time believe (or judge) that there are unicorns, and at a later time believe (or judge) that there are no unicorns. Though the two beliefs (or judgments) are clearly different, since they are in disagreement, still they have some things in common, and one common element is the concept *unicorn*. Concepts, as psychological entities, are always *in* minds or organisms. Whether an organism can "have" a concept which is not an ingredient in any belief or any judgment need not concern us here. It is certain, however, that no organism can hold a belief or make a judgment involving a given concept unless, in some sense, the organism "has" that concept.

It seems fair to say that there are no beliefs which are not held by some one or other and that there are no judgments which are not made by some one or other. Similarly, there are no concepts which are not "in" or "had by" some organism or other, so that concepts, as psychological entities, are mind-dependent. A concept can be "in" a number of different minds or organisms at the same time, of course. In fact, the sharing of concepts is a necessary condition for successful communication.

On the other hand, such remarks as "There are some beliefs which no one has ever held," and "There are some judgments which no one has ever made," are perfectly intelligible and probably true. These statements may conveniently be analysed as dealing with *propositions*, and as asserting that there are some propositions which no one has ever believed in (or judged to be true). Here propositions are conceived, not as psychological entities, but as logical ones, which have much the same relation to concepts in the logical sense as judgments and beliefs have to concepts in the psychological sense. The proposition *all men are mortal* contains as ingredients the concept *man* and the concept *mortal*. Both of these are class concepts.

When a logician speaks of a "class concept" he refers to the property which is common and peculiar to all the members of a class, and thereby defines it. In the logician's sense, a concept is a *property*, which may belong to all, or some, or just one, or to no entities of an appropriate type or sort. In case it belongs to or is exemplified by *no* entity, it is sometimes called an *empty* concept. Carnap has called a concept which belongs and is believed to belong to just one individual entity an *in-*

dividual concept. In the logician's sense, a concept is a *universal*, and definitely *not* a psychological entity.

From the point of view of traditional logic *and* of some distinguished modern logicians (Frege, Russell, Gödel, Church, and Fitch), concepts are *abstract* entities. These may or may not be exemplified by particular spatio-temporal objects but they themselves are not spatio-temporal. They are properties or *forms* which may be exemplified by different particulars at the same time or at different times. The doctrine that there are such abstract entities, independent of objects which exemplify them or persons who think of them, is traditionally called "Platonism" or "Platonic Realism."

There are several theories which involve a rejection of Platonism. One of these alternatives is *Aristotelian or moderate realism*, which admits the existence of universals, but denies that they can have any "independent" existence. There are concepts, on this view, only if they are exemplified by particulars or conceived by thinkers. Another theory is *conceptualism*, which (on some versions, at least) holds that universals exist only as conceived by thinkers, but cannot either exist independently or be exemplified by a plurality of particular objects. On the conceptualist view there is no distinction between logical and psychological concepts. Still another, and extreme, alternative is the doctrine called "nominalism." The nominalist position is that there are no universals at all: there are particular things, which do *not* share any common properties or universals, and there are particular words or utterances, which may, however, refer indifferently to a plurality of particular objects. In current discussions there is an antihistorical tendency to label as "nominalism" any view which constitutes a rejection of Platonism.

Since numbers have traditionally been regarded as universals, and since the importance of mathematics for the sciences is indisputable, contemporary anti-Platonists have sought to prove that Platonism is not necessarily involved in or presupposed by mathematics through developing adequate systems of mathematics on what they have called a "nominalistic" basis. These efforts, it is generally agreed today, have not been successful, and the program seems to have been dropped. Even when the nominalists believed their program to be workable, their *motivation* was unclear. They spoke of their "renunciation of abstract entities," [3] of their refusal to "countenance" abstract entities,[4] of their "aversion to queer entities like attributes," [5] and they have described abstract entities as "elusive" and "obscure." [6] Some writers have used even stronger language in derogating concepts; in fact, anti-Platonists have urged that the admission of concepts is sufficient grounds for the rejection of any theory. "Any system that countenances abstract entities we deem unsatisfactory as a final philosophy." [7]

This criterion has been challenged by Alonzo Church, who wrote:

To those who object to the introduction of abstract entities at all I would say that I believe that there are more important criteria by which a theory should be judged. The extreme demand for a simple prohibition of abstract entities under all circumstances perhaps arises from a desire to maintain the connection between theory and observation. But the preference of (say) *seeing* over *understanding* as a method of observation seems to me capricious. For just as an opaque body may be seen, so a concept may be understood or grasped. And the parallel between the two cases is indeed rather close. In both cases the observation is not direct but through intermediaries—light, lens of eye or optical instrument, and retina in the case of the visible body, linguistic expressions in the case of the concept. And in both cases there are or may be tenable theories according to which the entity in question, opaque body or concept, is not assumed, but only those things which would otherwise be called its effects.[8]

Enough has been said by now, I think, to show that there is *a* sense of "concept" in which concepts are not psychological or mind-dependent. Whether there *are* concepts in this logical sense or not is a matter over which philosophers are in disagreement. This logical sense of "concept" has been discussed at length because it is so frequently confused with the different, psychological sense which also attaches to the word. The confusion arises very largely from our language, especially when we recall that the term "idea" is often used as a synonym for "concept," and that besides its psychological use, the word "idea" is the usual term in which Plato's *non-psychological* "theory of ideas" is formulated.

What is the psychologist's sense of "concept"? That the long controversy over "imageless thought" has been abandoned rather than resolved testifies to the difficulty of adequately "defining" *concept* in the psychological sense. Older, more speculative psychologists often emphasized the conscious aspects of concept formation and use. But, according to Leeper, "Experiments on inductive concept formation have shown that . . . concepts may be formed, retained, and used unconsciously . . ." [9] A more functional approach to the study of concepts has tended to replace the method of introspection. Instead of attempting to grasp or describe concepts bare, so to speak, the psychologist investigates the way in which they function as ingredients in beliefs and in judgments. The ability to discriminate and to classify is taken as a cue to the possession of concepts, since concepts are involved in the beliefs manifested in consistent differential responses to different types of stimuli. "Thus it has become typical for experimenters on concept formation to use a criterion of 'correct naming of new examples' as the criterion of the attainment of concepts even when the subjects could not say why the name fitted that new stimulus." [10] There are, of course, other experiments on the formation of concepts which involve *sorting* rather than *naming*, in which the verbal aspect becomes still more subordinate.

Some writers have insisted upon a necessary connection between concepts and language. For example, Mrs. Grace De-Laguna has said: "If an animal cannot express its thoughts in language, that is because it has no thoughts to express; for thoughts which are not formulated are something less than thoughts." [11] And according to Ernst Cassirer:

By learning to name things a child does not simply add a list of artificial signs to his previous knowledge of ready-made empirical objects. He learns rather to form the concepts of these objects, to

come to terms with the objective world . . . Without the help of
the name every new advance in the process of objectification would
be lost again in the next moment.[12]

But there seem to be many cues to the possession of concepts
in an organism. These range from consistent differential behavior with respect to stimuli—which is exhibited by both
animals and humans—through grouping similar objects—which
is an experimental task given so far only to human subjects,
although it conceivably could be imposed upon animals—to
applying the same name to a number of similar objects, to the
actual verbalizing of the basis for such classification or naming.
The motive for restricting concepts to the human species would
seem to be the desire for some sharp differentiation between
human and nonhuman. This may or may not be an admirable
motive. But in the interest of greater generality, and for the
sake of a more fruitful conception of comparative psychology,
a broader use of the term "concept" is convenient. On the basis
of his careful survey of the field, Leeper concludes:

Inductive concept formation therefore must be understood in the
broader sense of the learning of concepts (the learning of repre-
sentations that have some generality of application) by means of
a process of recognition of some usually recurrent aspect of perceptual materials as a factor related to some other aspect. Inductive
concept formation therefore includes not merely the traditional concept formation experiments with human beings, but also conditioning
experiments, discrimination experiments, and many trial-and-error
experiments with animals.[13]

For human or for animal, it makes good sense to say, as
Piaget does, that "behavior . . . conceived in terms of functional interaction, presupposes two essential and closely interde-
pendent aspects: an affective aspect and a cognitive aspect." [14]
And it involves no obvious contradiction in terms for Piaget to
talk about "pre-verbal intelligence." We shall consider this in
some detail in the following section. Although we shall use
"psychological concept" in the general sense in which no necessary dependence on language is presupposed, in the following

sections the greater emphasis will be placed on *verbal cues* to the presence of concepts.

II. *The Development of Concepts in Children*

In discussing the way in which children acquire concepts, it is convenient to distinguish between two aspects or phases of the process. One is the acquisition of a brand new concept never had before; the other is the extension or development in the direction of greater adequacy of a concept already grasped. The term "adequacy," as we use it here, refers to a culturally determined norm. A child is said to achieve an adequate concept when he develops a *standard* concept, that is, one which is socially determined and shared by most adult members of a given culture. Children learn or acquire a standard concept by successive approximations. In a sense, they could be described as forming a series of new concepts, but it seems more natural to describe the process as one of first grasping or forming a somewhat inadequate concept, and then successively modifying it in the direction of greater conformity to the standard.

The acquisition of new concepts by experience confers "significance" upon new stimuli which are categorized in terms of that concept. On Walloch's account,[15] once the concept is acquired, a hammer is perceived, not just as a patch of certain form and color distribution, but as an object with which to drive a nail, or smash a vase, or the like. This learned function or significance is experienced as an objective fact, of equal status with the sensed color and form. This functional significance derives from previous experience with similar objects, and since it is not a physical quality of the object, it "must be furnished by a memory function."[16]

Thus, perceived meanings are the effect of a recall process, but the recall appears as part of a percept, i.e., it is not experienced *as recall*. Caused by a perceptual experience, it

. . . involves a process in which such an experience brings into function a memory trace of a similar experience of the past . . . Recall by association, then consists of two steps: A process of recall by similarity by which the present perceptual process makes contact

with the trace of a similar process of the past, and secondly, recall
of a content associated with this trace.[17]

What we take to be the same point is expressed by I. A.
Richards when he writes:

Thinking is radically metaphoric. Linkage by analogy is its constituent law or principle, its causal nexus, since meaning only arises
through the causal *contexts* by which a sign stands for (takes the
place of) an instance of a sort. To think of anything is to take it *as*
of a sort (as a such and such) and that 'as' brings in (openly or
in disguise) the analogy, the parallel, the metaphoric grapple or
ground or grasp or draw by which alone the mind takes hold. It
takes no hold if there is nothing for it to haul from, for its thinking
is the haul, the attraction of likes.[18]

The *development* of concepts in the direction of conformity
with the social norm has been extensively studied by psychologists. Schuessler and Strauss have investigated the development of the concept of money in children.[19] They developed
tests intended to investigate the child's recognition of coins,
his realization of their comparative values, and of their various
equivalents. These tests were devised to involve increasingly
complex levels of conceptualization about those subjects on the
part of the children. Their conclusion was that the organization
of the child's response to money develops from very simple to
highly complex modes, and they describe the change in terms
of such polar shifts as from concrete to abstract, discrete to
systematic, and gross to finely differentiated.

The terms "concrete" and "abstract" are of particular interest
here. The practical and dynamic character of the earliest concepts formed by children has been reported and emphasized
by Jean Piaget:

Every response, whether it be an act directed towards the outside world, or an act internalized as thought, takes the form of an
adaptation, or, better, of a re-adaptation. The individual acts only
if he experiences a need, i.e., if the equilibrium between the environment and the organism is momentarily upset, and action tends to
re-establish the equilibrium, i.e., to re-adapt the organism. A re-

sponse is thus a particular case of interaction between the external world and the subject . . .[20]

The term "concrete" is also applied, in much the same sense, to the regressive behavior of the schizophrenic. Goldstein [21] refers to a patient of Hanfmann who was "bound" to concrete reality and unable to make assumptions or accept fictitious situations as such. Not only was he bound to reality, but the reality was more dynamic than not—the patient having a tendency to *do* something, to prefer situations of activity, to experience objects as things for definite uses. Goldstein explicitly warns that we must not interpret such highly abstract words as 'God,' 'cosmos,' 'fate,' etc., as having their usual dictionary meanings when uttered by schizophrenics, who are more likely to use them in very concrete senses.

Unfortunately, Goldstein has not explained the precise sense in which he uses the term "concrete." In fact, he has characterized it in quite different and even incompatible terms on different occasions. In one place he asserts that the most concrete behavior is to be found when one reacts to only one property of an object or situation, the experienced property, as in reacting to the color of an object alone. This is contrasted with the less concrete, which is found when one reacts to the total configuration of an object or situation rather than to but one particularity of the total.[22] In another place, however, Goldstein characterizes concrete behavior as that which is confined to the immediate apprehension of a given thing or situation in its particular uniqueness.[23]

Various definitions of "concrete" are found in the ordinary dictionary. The two which seem at first to be most relevant to the data considered by Goldstein are first, "representing or applied to an actual substance or thing as opposed to an abstract quality," and second, "specific as opposed to general." The first of these corresponds to Goldstein's second definition, while the second corresponds more to the type of result reported by Schuessler and Strauss. It must be noted that the two senses of "concrete" taken from the dictionary are not entirely unconnected. To give an adequate description of something concrete in the first sense, i.e., particular, requires the use of terms which are concrete in the second sense, i.e., specific rather than general. But let us look again at Goldstein's two definitions, keeping in mind not merely the dictionary definitions but the kind of situation to which he wishes the words to apply.

That the second definition of Goldstein, that the concrete is the unique particular, is incompatible with the view that concrete behavior is regressive is shown by a common type of conditioning experiment on animals. When the sounding of a bell is followed by the administering of an electric shock which causes a leg lift, and the response is learned, it will be made to a wide range of stimuli, including buzzers as well as differently toned bells. It seems obvious that the animal's behavior here is very concrete, and just as obvious that it responds to the various stimuli in the same way rather than to each one in its "particular uniqueness." Nor is Goldstein's first characterization of concrete behavior very apt, since in one sense, at least, to respond to but one aspect of a total situation requires that one "abstract" that aspect from the total.

A somewhat different and perhaps more useful discussion of concrete and abstract is to be found in Dewey's *How We Think,* in which it is asserted that there is "a general line of cleavage which . . . marks off the concrete and the abstract . . . *the demands* of practical life." [24]

This is elaborated in the following way:

Things such as sticks and stones, meat and potatoes, houses and trees, are such constant features of the environment of which we have to take account in order to live, that their important meanings are soon learnt, and indissolubly associated with objects. We are acquainted with a thing (or it is familiar to us) when we have so much to do with it that its strange and unexpected corners are rubbed off. The necessities of social intercourse convey to adults a like concreteness upon such terms as *taxes, elections, wages, the law,* and so on. Things the meaning of which I personally do not take in directly, appliances of cook, carpenter, or weaver, for example, are nevertheless unhesitatingly classed as concrete, since they are so directly connected with our common social life.

By contrast, the abstract is the theoretical, or that not intimately associated with practical concerns. The abstract thinker (the man of pure science as he is sometimes called) deliberately abstracts from application in life; that is, he leaves practical uses out of account.[25]

Dewey's conception of concrete versus abstract appears to fit the facts referred to by Goldstein. Hanfmann's patient was regressive and childlike in being bound to familiar (concrete) reality. He refused to *theorize,* to make assumptions or to deal with fictitious situations as such. And Dewey's insistence on the connection between the familiar and the practical accounts for the patient's tendency to *do* something, to prefer situations of activity, and to experience objects as things for definite uses.

That children's concepts tend to be concrete in this sense is reported by Piaget.[26] When asked to define a word, he first simply points to an object which it denotes, or else defines things by their uses. For example, he will explain that a mother is for cooking dinner. But when the age of seven or eight years is attained, we find the first "logical" definitions being given. About this time the child can explain that a mother is a lady who has children. When we contrast these two definitions we observe that the earlier one is the more concrete, having to do with practical needs of which the child is aware, and having reference to a more dynamic situation (more dynamic within the child's range of experience, of course, not the mother's).

It should be noted that Dewey's sense of "concrete" is not completely new or altogether different. One straightforward dictionary meaning of "abstract" is *"theoretical; not applied,"* and "concrete" and "abstract" are standard antonyms. And "concrete" in the sense of practical is closely related to the two other senses previously noted, for practice always comes down to manipulating *individual objects* in terms of their *specific* characteristics—although Dewey would be the first to insist that *theoretical* considerations of their more general properties is a necessary means to that end.

More explicit agreement with Dewey's distinction is found in Goldstein's characterization of abstract:

The abstract attitude is basic for the ability:
1) To assume a mental set voluntarily. 2) To shift voluntarily from one aspect of the situation to another. 3) To keep in mind simultaneously various aspects. 4) To grasp the essential of a given whole; to break up a given whole into parts and to isolate them voluntarily. 5) To generalize; to abstract common properties; to plan ahead ideationally; to assume an attitude toward the 'mere possible,' and to think or perform symbolically. 6) To detach our ego from the outer world.[27]

A somewhat more elaborate description is given by Goldstein and Sheerer:

The abstract attitude is the basis for the following *conscious* and *volitional* modes of behavior. 1) To detach our ego from the outer world or from inner experience. 2) To assume a mental set. 3) To account for acts to oneself; to verbalize the account. 4) To shift reflectively from one aspect of the situation to another. 5) To hold in mind simultaneously various aspects. 6) To grasp the essential of a given whole; to break up a given whole into parts; to isolate and to synthesize them. 7) To abstract common properties reflectively; to form hierarchic concepts. 8) To plan ahead ideationally; to assume an attitude towards the "mere possible" and to think or perform symbolically.[28]

For a detailed account of the actual development of concepts in children from concrete to abstract, we may profitably examine the writings of Piaget. Piaget's essential concern is with describing the modes of generalizing response that appear in the child's behavior during the course of his development. It may be said that the ten stages he describes are all different ways of generalizing response, and are thus phases in the development of concepts—although Piaget himself uses the term "concept" in the somewhat more restricted sense in which concepts are necessarily tied to language.

These different modes are divided into those that partake of sensori-motor intelligence, and those partaking of conceptual intelligence (in Piaget's sense). The former consists in acts that co-ordinate successive perceptions and actions, acts that are in themselves a bare succession of separate states linked only by anticipations and memories, never grasped as wholes. They lead merely to the success of practical action and deal only with concrete entities. Conceptual intelligence, on the other hand, consists in states considered apart from their temporal sequence, states that expand infinitely the spatio-temporal distances between subject and object. Since conceptual intelligence begins, according to Piaget, only when language is acquired, he believes that only humans can attain it. The stages of development are as follows:

Sensori-motor intelligence (perception and habit):

1) The earliest nonhereditary behavior is the consolidation of the sucking reflex by means of practice, discriminating between situations, and extending the reflex to new objects. Skill at sucking improves, the infant learns to reject the finger in favor of the nipple, etc. Using the example of the child's behavior toward objects to illustrate the first six stages, we may say here that no object yet exists.

2) The first addition to generalized behavior that is due to experience comes when the scope of a reflex is extended by new co-ordinations, as in thumb-sucking. No object exists here, either.

3) Between three and six months we find co-ordination of vision and prehension so that objects may be affected by the infant's behavior, as in shaking a rattle by pulling a string. But an object *qua* object does not exist even here, for the child does not remove a cloth that is placed over a desired object. The object exists only in action and perception.

4) Between eight and ten months we find the co-ordination of previous organizations of behavior in terms of means and ends (or goals). The child can remove a screen in order to obtain (reach for) a desired object. But here the object is still tied to action. If the child is looking for a desired object under a cushion on his right, and the object is removed *in his sight* and placed under a cushion on his left, he first turns to the right and attempts to find it there.

5) The differentiation of behavior is now made in order to discover new means of arriving at a goal (new kinds of acts or new uses of old acts); e.g., having seen an object fall, the child tries to drop it in different ways or from different positions. The object has now apparently attained complete individuality.

6) During the second year sensori-motor intelligence is complete when, instead of active experimentation, new means to an end may be discovered by internal co-ordination of processes so rapid that we may term them sudden insight; e.g., interruption of random attempts to open a box, a pause and a thoughtful look, and then immediate opening of the box without any indication of randomness of behavior.

Conceptual intelligence follows:

7) From the time language appears to the age of four years, we find the child generalizing his responses according to what Piaget calls imaginal symbols (and what the translators note to be, in Morris' term, iconic signs). In this stage those individual symbols are formed by the active copying (through imitation) of perceived objects. But since this is an assimilation of reality to his own action alone, these symbols are wrapped up in the objects themselves despite the child's growing capacity to distinguish between reference and referent; e.g., a shadow in a closed room will be explained by the child in terms of what is found under a tree.

8) Between four and seven we find intuitive thought in which representative symbolism is still used, but in a far more refined manner. E.g., a shadow in a closed room might be explained in terms of what it is underneath rather than in terms of what is underneath a tree, but with no recognition of what unites the different shadows.

9) Between seven and twelve we find concrete operations. Although "logical" concepts arise in concrete behavior and language, those concepts cannot be manipulated in the abstract, i.e., presumably the class-concept "shadow" arises here in concrete instances of experience, but the child cannot use the concept abstractly. When it is divorced from his actual experience, he cannot reason with simple *verbal* propositions

about shadows. Children at this stage cannot say which of the statements, "*all* trees' shadows are round," "*some* are round," "*none* is round" is true, given the verbal proposition, "some of the shadows of the trees in my orchard are round."

10) From twelve on we find true formal operations of structuring behavior and experience by logical concepts. The child can now reason in the abstract, arriving at accurate conclusions from purely verbal abstract propositions.

There are several aspects of this classification of the modes of generalizing responses that are quite important in Piaget's view. One point to be emphasized is that Piaget does not see these ten stages as something one simply goes through, but rather as definite steps towards a logical way of thinking. They are cumulative, and not simply sloughed off as one advances to another stage. Beginning with the consolidation of the simple sucking reflex, all activity moves toward and prepares for logical thought.

Piaget classifies these modes of generalization of activity in several ways. Language is the most important implying the major distinction between sensori-motor and conceptual. The sensori-motor is nonverbal, while the conceptual is verbal. Within this major distinction, there are those of individual-social (or conventional); incommunicable-communicable; ego-centric-logical. These three apply to the differences between (7) and (8), and (9) and (10), and in fact imply each other.

Before (8) may be passed and (9) attained the ability to take other people's points of view must be attained. The relativism gained from that ability is crucial to the development of abstract concepts completely dissociated from the individual's idiosyncratic point of view.

The general characterization of abstract thinking, or the abstract attitude, which was given by Goldstein and Sheerer [29] finds application in the developmental studies of Piaget. Thus the criterion of being able to ". . . grasp the essential of a given whole, to break up a given whole into parts; to isolate and to synthesize them" is embodied in the power to give definitions by genus and difference, which comes at a later stage than definition by example or by reference to practical use.

In his *Judgment and Reasoning in the Child* Piaget makes much of the fact that logical skill is not achieved until the child advances beyond the egocentrism that characterizes his early years. This is also mentioned as the first mode of behavior characteristic of the abstract attitude in the list of eight modes set forth by Goldstein and Sheerer: "To detach our ego from the outer world or from inner experience." That adequate concepts are only achieved when the child becomes socialized is easily explained. And that his learning of language is a necessary condition for this comes to much the same thing. It should be mentioned that Piaget's methods have been criticized and some of his conclusions challenged by other investigators.[30]

Language is a social phenomenon. Hoijer has defined a *language* as "an historically derived system of explicit and implicit designs for speaking which tend to be shared by all or specifically designated members of a group."[31] Shared concepts are the meanings expressed in the common language. To learn a language involves forming the concepts expressed by or in it. These concepts, being historically determined, are presumably more adequate theoretically than those which an individual will develop in the course of his own maturation if unassisted. Those concepts arise, not in the course of his own individual, personal experience with his limited environment, but have arisen out of the cumulative experiences of many individuals within a presumably wider environment. When the individual learns a language, he acquires concepts which grew not out of his own experiences alone but from those of others as well.

We have already indicated how concepts are formed by an individual on the basis of his own experience. The way in which social concepts or meanings are acquired has been described by Bloomfield,[32] who has observed that learning of language may take place in several ways. The most elementary process is that of *demonstration*, in which the learner responds to the observation of the gross features of an utterance in its context by hypothesizing the meaning, then waiting for confirmation or destruction of his hypothesis by further observation of the utterance in other contexts. The process is actively used by the teacher of language in repetition of the utterance with simultaneous emphasis upon the relevant features of situation and response. Another way of learning is by observation of speech-forms in contexts whose components are familiar (e.g., such function words as 'and,' 'or,' 'because,' 'the').

Finally, Bloomfield continues, the process of *definition* is used in learning a language. The most generally used definition is *informal*, in which rough synonyms are given (rapid: fast; *cheval*: horse) and the rest of the learning process left to demonstration. *Formal* definition exists when, for a given sphere of discourse, two terms are freely and completely interchangeable (e.g., eight: seven plus one). But even in formal definition, uniformity and consistency will be limited by the degree of uncertainty as to the meaning of speech forms used in definition. Whatever terms cannot be formally defined will contain individual variations which can be reduced, but not eliminated, by statistical observations or by copious discussion among the users of the language.

Learning a language involves acquiring a whole set of concepts. If it is true, as was urged by Walloch, that the concepts we have influence our perception, then the possession of a given language determines, to some extent, at least, what kind of world we perceive around us. The bearing of language in experience has been described by Sapir in these terms:

The relation between language and experience is often misunderstood. Language is not merely a more or less systematic inventory of the various items of experience which seem relevant to the individual, as is so often naively assumed, but is also a self contained, creative symbolic organization, which not only refers to the experience largely acquired without its help, but actually defines experience for us by reason of its formal completeness and because of our unconscious projection of its implicit expectations into the field of experience.[33]

The thesis that a language has important influence on the experience and the thinking of its users is an important one, and has been discussed at length in Chapter 1. One of its implications is that any development or growth of concepts in a culture will be accompanied, perhaps even be effected by, changes in the language of that culture. The dynamics of this process will be discussed in the following section.

III. The Development of Concepts in a Culture

In speaking of the growth of concepts in a culture we shall be concerned, not with new patterns of response which may occur to one or another individual member of society, but only with those which are accepted by all or most members of the group. As in the preceding section, we shall be concerned with growth or development of concepts in the direction of increased theoretical scope or adequacy. One key to the concepts which are shared by the members of a given culture is the common language used by them, and we can take changes in their language as evidence (though perhaps not conclusive proof) of changes in the concepts they share.

By changes in a language we refer not only to the introduction of new terms not synonymous with any older ones, but also changes in meaning of the same term. There is nothing mysterious in this process: as Bloomfield says:

> We can easily see today that a change in the meaning of a speech-form is merely the result of a change in the use of it and other, semantically related speech-forms.[34]

The historical interest that attaches to philological studies is obvious. As Bloomfield explains,

> . . . a change of meaning may imply a connection between practical things and thereby throw light on the life of older times. English *fee* is the modern form of the paradigm of Old English *feoh*, which meant 'live-stock, cattle, property, money.' Among the Germanic cognates, only Gothic *faihu* means 'property'; all the others, such as German *Vieh* or Swedish *fä*, have meanings like '(head of) cattle, (head of) live-stock.' The same is true of the cognates in the other Indo-European languages, such as Sanscrit ['pacu] or Latin *pecu;* but Latin has the derived words *pecunia* 'money' and

peculium 'savings, property.' This confirms our belief that live-stock served in ancient times as a medium of exchange.[35]

As has been argued by Goldstein and Sheerer, and Piaget, the abstract attitude is more adequate, both theoretically and socially, than the concrete. The historical development of Indo-European languages seems to have followed this pattern, at least in part. To quote again from Bloomfield:

> The surface study of semantic change indicates that refined and ab-stract meanings largely grow out of more concrete meanings. Mean-ings of the type 'respond accurately to (things or speech)' develop again and again from meanings like 'be near to' or 'get hold of.' Thus, *understand,* as we say, seems to have meant 'stand close to' or 'stand among.' German *verstehen* [fer'šte:en] 'understand' seems to have meant 'stand round' or 'stand before'; the Old English equiv-alent *forstandan* appears both for 'understand' and for 'protect, de-fend.' Ancient Greek [e'pistamaj] 'I understand' is literally 'I stand upon' and Sanskrit [ava'gaččhati] is both 'he goes down into' and 'he understands. Italian *capire* [ka'pire] 'to understand' is an analogic new-formation based on Latin *capere* 'to seize, grasp.' Latin *com-prehendere* 'to understand' means also 'to take hold of.' The Slavic word for 'understand,' as in Russian [po'nat] is a compound of an old verb that meant 'seize, take.' A marginal meaning of 'under-stand' appears in our words *grasp, catch on, get* (as in *I don't get that*). Most of our abstract vocabulary consists of borrowings from Latin, through French or in gallicized form; the Latin originals can largely be traced to concrete meanings. Thus Latin *dēfinīre* 'to define' is literally 'to set bounds to' (*finis* 'end, boundary'). Our *eliminate* has in Latin only the concrete meaning 'put out of the house,' in accordance with its derivative character, since Latin *ēlimināre* is structurally a synthetic compound of *ex* 'out of, out from' and *limen* 'threshold.' [36]

The mere achievement of abstraction is not the pinnacle of linguistic or conceptual excellence, however. To say that, on one set of definitions of 'abstract' and 'concrete,' would commit one to the view that the highest level of language development would be one in which all words had universal scope, such as the term 'entity,' 'object,' or 'thing.' On another set of defini-tions, one would have to say that the "best" language would contain words for qualities only, and none for particular individual objects. And on Dewey's view, an absolute preference of abstract over concrete would amount to abandoning practice for pure theory with no connection possible between theory and what the theory is "about." None of these is in any way satisfactory. Instead, we must say that the well-developed language possesses terms of all degrees of abstractness, in all three senses. The terms of such a language will have as their meanings, not only individual concepts, but also those which are appropriate to the various groupings, wide and narrow, of objects which it is practically or theoretically desirable to consider together. A speech-form also may have a very concrete meaning initially, then come to be used in a much more abstract sense, and finally have its meaning narrowed so that its use is exactly appropriate to a situation which was not previously conceptualized. Thus Bloomfield writes:

The shift into a new meaning is intelligible when it merely reproduces a shift in the practical world. A form like *ship* or *hat* or *hose* designates a shifting series of objects because of changes in the practical world. If cattle were used as a medium of exchange, the word *fee* 'cattle' would naturally be used in the meaning 'money,' and if one wrote with a goose-feather, the word for 'feather' would naturally be used of this writing-implement. At this point, however, there has been no shift in the lexical structure of the language. This comes only when a learned loan-word *pen* is distinct from *feather*, or when *fee* on the one hand is no longer used of cattle and, on the other hand, loses ground in the domain of 'money' until it retains only the specialized value of 'sum of money paid for a service or privilege.' [37]

Bloomfield gives credit to H. Sperber for first pointing out

. . . that extensions of meaning are by no means to be taken for granted, and that the first step toward understanding them must be to find, if we can, the context in which the new meaning first appears. This will always be difficult, because it demands that the student observe very closely the meanings of the form in all older occurrences; it is especially hard to make sure of negative features, such as the absence, up to a certain date, of a certain shade of meaning. In most cases, moreover, the attempt is bound to fail because the records do not contain the critical locutions.[38]

Professor Eric Havelock has described the growth of concepts as reflected in semantic change in the direction of greater abstractness (both in the senses of "general" and "theoretical") in the Greek vocabulary from the time of Homer to the Periclean Age.[39] According to Havelock, the Homeric vocabulary contained the seeds of abstraction, betraying a tendency to generalise. But the most that it achieved was "semi-abstraction." To take the commonest example, a Homeric god can symbolise a psychic state or a phenomenon of nature. But he remains a god, appearing as event or object, not as principle. Even at the Hesiodic level, a cosmo*gony* is not a cosmo*logy*. The one is a narrative sequence in time, the other a pattern of timeless concepts. Between them lay a gulf which only strenuous conceptual effort could bridge. In the Ionian philosophers we find a continuous struggle to build such a bridge for the Greek vocabulary and the Greek mind.

The Ionian thinkers attempted to achieve abstraction by merely aggrandizing words already available for them. For example, the history of the word "cosmos" reveals the psychology of the abstracting process. 'Cosmos' has denoted such phenomena as a woman's headdress or the trappings of a horse's harness. It connoted a pleasing decorative effect, concrete and particular, and even dynamic in the sense that it caught the effect of a moving cluster. But it had already begun its ascent toward semi-abstraction in two different ways, by being applied adverbially in the sense of 'decoratively' and by being stretched a little so as to identify the ranks of an army. It thus came close to the sense of 'order,' but was still concrete, still restricted to an aspect of human behavior. The Ionian thinkers stretched it still further to identify some over-all "world" which they wished to discuss. They therefore approached close to the abstract concept of a (physical) order. They did not make their initial steps toward abstraction by neologism. Rather, an existing semi-abstraction was placed in an enlarged context, which generalised the application of the word. It was stretched until it covered everything.

But even in the term 'cosmos,' the process is incomplete. The term retains a deictic and concrete quality: it is still close to the visual. It is *this* world or *a* world, but not yet the physical universe. An array or order, like any other available symbol, is particular; that is, there can be more than one; to be genuinely conceptual, it must be single, solitary, unique and total. Or more correctly, the concepts of unity and uniqueness and totality must be discovered. The pre-Socratics, therefore, in their search for a vocabulary abstracted from the concrete and particular, were driven to exploit the resources of the words 'one,' 'common,' 'alone,' 'whole,' 'all.'

Such an exploitation of the resources of these words can be illustrated by considering Heracleitus' use of the word 'one' in the neuter singular. He no longer speaks of one god but simply of a 'one.' This intuitive decision to exploit the severity of the impersonal absolute as a terminological resource was quite decisive. By stripping from the one god all "godliness," so to speak, the mind was prepared to accommodate the unfamiliar idea of oneness, or unity. The linguistic device was a symptom of an effort toward genuine abstraction, and it was rapidly extended to several other symbols. Indeed, we can say that the usage of impersonal forms, whether applied to adjective, to participle, or to a verb, a usage which lends to so many of Heracleitus' aphorisms their cryptic quality, simply marks the first organised attempt in Greek thought to reach a mental level which is consistently abstract, and to devise a suitable vocabulary for theoretical speculation. The whole philosophy of Heracleitus can be viewed simply as an extended attempt so to twist the limited resources of concrete language as to destroy its concrete references and thereby to express ideas of what we would call unity, identity, difference, process, and change. These now seem so elementary that it requires a strong effort of imagination to realise what an expenditure of mental energies was required for this program, and how the effort could monopolise the attention of a thinker to the exclusion of any so-called "systems" of thought. Heracleitus and Parmenides are both "dark philosophers" only because they grapple with an inherited idiom wholly imagistic and concrete and try to empty it of images. No wonder the language looked queer when they had finished with it.

The initial stage in abstraction is to select out pairs of opposites; e.g., in Empedocles we have "Mistress Hurry" and "Mistress Slow." In Heracleitus we have "day-night," "war-peace," etc. This pairing habit, as it grows, begins to suggest a law of organization. The concealed assumption here is that such pairs are "natural pairs." There is not as yet pure abstraction, isolated per se. Rather there is only the semi-abstraction of hot and cold "things" being turned into one other. A higher level of abstraction is not achieved until the Eleatics. By the time of Anaxagoras, Greek language is close to recognizing temperature, humidity, etc. The word for quality does not appear until Plato and Aristotle.

In Homer we find a rich vocabulary of consciousness, but we also find that the vocabulary "confuses" categories of experience whose distinctness we take for granted (e.g., blending acts of perception with acts of cognition, emotion with cognition). One cannot think about thought in Homeric language. The pre-Socratics tried to describe how the Homeric "wits and senses of total experience" functioned. They tried to formulate them as a total physical phenomenon, a mixture of ingredients or a by-product of physical conditions of body or as something drawn in from atmosphere. But the pre-Socratics did not fully succeed in formulating a vocabulary to symbolize the complex processes of intellection and analysis. Only the Sophists and Plato finally succeeded in coining an adequate symbolism.

We have seen that there are three distinct but allied senses which attach to the concrete-abstract division of concepts: these are first, object *versus* property; second, specific *versus* general; and third, practical *versus* theoretical. There are three different areas in which the words 'concrete' and 'abstract' are applied: child development, mental disorders (schizophrenia and aphasia), and cultural-linguistic evolution. It can legitimately be questioned whether the terms 'concrete' and 'abstract' are used in the same senses in all three areas, or even whether a single investigator uses them consistently in the same sense in just one of these areas. The situation is made more difficult because the three pairs of terms are not mere homonyms, but have meanings which are quite closely linked. In the absence of behavioral definitions whose applications can be objectively tested in the different contexts of the three areas, no definitive answer to the question of their usage can be determined. It seems very plausible, however, to take Dewey's senses of 'practical' and 'theoretical' for 'concrete' and 'abstract,' since they do seem to fit the data at hand.

On this interpretation, a sort of psychogenetic law suggests itself as a parallel to the biologist's "ontogony recapitulates phylogeny." Western culture is far advanced in the direction of abstract theory. This does not mean that every man is a philosopher or pure scientist, but that the value of theory is generally recognized. The secular intelligentsia constitutes a larger segment of the total population than in any other society at any other time and has a higher status than ever before. This is, of course, made possible only by a highly developed socialized economy. As the child grows from infancy to adulthood in our culture, his development recapitulates the gamut of conceptual levels. From what Piaget calls the infrahuman sensori-motor responses (e.g., sucking), his attitude, concepts, and language grow in the direction of greater theoretical adequacy. This suggested "law" cannot be sufficiently qualified at the present stage of our knowledge, and is proposed with great diffidence. But it points in the direction of further research in a number of areas.

Chapter 3

A STIMULUS-RESPONSE ANALYSIS
OF LANGUAGE AND MEANING

Apparently, there is no language that can be counted among our innate ideas or, if there is, it has been thoroughly obscured by individual linguistic training. Apparently, too, the linguistic capacities of a child are independent of the race of his parents and the speech they practice. Every child learns to speak the language of the significant adults in his milieu. Does this learning follow familiar behavioristic principles, or are there complications in language that require a different approach?

There are reasons for believing that the process of learning to produce and comprehend language is the kind of process to which conditioning principles apply. Psychological theorists like Wertheimer, Maier, and Koehler who have emphasized productive thinking, reasoning, and insight have never denied human conditioning. They simply place it in the category of "nonsense learning" where the relationships between items to be learned are purely arbitrary or "external," i.e., where possibility of insight is ruled out by the nature of the problem. Because these authors believe that insightful learning is most characteristically human, they hold that conditioning experiments are not very important in human psychology.

In spite of this judgment we submit that semantic connections, relations between signs and their denotata, are, for the most part, arbitrary connections. There are a great many languages and codes and none of them seems any more appropriate than any other. It is unlikely that a child enjoys any "Aha!" experience on learning that a particular physical object is called a window. It is no more window-ish than it is *Fenster-*

ish. There seems to be little opportunity for insight in the acquisition of a lexicon.

On the other hand, a language is not completely described by its semantic rules. There are, in addition, rules of syntax which make it possible to create unfamiliar combinations of lexical elements and to understand, immediately, the meaning of such combinations. Linguistic utterances are, furthermore, apprehended as Gestalten in which the meaning of the elements depends upon the combinations and sequences in which they occur. There are many who seriously doubt that it is possible to comprehend the "structure" of language within conditioning theory.

There now follows in this chapter a brief characterization of the speech act. A second section presents general principles of behavior derived from experiments with both animal and human subjects. These principles are then extended to some of the problems involved in learning to produce speech and in learning to respond to speech. In a final section there is a discussion of the nature of language and an evaluation of the adequacy of learning theory as an explanation of linguistic functions.[1]

I

The Speech Act

Leonard Bloomfield [2] has described the stimulus-response sequences that are involved in a speech act. One organism produces a verbal response (r) to an external stimulus (S). A second organism hears that verbalization (s) and responds to it (R).

ORGANISM 1   ORGANISM 2

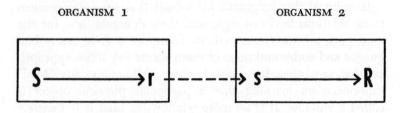

This diagram is obviously a minimal characterization that excludes such things as the effect of speech on the organism producing it, the intentions of the producing organism and the noncommunicative use of language in private contemplation. However, it will serve as a useful frame for the first stage of our investigation because it clearly makes two important points. First, Bloomfield stresses the social nature of speech. For him, as for Pillsbury and Meader and John Dewey, speech is a communication, a connection between nervous systems. We should like to preserve this stress on communication because it is essential to a stimulus-response analysis. The second point of emphasis is the recognition of two functions—the production of speech and the response to speech. Much the same distinction appears in communications engineering as the encoding and decoding processes. It is paralleled again in the clinician's classification of expressive and receptive aphasia, and in the familiar distinction between active and passive vocabularies. We shall discuss the learning of language under the same two headings—the production of speech and the response to speech.

II

Principles of Behavior

There is a distinction made with regard to animal learning situations that may help us to understand the functions of speech production and of the response to speech. The distinction was first made in the Russian laboratories devoted to the investigation of the conditioned reflex. The students of Pavlov developed a training technique that differed in several important respects from Pavlov's original procedure. Hilgard and Marquis have called the two learning situations classical conditioning and instrumental conditioning.[3] We shall use these terms because they describe different learning conditions without taking any stand on the learning mechanisms involved.[4]

Classical Conditioning.—Classical conditioning has usually been demonstrated for glandular or smooth muscle responses. Following Hilgard and Marquis we accept several experiments as instances of the classical conditioning of skeletal responses. As a paradigm of the process, however, we select the reflex with which Pavlov began his work—salivation in the dog.

A dog is presented with food powder which causes him to salivate. The food powder functions, therefore, as an unconditioned stimulus to that unconditioned response. The term unconditioned does not necessarily mean congenital. It refers to a stimulus-response connection that will operate at the beginning of the training period. The unconditioned response is a response that the trainer knows how to elicit. He knows which sensory button to push.

The sound of a bell is a stimulus that does not originally cause the dog to salivate. Because it does so after occurring a number of times simultaneously with, just prior to, or just subsequent to the unconditioned stimulus, the bell is a conditioned stimulus. The salivation following the presentation of the bell alone is a conditioned response.

'Reinforcement' is a name for that aspect of the training procedure which is essential if the conditioned response is to be elicited by the conditioned stimulus. In the classical procedure the unconditioned stimulus is the reinforcement. Repeated presentation of the conditioned stimulus without the unconditioned stimulus is the technique of extinction. It causes the conditioned stimulus to lose (extinguish) its ability to elicit the conditioned response.

One point of emphasis is to be picked up later in our discussion of the response to speech: The conditioned response is almost never identical with the unconditioned response. In our present example, it is only a fractional component of the unconditioned response. Pavlov's dog learned to salivate to the bell but not to chew and swallow, although these activities were part of the unconditioned response. In the other cases, the conditioned response has been described as preparing for the appearance of the unconditioned stimulus or manifesting an expectation of it. Classical conditioning cannot then, be represented as the simple transfer of a response from one stimulus to another. The conditioned response must be defined as any change in the response to the conditioned stimulus that occurs as a result of the association of that stimulus with the unconditioned stimulus.

Instrumental Learning.—In describing the conditions that define instrumental learning we shall talk about a kind of experiment developed by B. F. Skinner.[5] A hungry rat is placed in a closed box. From one wall of the box a lever protrudes and directly beneath the lever there is a tray. If the rat will press the lever a pellet of food will bounce into the tray. But the experimenter cannot elicit this response from the animal. The fact that the rat is hungry restricts its behavior to a certain family of responses—running, jumping, squealing, etc. Sleep, prolonged waiting, and quiet contemplation are pretty well ruled out. The box further limits the possible responses: the animal can't run far or climb very high. Still, when all this has been done the experimenter must wait for the response to take place. All his efforts serve only to reduce the waiting time. This is the first contrast with classical conditioning; the response is *emitted* rather than *elicited*.

When the lever is pressed the pellet appears and is devoured. The edible pellet is essential to learning and is called the reinforcement. In this case the animal's response is *instrumental* in producing the reinforcement. This provides a second contrast with classical conditioning where the unconditioned stimulus, the appearance of the powder, which was also the reinforcement, preceded the conditioned response and was in no sense contingent upon it. With instrumental learning, as with classical conditioning, omission of the reinforcement results in extinction of the conditioned response. However, the reinforcement is not the stimulus that originally produced the response, but rather a consequence of the conditioned response.

Four varieties of instrumental learning are distinguished by Hilgard and Marquis.[6] (1) The situation we have just described is an instance of reward training. (2) Secondary reward training is a variant on the procedure in which an initially neutral stimulus acquires the ability to reinforce learning. Exemplifying secondary reward training is the famous experiment of Wolfe [7] in which chimpanzees learned that tokens of various colors could be placed in vending machines to obtain grapes. With this prior experience they learned a variety of new tasks simply in order to obtain tokens even though the vending machines were removed and the tokens could not immediately be exchanged for grapes. Tokens of one color produced more grapes than tokens of another color and the chimpanzees learned to value them accordingly. The tokens are described as secondary rewards, deriving their power of reinforcement from association with the primary reward of the grape. There are several points of analogy between these tokens and money. Both are intrinsically valueless objects that become important because they can be exchanged for primary rewards. Extinction of this acquired reinforcing power occurs when the token loses its exchange value as was the case with German currency at the height of the inflation after World War I. (3) Suppose an animal is imprisoned in a box in one corner of which there is a small paddle wheel. A shock is administered through the floor grid. It can be turned off by spinning the wheel. The process by which this act is learned is called escape training. Reinforcement here involves the termination of some unpleasant stimulus. (4) If a buzzer is sounded somewhat before the shock is turned on in escape training the animal can learn to spin the wheel in response to the buzzer. If he does this quickly he can completely avoid the shock and such learning is called avoidance training.

In this presentation reinforcement has not been defined independently of its effect, which is the production of learning. Behavior theorists have suggested several different independent definitions in terms of the reduction of tissue needs, stimulus-response, contiguity, and the confirmation of expectancy. We prefer not to choose among these formulations but to work for the present with lower order empirical constructs. Many reinforcing conditions have been identified by their ability to produce and preserve learning in experimental situations. These recognized reinforcers can be used to explain learning in new situations (the acquisition of speech) without any vicious circularity. They are independently defined by their demonstrated effect in other situations.

Generalization and Discrimination.[8]—Sensory generalization occurs in both classical conditioning and instrumental learning. When the dog in our example of classical conditioning has been trained the experimenter is likely to conclude that he has learned to salivate in response to a bell. But the bell exists as such in the consciousness of the experimenter and there is no good reason why the dog should learn what the experimenter has in mind. And, in a sense, the dog does not. For if a buzzer is sounded he salivates again; if a pane of glass is broken or a drum is rattled he may salivate. This phenomenon has been called primary sensory generalization. It has been interpreted to mean that no animal responds to all the properties of a stimulus which make it a unique occurrence. The very notion of learning implies some equivalence of stimuli making possible the transfer of experience from one situation to another.

Presumably, the animal categorizes the stimulus in terms of its most striking attribute. The conditioned dog, for example, might respond with salivation to any steep auditory gradient. He may not distinguish the timbre of a buzzer from that of a bell. Similarly a monkey who is trained to run to a red triangle does not, perhaps, run to a triangle at all. Size, shape, and position may be indifferent to him. He may be running to redness. It would be possible to find a way into the monkey's consciousness with the proper tests. If he should run to red circles and red squares as well as to red triangles, but not to circles, squares, or triangles of other colors, then it would be fairly safe to infer that he is running to redness.

Although the dog does not, at first, distinguish buzzers from bells he is capable of doing so if it is required of him by the technique of discrimination training. If the bell is consistently reinforced with the food powder while the buzzer is not, the dog will eventually distinguish between the two by responding to the bell and extinguishing the response to the buzzer. Finer discriminations can be achieved such as that between two pure tones that differ slightly in pitch. With the method of selective reinforcement, the limits of the animal's sensory acuity can be determined.

In the case described above the two stimuli are successively presented. Discrimination training is often conducted, however, with simultaneously presented stimuli. With rats, the Lashley jumping apparatus is employed. The animal is placed on a stand facing a screen with two doors. One door may be marked with a circle, the other door with a triangle. If the rat jumps at the circle, that door will fly open and the animal will land happily in a plate of food. If he chooses the triangle, that door proves to be locked. He receives a bump on the nose and falls into a net. It is to his advantage to learn to select the open door. This can be done only by learning to discriminate the triangle from the circle.

Hull [9] and others have adapted the methods of discrimination learning to human subjects for the purpose of studying conceptual behavior. Paired stimuli may be presented and the subject be told to choose one of them. He is then told whether or not he has chosen correctly. There is a principle which, if he discovers it, will enable him to make the proper choice in every case. In this way the subject's ability to abstract some property from many situations can be tested.

The behavior principles discussed in this section were selected because they could be accepted by many learning theorists and because they appear to be relevant to the problems involved in acquiring language. We now turn to the first of these problems—the production of speech.

III

Speech Production

No attempt will be made in this section to summarize the great quantity of research on the acquisition of speech. Dorothea McCarthy has excellently performed that task as recently as 1946.[10] Neither does the following discussion constitute a completely worked out theory of the acquisition of speech.

It attempts merely to illustrate the usefulness of the learning principles described in the last section and to suggest the lines along which a theory might be developed. Four possible objections to this approach are then presented and discussed.

Speech—An Act with Social Instrumentality.—Learning to produce speech seems to be a variety of instrumental learning. Certainly one cannot *elicit* a particular speech sound from an infant but must wait for it to be emitted. The infant often vocalizes in a state of need and the vocalization may be instrumental in procuring satisfaction. It becomes a means of environmental control. Probably speech is learned by all the instrumental techniques. A child may learn to call its mother because that act results in *escape* from the crib, the *primary reward* of food, the *avoidance* of discomfort, or the sight of mother's smiling (and *secondarily rewarding*) face.

Speech differs from many other instrumental responses in that the instrumentality of the response is dependent upon its functioning as a sign for someone else. The food pellet follows directly from pressing the lever with only mechanical mediation. But a request for food does not produce food unless there is some well-intentioned and capable individual who correctly interprets the request.[11]

If we accept Kenneth Burke's [12] characterization of rhetoric as a technique for moving men to action, then the cries of the infant are a form of rhetoric. The rhetoric of the politician is primarily concerned with persuading an audience to identify its welfare with his welfare, to take his cause as its own. The infant's task is easier since his audience is predisposed to sympathize with his needs. Thus, language is very essentially a social process. As Malinowski said: "In its primitive uses language functions as a link in concerted human activity, as a piece of human behavior. *It is a mode of action* and not an instrument of reflection." [13]

The theory of instrumental learning (and of its predecessor "trial and error learning") appears to have been formed on the model of Darwin's natural selection. The genetic traits that characterize a species originate as mutations, as random genetic variations which are selected for preservation because of their survival value. The acquisition of instrumental acts depends upon the emission of a variety of responses some of which are selected to become increasingly probable responses, because of their ability to produce reinforcement in a particular kind of situation. Particular mutations and particular responses must be emitted and cannot be elicited. Both are selected because of their consequences. Although genetic selection works toward survival of a species and behavioral selection works toward individual adjustment, neither system is teleological. It has frequently been postulated that phylogenetic advance is marked by an increase in the importance of the learning mechanism and a decline in the importance of the genetic mechanism (instinct). Man is more helpless as an infant, but in maturity he has a plastic adaptability exceeding that of any other animal. The infant organism cannot interact with the inanimate environment to satisfy its vital needs. By contrast, a mechanism has been built into the turtle that causes him to move down hill when he is thirsty. This action brings him to water. The mechanism works because environments of turtles are much the same and are seldom very far from water. Nothing of the kind will work for man. We should all end up in our cellars, dying of thirst. We have instead an instinct to vocalize and a linguistic community intent upon interpreting our vocalizations.

In the genetic problems of biology and psychology it is usually possible to emphasize either the integration of elements or the differentiation of wholes. The elements of speech—the speech sounds—make a sequential appearance that has been charted by many observers with general agreement as to the priority of the vowels and some disagreement as to the order in which they are followed by the various consonants. In later stages there is a gradual acquisition of single words, the growth of vocabulary, and finally the appearance of sentences. The ages at which various parts of speech emerge have been determined. The increasing frequency of grammatically compound and complex sentences has been plotted. These are facts. They suggest, but do not compel, a synthetic theory of speech acquisition according to which elementary sounds are combined to form words and words are put together to make sentences. The next step is a developmental chemistry in which simple ideas of objects (nouns), actions (verbs), and relations (prepositions, conjunctions) are compounded into higher units of thought (sentences).

If speech production is to be identified with instrumental learning, however, the developmental facts must be described as a selection process. By about the end of the fifth month the infant is producing a great variety of speech sounds. These may extend beyond the language of his parents to include sounds from other languages as well as noises that challenge phonetic transcription. These early vocalizations are used quite unselectively to express many different needs and affective states. Learning to speak the language of a community must involve the selection of a restricted group of sounds and the further selection from this group of the combinations and sequences appropriate to each situation.

The child's extensive phonetic repertoire narrows down to those sounds which are produced in the language of his community. Sounds that are not heard in the speech of his parents tend to be excluded from his vocalizations. When, in our paradigm of instrumental learning, the hungry rat is put in the Skinner box, he responds with a wide variety of behaviors. Still this variety is considerably less than that represented in his total repertoire. In general he produces "food seeking" activities, either because these are innately connected with the hunger drive or because he has learned that some member of this family of responses generally produces food. In the early stages of training some further selection takes place. The animal begins to concentrate its activities in the region of the box in which the lever is located. Working in this region has been reinforced by the food pellet. Selection, ultimately, narrows still further and the rat presses the lever that is directly instrumental in producing food. The vocalizing child in our society may, similarly, be expected to make a preliminary selection of sounds in the English language which are more effective, as a class, than non-English sounds. Later, he will find the particular pattern for every occasion.

In the first months of life the child's speech sounds are rather unselectively employed. He may run through much the same set of cries whether he is hungry, thirsty, or afflicted with a pain in the leg caused by the jab of an open pin. If it is the last of these which causes a child to cry, he may be fed, hugged, bounced, and only belatedly relieved of the offending pin. Reinforcement is greatly delayed. The parents will respond more rapidly and accurately as vocalizations come to be more like the patterns prescribed by their language. It is, of course, well established that when two responses are followed by a differential delay prior to reinforcement, the one which involves the lesser delay will be favored. The child's vocalizations, therefore, will be modified into an ever improving approximation of speech. He will learn to employ distinct cries for pains that call for distinct treatment, eventually to indicate whether the pain is inside or outside, high or low. Later, he may learn that assistance is more rapidly forthcoming from some people when the request is prefaced with the word "please." Without that ingratiating element, reinforcement will be delayed by a long sermon on courtesy. Is it possible that all the refinements and complications of language are learned because of their superior instrumentality?

To sum up, the vocal responses to a stimulus situation are initially more or less indiscriminate. Social selection gradually differentiates out of the response mass those sequences that are approved by the linguistic community. These sequences become increasingly numerous and increasingly complex. They are the "data" of linguistic development—the growth of vocabulary and the complication of sentence structure. According to the theory of instrumental learning the data result from a great many processes of differentiation by social selection.

Learning to speak a language, like other motor skills, involves considerable perceptual training. Being able to vocalize speech sounds is not enough. One must pattern the sounds as they are patterned in the linguistic community. For the child learning his native language this probably is not simply a matter of memorizing the names for familiar objects and events. He must learn to "see" the circumstances that govern the usage of speech sounds. The need to speak the language is one of the cultural forces molding the structure of perception and conception. The child will, at first, structure the world somewhat differently from the adult members of his community. Following Gestalt theory, we are inclined to believe that some aspects of this structure result from the interaction of stimulus energies and the human sensory apparatus quite independently of any learning. In particular, the "units" [14] of the perceptual field, the unidentified "things" or coherences, are probably sensorily determined. The child who sees, for the first time, a set of wooden blocks probably does not have to learn to see each block as a unit, distinct from the floor beneath and the wall behind. However, he may not distinguish one block from another; they may all be equivalent in his eyes. If now his father comes along to play a game in which all of the green blocks are to be used in building a house and all of the red blocks are for a barn, the child must break down the primitive equivalence of the blocks in order to join the game. If he does not discriminate properly, his father will tell him that he is not using the blocks correctly. In this case a perceptual change is required by the rules of the game. The same change could have been required by the semantic rules governing the use of the words 'red' and 'green.' Every addition to his vocabulary involves some perceptual restructuring. He cannot learn the language of a community without learning to make the perceptual discriminations that are made by the community. To use the English word 'snow' properly one must distinguish snow from grass and earth and one must perceive the equivalence of dry, cold snow and soft, packing snow. Learning a language is not simply learning to produce a set of vocal skills, it is learning to use these skills in ways and on occasions that are defined as appropriate by a community. It is necessarily the case, then, that language influences perception and conception (see Chapter

1) in at least this minimal sense. Mere exposure to the sounds of a language exerts no such influence. But as soon as one undertakes to learn to speak a language he undertakes, as part of this task, to form a perceptual structure.

Conceptualizing speech production as an instrumental act that is socially reinforced, we have suggested the lines along which a learning theory might be developed. Four problems which would seem seriously to limit such a theory are:

1. Speech is not always used to ask for a glass of water or a bite to eat. How are those verbalizations acquired that do not receive primary reinforcement?

2. Certain features of speech (allophones) are nondistinctive; they are not used to signal differences of meaning. Adult speakers of a language are commonly unaware of allophonic variations. How can their usage be socially reinforced if speakers of language are unaware of these nondistinctive features?

3. Many words and phrases refer to "private states of mind" rather than to objects or events in the external world. Children learn to use such verbalizations appropriately. How can this usage be socially reinforced when the correctness of the usage can hardly be judged by adults who have no access to the child's private states of mind?

4. If speech is learned by a selection process how can one account for the occurrence in mature speech of novel linguistic combinations which have not occurred in random vocalization nor in imitation of any model?

These four questions are discussed in the remainder of this section.

1. The Secondary Reinforcement of Speech.—Our account of the development of speech may seem unrealistic in that it relies too heavily on the satisfaction of hunger and thirst as learning mechanisms. For speech acts are not always requests for primary rewards. Parents do not teach their child language by popping a chocolate in his mouth every time he speaks correctly. Infants are often reported to vocalize for their own

pleasure or in imitation of an adult. Are these observations to be denied? The theory is rescued from that particular absurdity by the concept of secondary reinforcement. Any stimulus concomitant of primary reinforcement acquires the ability to produce learning. Parents supply most of the child's primary reinforcement and they are likely to talk to him while doing so. The quality of the parental voice and the sounds of the parental language should, under these circumstances, acquire secondary reinforcing powers.[15] Insofar as the child copies these sounds he reinforces their production with a resultant increment to the tendency to use them. Miller and Dollard [16] have suggested that this is the mechanism of babbling. This formulation is preferable to the assumption that the child takes aesthetic delight in the sound of his own voice, in playing with words, because it helps to explain why these vocalizations change in the direction of the speech he hears. The "aesthetic delight" assumption accounts for the great flood of sound but not for its systematic drift in the direction of language.

This change can be accounted for by assuming a tendency to imitate. Miller and Dollard [17] have suggested that imitation is an instrumental technique learned in accordance with familiar principles. If the younger brother imitates his older brother it is because this mode of behavior is reinforced. He will extinguish his imitative tendency when it is no longer instrumental in this way. Miller and Dollard [18] have demonstrated the acquisition of generalized imitative tendencies in both animals and children. On this theory, we should not expect imitation to appear in the first months of life as it would presumably take some time to accomplish this rather difficult learning. We should, in fact, anticipate something like Lewis' [19] conclusion that imitation, in the sense of an improving approximation to the behavior of a model, does not occur until the ninth month of life. We should also expect imitation to be selective—the child would imitate some people at some times—following the selective administration of reinforcements. This, also, appears to be the case. The assumption of an imitative instinct would

be gratuitous since Miller and Dollard have provided a theory
that fits more of the facts and yet follows familiar principles of
behavior.

One of the things involved in learning to imitate is learning
to be rewarded by a perceived correspondence between one's
own behavior and the behavior of a model. This is another instance of secondary or derived reinforcement. If any stimulus
concomitant of primary reinforcement acquires the ability to
produce learning, the child's speech can be reinforced by a
smile, a pat on the head, a warm look, or a wink. In adult conversation, the listener ordinarily feeds this kind of subtle reinforcement to the speaker. Charles Fries [20] has listed some of
the responses by which continued attention is conventionally
signalled. The listener may interpolate a nod at one point, a
comprehending "unh-hunh" at another. When we speak we
look for these cues and wait for them. What would happen if
they failed to appear has not been experimentally determined.
Quite probably conversation would be disrupted.

Greenspoon [21] had subjects speak single words in a free association task. He controlled the interpolation of an encouraging
"unh-hunh"—using it only after plural nouns. He was able to
demonstrate that plurals increased in frequency under these
circumstances even though subjects were unaware of any selective encouragement. In most cases remarks that are reinforced
by a nod are not immediately repeated. It may be that these
conversational reinforcers affect larger response units, increasing the tendency to express a particular sentiment, to adopt a
certain mode of address or just to continue conversing.

In communication theory [22] a distinction is made between
primary information and secondary information. Primary information is the message the speaker is attempting to circulate.
Secondary information is given to the talker by the recipient's
response. It tells him whether or not the message has been
correctly received. The confirming signals of secondary information are what we have called secondary reinforcement.
Radio communications between an operator at a landing field
and a pilot in the air are heavily loaded with such secondary

information, assuring the pilot that the man on the ground knows he is there and is looking out for him. Cutting off these assurances brings immediate frantic questions from the pilot. Heise and Miller [23] have shown that curtailment of secondary information greatly reduces the operating efficiency of certain kinds of small group communication.

Festinger [24] has recently pointed out that expressive messages are "consummatory" rather than "instrumental." Instrumental communication requires secondary information from the listener. The talker wants to check the effect of his message. Consummatory communication is its own reward. The talker is not interested in the reactions of the listener. This distinction is similar to that made by Piaget [25] between egocentric and socialized speech. These concepts need not be restricted to the small group conversation. The speaker who addresses an audience can also be more or less concerned with secondary information coming from that audience. Some teachers are enthusiastically in favor of having students evaluate their work while others are violently opposed to any such scheme. The studio audience is more important to some radio and television performers than to others. The egocentricity of the film maker is limited by sneak preview reactions, critical reviews, and box office receipts. The speech of the schizophrene is altogether consummatory since he is insulated against any secondary information. What determines an individual's sensitivity to secondary information? Under what conditions does speech become consummatory? These questions raise empirical problems of very great interest.

2. The Acquisition of Nondistinctive Features.—Experiments in perception and learning as well as cross cultural linguistic studies (see Chapter 1) suggest that animals and human beings do not make perceptual discriminations unless these discriminations are required of them. Speakers of English immediately recognize the distinctive or phonemic contrasts of their language. No one doubts that [p] is different from [t]. This is a contrast capable of distinguishing one meaning from another, as in 'pin' and 'tin.' There are, in addition, nondistinctive differ-

ences in English utterances that do not contrast with one another and, consequently, are not used to distinguish meanings. Thus, although the [e] of 'heed' has a greater duration that the [e] of 'deep' there are not two words in English which are identical except for this feature. The feature is, therefore, non-distinctive and the variations of [e] that occur in different phonetic environments are called the allophones of a single phoneme. We are, most of us, surprised to learn of these allophonic variations. It may be necessary to say the words over several times before the distinct allophones can be heard although the words themselves are, of course, immediately distinguished by their phonemic contrasts, the differences between [h] and [d] and between [d] and [p]. Bloch and Trager [26] say: "The ordinary speaker of English . . . feels that the [p'] of 'pin' and the [p-] of upper are alike and both different from the [b] of 'bin,' he feels or conceives of the two l's in 'little' as the same sound." Bloomfield [27] put it this way: "The speaker has been trained to make sound-producing movements in such a way that the phoneme features will be present in the sound-waves and he has been trained to respond only to these features and to ignore the rest of the gross acoustic mass that reaches his ears."

The child in learning English learns to reproduce its allophonic variations. If the adult speakers of the language are unaware of these nondistinctive features, how can they provide the selective reinforcements which our theory assumes to be prerequisite to perceptual discrimination and differential response? If the child makes an allophonic error (as in prolonging the [e] of 'deep,') he does not thereby produce another word and his meaning is not misunderstood. What consequences can this error have which will eventually cause it to be corrected? If there are no consequences then we must find some other principle of learning since the errors definitely are corrected. A clue to the answer derives from this statement by Bloomfield: "When a foreign speaker reproduces the phonemic values of our language so as to make himself understood, but does not distribute the non-distinctive features in accordance with our habit, we say that he speaks the language well enough but with a foreign accent." [28] For although we may not have thought of the [e] in heed as longer than the [e] in deep it does not follow that we should fail to detect a peculiarity in speech of a person who prolonged the [e] in deep. In fact we notice it at once. And so the parent who hears the child's allophonic error may not mistake his meaning, but is likely to laugh at his accent and motivate him to change. These differences in response may be distinguishable from those caused by phonemic errors in terms of the secondary information. Phonemic errors produce misunderstandings or requests that an apparent nonsense word be repeated. Allophonic errors may occasion somewhat different reactions, but what these are has not been reported to our knowledge.

There is another reason for believing that allophonic deviations are detected. The allophonic variation between the two [e] sounds of 'heed' and 'deep' is redundant because the difference in meaning is carried by another feature, the phonemic distinction between [d] and [p]. Wherever the two allophones of [e] occur differences are conveyed by at least one other feature of the word. Consider the case of 'heed' and 'heap.' In actual conversation the [d] and [p] distinction might occasionally be lost. The words would still not be confused because the ordinarily redundant allophone is there to signal the difference. But in such a case the allophone would make a difference in meaning. Allophonic errors will then occasionally cause an error of interpretation, for when the other features are missed the meaning will be carried by the allophone. This is one reason for correcting such errors in children. Once it is recognized that there are good reasons for noticing allophonic deviations, the learning of allophones presents no special difficulties.

3. Describing Private States of Mind.—It is not so very difficult to see how we learn to use words like 'mamma,' 'book,' and 'milk.' In each of these cases there is a stimulus object perceived by both tutor and tutee. The tutor has no great difficulty deciding when these words are appropriately used,

and thus knows when to reinforce and when not to reinforce. But there are other, private, events, introspectively available only to the speaker, which are expressed in such phrases as "I am depressed," "I have a toothache." If a child speaks in this way how can one judge whether or not he is speaking correctly?

There are two kinds of cues [29] that are very likely to guide the administration of reinforcement.

a) The tutor may know that some event has occurred which normally occasions depression in a child. His dog has died or his mother has gone away. Under the circumstances the tutor is likely to approve the child's usage. There is, after all, reason to be depressed.

b) On the other hand there may be overt symptoms of depression, a hanging head and scowling countenance. Again the tutor will reinforce the child's usage. His words are confirmed by his depressed appearance.

This answer violates the "privacy" of the speaker's states of mind. It suggests that there are cues which make it possible to judge whether or not verbalizations that refer to the "inner man" are being used appropriately. These cues are of the same sort as those involved in learning the names of external objects or events. If a child says "milk" when there is a glass of milk before him we reinforce that usage, because it is likely that he is perceiving the milk set before him (*a* above) or because the direction of his glance suggests that this is the case (*b* above). There is, even here, the possibility of a failure of communication. To use the word 'milk' correctly in all circumstances, the child must abstract the qualities of whiteness and density that characterize this liquid. In the present case he could very well be attending to the glass that contains the milk. So long as he is presented with milk in a glass container his usage will seem to be correct; but the error will be revealed in certain critical cases. Milk is sometimes placed in a bowl, water is sometimes placed in a glass. In both of these situations he is likely to say the wrong thing and to be corrected. When the statement "I feel depressed" is pronounced under circumstances that cause the usage to be approved there is a very great chance that the speaker has not identified the internal cues that should trigger that response. Correction by nonreinforcement is now a very clumsy business. There is no set of external circumstances that can be guaranteed to induce depression. There are no inevitable overt symptoms of the state. The tutor recognizes that, in the last analysis, the speaker knows best whether or not he is depressed. Because the rules for reinforcement are not clear the chances are very great that this expression will be employed with different "meaning" by different people.

There are in English many expressions for which the rules of application are not clear. Suppose a professor of English literature wants his students to learn to recognize great poetry on the basis of their aesthetic reaction to it. His notion is that the term 'great poetry' is appropriate whenever a certain kind of aesthetic appreciation is engendered. He has no idea what the external manifestations of an aesthetic state would be. His technique is to expose them to a succession of great poems— poems of Shakespeare, Milton, Wordsworth—a set of stimuli ordinarily considered adequate to the arousal of an aesthetic state. It is his hope that each student will extract from his experiences with these poems some common element that will give him a feeling for great poetry.

This is something like the problem of learning when to use the word 'red.' One way of conveying this knowledge is by pointing to a succession of red objects and hoping that some common quale will be detected. Now if the problem is to test the subject's knowledge of "red" it won't do to point to a number of familiar objects and ask whether they are red because it would be possible for the subject to answer correctly either because of an actual ability to recognize red or because of a good memory for the color names applied to familiar objects. So a color blindness test is set up in which the correct discriminations can only be made on the basis of sensory capacity.

What would happen if an aesthetic blindness test were constructed along similar lines? Instead of asking students to evaluate poems by Shakespeare and Ella Wheeler Wilcox we should provide them with samples of poetry, unidentified by title or author, and ask that they be evaluated in terms of aesthetic merit. This is more or less what I. A. Richards [30] did with Cambridge undergraduates and found that their evaluations did not agree with his own nor did the students agree among themselves. Probably very different things can be abstracted from repeated exposures to examples of great poetry. The ostensive definition does not guarantee that what the teacher finds in his examples will be found there by his students. For one student these experiences may have nothing in common but a suffocating dullness. Another enjoys an autonomic upheaval, a third feels an expanded awareness. Asked to evaluate unfamiliar poetry they will naturally hit upon quite different rankings.

When the authors' names were attached to the poems in Richards' study the students were quite able to match his ranking. This suggests that they had all discovered one set of semantic cues for using the expression 'great poetry,' namely a list of the recognized great poets of English literature. It is as if the students had memorized the names of a number of red objects and could agree very well within this list but somehow they had found quite different qualia in these experiences and so could not agree at all on the identification of new examples.

The names of the emotions and other states of mind are not necessarily semantically confused any more than the names of external objects and events are necessarily semantically clear. A toothache is a private experience and yet the expression "I have a toothache" is quite univocally applied. The tutor has a clear set of cues for identifying appropriate usage. A deep cavity may be confidently expected to produce toothache, whereas a reading of Shakespeare is not necessarily the adequate stimulus to aesthetic emotion. A swollen jaw, an agonized moan, are clear symptoms of this inner state, but a watery eye and tremulous voice are not certain indications of an aesthetic state. Reinforcing usage that satisfied these external cues, the tutor can be confident that the speaker will identify the feelings that are the proper stimulus to his statement—which is to say there is no mistaking a toothache. It imposes itself upon our attention in a way that aesthetic pleasure does not.

These are, of course, extraordinarily complicated problems, but they probably need not remain forever refractory to empirical investigation. The first step is their general assimilation to other problems of linguistic learning. The next step is the identification of the peculiar circumstances that attend learning to say "I feel depressed" or "That is a great poem."

4. Production of Novel Combinations.—It is possible to believe that English sounds are selected out of a larger vocalization repertoire because of their superior instrumentality in the life of a child reared in an English-speaking household. The sounds may be detected in the infant's early unselective babbling. It is even possible to believe that some words and phrases are so learned. A vocabulary of words and phrases that have not appeared in the random vocalization of the child begins to grow rapidly around the ninth month and, we have seen, has been attributed to a general learned drive to imitate. However, the linguistically mature human being produces novel utterances that cannot be regarded as either random or imitative. These utterances appear to be systematic and patterned, their novelty constrained by the structural rules of the language. How can such utterances be explained by a selection mechanism? Where is the practice period? What are the responses to be differentially reinforced?

We can only suggest the lines along which answers to these questions may eventually be formulated. The grammar of a language has been described by Fries as consisting of "the devices that signal structural meanings." [31] The young child, and indeed many adults, cannot be said to know the grammar of a language in the sense of being able to verbalize its grammatical rules in a generalized form. However, even the young child "knows" the grammar in the sense of being capable of producing the devices that signal structural meanings. He is also capable, somewhat earlier it appears, of responding to the indications of structural meanings.

We should suppose that the child learns certain general habits of form and arrangement which are the combinations of form classes and function words that signal structural meanings. We might also suppose that the learning of these general habits occurs by a process of selective reinforcement. Utterances consisting of combinations of forms that obey the structural rules, as manifested in the linguistic behavior of the parents, will be reinforced. Other combinations will be judged "improper" or will fail to communicate and hence will not be reinforced. Once these general habits are learned, they seem to be retained and usable independently of the particular forms which in combination obey the structural rules. Those words that can fill a given position in an utterance, the members of a form class, are in some way substitutable, giving rise to the occurrence in mature speech of novel combinations of words. At some level beyond mimicry and selection from random vocalization, novel utterances occur not by chance but by design. An explication of this design in terms of learning and behavior principles is yet to be accomplished. The instrumental learning theory cannot handle such problems without complicating its structure beyond that presented here.

The difficulty with explaining the production of novel linguistic combinations raises the parallel difficulty of explaining how such combinations can be understood for the first time. This question is reserved for discussion in the final section of this chapter.

To summarize, this entire section on speech production has described a process by which a child might acquire a set of skills universally employed among the adults of his community. These skills differ from such other motor skills as walking and grasping in a great many ways. For one thing they are executed by the fine musculature of the vocal apparatus. This is certainly a salient feature of most human language, but hardly necessary since there are also gesture languages and written languages. Too great a stress on vocal production has led some comparative psychologists to teach chimpanzees to say 'cup' in the belief that they were investigating the animal's linguistic capacities. The chimpanzee may have rudimentary vocal skills and still be unable to speak English.

A more important characteristic of language skills is the fact that their instrumentality is socially mediated. This distinguishes them from those behaviors that are learned because of their effects on the inanimate environment. This latter category is more important for animals other than man. However, the child does learn to avoid the burning stove, to reach for a cookie, to climb down from his crib. His gestures and cues, on the other hand, accomplish their effects because they function as signs for others. The present chapter will not be a discussion of language until some attempt is made to explicate the sign function. A stimulus functions as a sign when it causes an interpreter to take account, in some ways, of the object or event signified. Spelling out this sign function in behavioral terms is the problem of the response to language, the subject of the next section.

IV

The Response to Language

Before the child can appropriately respond to language he must appropriately perceive it. The sign must be discriminated before it can function. Just as there is a perceptual education that develops with the ability to produce speech so there is much perceptual learning involved in the response to speech. It is not certain which aspects of audible speech are most impressive to the child. Probably these are not the finicking contrasts that interest the phonetician and which are the principal bearers of meaning in mature speech. The initially impressive aspects are more likely to be the patterns of stress, the melodies, or affective tones of speech, all of which are likely to represent greater variations in the sound spectrum than many phonemic contrasts. Lewis,[32] among others, has suggested that intonation is the first aspect of speech to which the child shows consistent response. Meumann [33] reports Tappolet's experiment with his son who would, at a very early age, turn in the direction of the window when asked *"Wo ist das Fenster?"* or *"Où est la fenêtre?"* Had the child learned to understand French as well as German? Such an extravagant conclusion could be refuted by asking the child to locate the ceiling. He would turn, as before, to the window. In all of these questions the intonation pattern (as it can be described with Kenneth Pike's symbols) [34] is the same, and it was presumably to this speech melody that Tappolet's son responded. Actually, there was also a pattern of stresses common to all these questions and it remains possible that stress was the decisive attribute.

Tappolet could have directed the child's attention to phonemic elements by informing him that it was a mistake to turn to the window when asked to locate the ceiling. Intonation and stress would be equated in the two sentences and so for the child, the two sentences would be perceptually equivalent. However, it would sometimes be correct to turn to the window and sometimes not. His attention would be redirected to the speech sounds in which perceptible differences exist and would eventually be found. In some such way, the child is required to give up his first perceptual predilections in favor of smaller differences of greater consequence. This can be accomplished by discrimination training involving selective reinforcement.

The Identification of Signs.—Any theory of language must explain how some stimuli, from the multitude of stimulus patterns that we discriminate, come to be signs of others. There have been suggestions that one stimulus pattern is the sign of another when there is some relation of similarity or identity between the overt behaviors evoked by the one with those evoked by the other or when the two are linked by some common mediator—or that both overt behaviors and a mediator are necessary to define the sign relation. Is it feasible to require that the same behavior be produced by both the sign and denotatum? If not, perhaps it would be sensible to require that only some of the responses produced by the denotatum be also produced by the sign. As a third possibility, signs might be distinguished by their capacity to elicit behavior that is in some way appropriate to the denotatum. Should none of these relations between overt behaviors obtain it will be necessary to look to implicit, mediating responses.

The Role of Overt Responses in the Sign Process.—Recall the familiar story of the prankish boy who cried "Wolf." The villagers ran to the fields to rescue him, only to find that he had amused himself by sounding a false alarm. The behavior of the villagers seems to be much as it would have been if they had actually seen a wolf menacing the sheep. In this story the cry "Wolf" would appear to function as a sign, if the sign process were defined in accordance with an earlier Watsonian understanding [35] of conditioning. According to this view a stimulus is a sign if it evokes the same response as a denotatum. The word 'book' will mean the object book only if we respond in the same way to both. This is a simple substitution of stimuli view of classical conditioning that holds the conditioned response to be identical with the unconditioned. The question is does this ever happen either in the response to language or in the conditioning of animals. Even in the fable discussed, the villagers do not behave exactly as if the wolf were really present. They may rush to battle but they don't actually battle. In the same way the word 'Napoleon' has meaning, as Langer [36] has pointed out without inducing the awful surprise that would follow upon the materialization of the man himself. Certainly, there is something wrong with a definition of the sign function that renders inevitable those confusions of sign with object which constitute the "word-magic" so deplored by the reforming semanticist. A sign is seldom, if ever, a simple proxy for its referent.

In an earlier section of this chapter we pointed out that in both classical and instrumental learning the conditioned response is rarely identical with the unconditioned response. Even in classical conditioning Zener's [37] observations argue that the apparent simplicity of the response learned is due to the behavioral limitations placed on the experimental animal. A dog does not simply learn to salivate to a bell. If he is trained in a standard harness and, then, taken out and placed on a nearby table, he will, upon hearing the bell, bound over to the original table and stand poised over his food. This is clearly not the response evoked by the unconditioned stimulus of meat powder on the tongue. Were we to accept this severe qualifying test for sign functions the range of sign behaviors would be restricted to a very few perfectly reintegrative conditioned responses—perhaps the pupillary contraction and eye wink.

There are those who do not subscribe to this naïve understanding of conditioning, but do identify meaning with the overt responses to signs. They must further specify the relation between the overt responses made to signs and those made to the denotata, if the class of signs is to be differentiated out of the very broad class of stimuli that evoke responses. Charles Morris suggests a relation between behaviors produced by signs and denotata that is less stringent than identity. The notion of a "disposition" to respond, produced by a sign as it is described in Morris' [38] later work, retains the essentials of his concept of "interpretant" presented in an earlier monograph.[39] This disposition is still a reaction to a sign that mediately takes account of the object signified but this "taking account of" is now defined in terms of the conditions under which a common response to both sign and denotatum may be identified.

Suppose we take an example of a meaningful reaction to language and note what operations Morris seems to suggest for identifying this reaction as sign behavior. As someone is about to leave the house he may be warned, "It is raining out-of-doors." He may very well respond by putting on a raincoat, fetching an umbrella, or possibly postponing his outdoor errand until a more propitious time. Clearly there is no single overt response attached to the sign. By adopting the concept of "habit family hierarchy" from Hull's [40] behavior theory, Morris is able to suggest a basis for continuity between responses produced by signs and denotata. Basically a "behavior family" is a group of alternative response sequences such as running a maze, swimming a maze, etc., initiated by a particular stimulus and terminated by a particular goal response.[41] A stimulus, then, is a sign of an object if it produces a disposition to respond under certain conditions with response sequences that are also cued by the object. This is something like Watson's notion of stimulus substitution but it is more complicated. An entire family of response sequences is transferred to the substitute stimulus. Which one of the response sequences is actually to occur will depend upon the total context of cues. Morris' theory commits us to discovering an identity between a response produced by the denotatum and some response an organism is *disposed* to make to the sign, a response that it will make when and if the shifting context of cues is propitious. Apart from the practical difficulty this would impose upon identifying signs and meaningful relations, there is a prior question as to whether or not the sign and its denotatum actually do cue the same behavior family.

The response family evoked by rain is instrumental in that it provides an *escape* from unpleasant stimulation while the response family cued by the linguistic warning is instrumental in *avoiding* rain. These facts suggest that it may be profitable to reintroduce the avoidance-learning experiment mentioned in a previous section. As we have seen, the avoidance-learning experiment typically begins with a brief training period during which a cue, perhaps a buzzer, a tone, or simply the visual stimuli of the training box is presented just prior to electric shock. In an effort to escape the shock in one way or another the animal may dart off the grill or jump into another compartment or may dance gingerly on the grill thereby reducing the shock. The apparatus may allow several such instrumental responses to occur. We may think of these responses as part of a behavior family, each of the alternative response sequences being cued to the shock and terminated by escape from the shock, the condition which reinforces the escape responses. Now, according to Morris, it is the behavior family of which these responses are a part that must become dispositionally attached to the buzzer, if the buzzer is to function as a sign.

Let us look more carefully at what happens in this experiment. It is generally accepted that an electric shock will arouse the animal's autonomic system, producing a fear reaction. This response requires no training and is, therefore, an unconditioned response. If the same cue regularly precedes the shock the fear response will tend to anticipate the shock and occur in response to that cue. Neal Miller [42] and others employing a similar procedure have used this fear conditioned to visual stimuli of the shock compartment to motivate a variety of instrumental responses. The animal will, for example, learn to spin a wheel if that response permits an escape from the fear-producing cue into an adjoining compartment. It may, alternatively, learn to press a lever if that response reduces the conditioned fear. The range of avoidance responses that can become attached to the cues is in no way limited to the family of escape responses evoked by the shock. Only the animal's response repertory and the experimenter's ingenuity and patience set any limits. Of course, it is possible that some responses may occur both as an escape reaction to the shock and as an avoidance reaction to the cue. A high-priority escape response like running will be high in the animal's hierarchy of responses to the cue. But this response will not be retained unless the experimenter allows it to be reinforced. The crucial point against Morris' theory is that the cue need not produce a disposition to any of the responses that are evoked by the shock. Neither is it necessarily the case that any of the instrumental responses made to the rain itself will occur to the word 'rain.' Indeed, none of the responses needs be the same.

Of course, not all sign learning will fit an avoidance-training paradigm. Denotata are not always rain, wolves, or other threats to our weal. The avoidance training example was reviewed because it points up some important distinctions—between response families produced by denotata and signs, between the classically conditioned fear and the instrumentally learned avoidance response. However, the unconditioned stimulus in classical conditioning need not be noxious and in the very famous work of Pavlov it usually was not. That Pavlov's metronome comes to "mean" food rather than simply acquiring the ability to elicit a highly specific salivary response is argued by Zener's [43] observations. This procedure could serve as a model for many sign learning situations.

If meaning is to be identified with overt behavior, it is necessary to specify some linkage or continuity between behaviors produced by signs and denotata. We have seen that Morris' attempt to provide this connection through the habit family hierarchy does not seem to truly describe many sign situations. There are, of course, additional drawbacks to the theory.[44] One of these involves the difficulty in recognizing habit families. This can be done in simple cases as that in which a rat negotiates a maze. Swimming the maze when it is flooded, running the course with the waltzing, twirling movements produced by certain lesions, running over alternative routes could all be accepted as members of a single habit family. But human responses to language do not show such obvious ties. When the denotatum is a goal, there is some possibility of identifying a behavior family by the common goal response. But it would be difficult to specify the goal response that binds together all the reactions to a simple greeting like "Good morning" or the reactions to a statement such as "This is red." In short the meaning of habit family hierarchy is not at all clear in human responses to language since the observations that define it in certain elementary animal situations are simply not possible in most of the more interesting cases. Even where habit families might be identified, it would still be difficult to distinguish signs from nonsigns. The claim could be made that any stimulus is a sign of any other. All challenges could then be met by asserting that the disposition had just not yet been realized. As stimulus-response theories of the sign function grow sophisticated and more adequate to human language, their behaviorism fades into the promise of a program, and the statements of the theory lose vulnerability.

There are other approaches less open to objection than Morris', primarily because they are less ambitious. Stevenson [45] identifies meaning with a disposition to respond in regular fashion to other stimuli. This dispositional definition must certainly be correct, but its value to the psychologist is limited by the failure to describe these responses, their relation to the responses produced by the denotatum and the manner of their acquisition.

The Role of Implicit Reactions in the Sign Process.—Watson believed that sign value or meaning attaches to a word by a process of simple substitution. The meaning would be that overt response which was evoked by both sign and denotatum. When unable to find overt responses he postulated implicit ones—slight muscle movements or—the favorite—subvocal speech. When someone reads a book an observer may be unable to detect any overt responses at all. It would still be possible, however, that various implicit responses were occurring. Watson's view is typically peripheralist. From this standpoint deaf mutes dream with their fingers. There is some substantiation of such a view in Max's [46] discovery that there are greater action potentials obtainable from the fingers of such handicapped people when they are dreaming than from the fingers of normal subjects. These may, of course, simply be unreliable peripheral accompaniments of central meaning processes. We have no assurance that such muscular activity inevitably accompanies meaning. Even if there should be such reliable implicit muscular reactions there are no instruments that would allow us to read off the meaning of a sign or discriminate among different meanings. We should still be dependent on the report of the subject. As Osgood says: "The subject . . . verbalizes meaning while the experimenter scurries about his periphery trying to pick it up on instruments." [47]

Morris' concept of a disposition is that of a kind of mediator between sign and overt behavior, the "interpretant" of the sign. The sign need not actually produce responses of a given behavior family; it must simply produce a disposition to perform certain responses, a disposition that will be translated into action under proper circumstances. The disposition, however, is not a common feature of response to both sign and denotatum. Nothing is said about its origin, the method of its acquisition. Apparently, the buzzer becomes a sign of the shock that galvanizes the animal and the disposition is some-how created. To be useful the mediating process must be further explicated.

Osgood builds on a mechanism of Hull's learning theory in developing a mediation theory of meaning. The problem of a linkage between responses to sign and denotatum is handled by asserting that "when stimuli, other than the stimulus ob-ject, but previously associated with it are later presented with-out its support, they tend to elicit some reduced portion of the total behavior elicited by the stimulus object." [48] Thus the fear produced by the buzzer, in avoidance training, is some frac-tional component of the total response to the shock. The sign produced response, then, has its origin in the relatively "de-tachable" portions of the response to the denotatum. Follow-ing Hull's [49] conception of the "pure stimulus act" these re-sponses would tend toward a minimum, their sole function being to participate in the selection of instrumental behaviors.

Confronted with the facts of linguistic behavior, a response theory is forced under the skin. If such implicit reactions are to be identified with meaning we should like to know whether they are classically conditioned or instrumentally learned. Most definitions of the sign process agree that the sign must "stand for something" and that the response to the sign is by virtue of this "signifying" relation. In classical conditioning the con-ditioned stimulus may be said to "stand for" the unconditioned stimulus. The whole procedure of presenting the two in close contiguity is a kind of ostensive definition. It is a way of saying that one stimulus stands for another as we might do it if we were teaching our language to someone who knew noth-ing of any language. No unconditioned stimulus can be identi-fied in instrumental learning and so there is nothing to serve as denotatum for the sign. This is one reason for believing that learning signs is a case of classical conditioning.

In classical conditioning a conditioned response extinguishes when the unconditioned stimulus (which is the reinforcement) is omitted. If sign learning is classical conditioning we should expect the meanings of signs to extinguish when the denotatum

is omitted. It has been experimentally demonstrated[50] that
when a word is read over and over again it becomes a mark
on paper, devoid of meaning. With the omission of denotata
and supportive context the meaning would seem to extinguish.
In the story of the boy who cried "Wolf" the villagers disregarded that call after they had repeatedly found that no real
wolf, the denotatum of the sign, ever appeared. It would be
possible to say that a part of the total meaning of the word
had extinguished. The villagers learned to interpret the call as
a sign of the boy's desire to amuse himself. Because meanings
extinguish under conditions parallel to those that produce classical response extinction, we become more confident that sign
learning is classical conditioning.[51]

We have some reason for identifying meaning with implicit
conditioned responses. Of course, linguistic signs also produce
instrumental acts. How are these related to the conditioned
responses? The names of some men have terrorized entire pop-
ulations. In the recent past, 'Hitler' has been such a name.
When the name of a tyrant is shouted out, his oppressed people
will experience something of the fear that was originally
elicited by a report of the man's bloody deeds. This primarily
autonomic reaction—a thump of the heart, a catch of the breath
—is the implicit conditioned response. But the name of the
tyrant will also cause his potential victims to lock their doors
and hide themselves away. These acts will extinguish when
they are no longer effective. Those who fear the tyrant will not
lock the door and hide if the soldiers always break in and
beat them. They will try other methods of escape. Yet we
probably should not like to say that the meaning of the
tyrant's name has changed. It is as frightful as ever. In the case
of the boy who cried "Wolf" if the villagers had arrived to find
a real wolf standing over a dead sheep their instrumental acts
would have extinguished. Running to the scene when called
by the shepherd had proved to be ineffective. Very likely they
would have installed a sentry to shoot marauding wolves. The
instrumental sequence would have changed but the cry "Wolf"
would signify as before. Finally, in the avoidance learning

paradigm suppose a rat has learned to spin a wheel in order to prevent shock. If that wheel is disconnected so that it no longer has this effect the response will extinguish. The buzzer will continue to evoke the fear reaction and new instrumental acts will be learned. In summary, of all these observations it appears to be true that instrumental responses extinguish when they are not followed by reinforcement but this extinction does not affect the implicit conditioned responses that have been identified with meaning.

As we have seen, the implicit responses will extinguish when the denotatum is omitted. If the tyrant devotes himself to deeds of charity his name will no longer be feared. A part of the meaning of the name may then be said to have extinguished.[52] When a tyrant is no longer feared his subjects will no longer run and hide. Similarly, when the cry "Wolf" loses its critical meaning the villagers stop running to the rescue. If the buzzer, in avoidance training, is no longer followed by shock the fear will extinguish and so will the instrumental act of spinning the wheel. In summary of these observations it can be said that the implicit conditioned response, identified with meaning, extinguishes when the unconditioned stimulus identified with the denotatum is omitted and that the instrumental acts then also extinguish. This is presumably because these overt acts are cued by the mediating response. A nontechnical paraphrase of these conclusions would say that what one does in response to a sign depends on the meaning it conveys to him. Our confidence in this formulation is increased by the discovery that it leads us to say such very sensible things.

Osgood makes no attempt to describe the substantive properties of his mediating responses. Certainly they need not be restricted to peripheral muscle movements as in the Watsonian theory. Perhaps they involve autonomic arousal, or central nervous activity, or all of these together. In what sense is this mediating process a response? It is an unobservable. As Osgood has recognized, there are no direct measures available. Meaning has been pushed to a place in the organism where it eludes the most sensitive instruments now available. We appear to

have here a conception that adds little to the usefulness and
subtracts little from the caprice of Titchener's "images" or
Ogden and Richards' "thoughts" or "reference." We submit,
however, that hypothetical constructs not directly measured,
are useful when the properties imputed to them make it possible to deduce and interpret meaning reaction as functionally
a response,[53] without attempting to specify what it may be
substantively. We have seen that meanings may be conditioned [54] and extinguished. We have seen that the laws of
extinction are congruent with facts concerning changes in
meaning. We are led to wonder whether meanings follow
principles of generalization and discrimination, whether they
manifest spontaneous recovery, whether the latency of meaning is a function of the number of reinforced trials, and so
forth. Evaluation of the implicit response theory depends, in
the long run, on the number of experimental problems it suggests and on the outcome of the experiments performed.

In this section arguments have been advanced that militate
against the identification of meaning with acts that are either
overt or instrumental.

1) It appears that not all of the overt responses to the sign
and denotatum are the same. It is not even always true that
some of the overt responses are the same. The overt responses
to the two stimuli may show no overlapping at all.

2) There is nothing in instrumental learning that is parallel
to the denotatum of sign theory. Instrumental responses often
extinguish in cases where we should not want to say that meaning had extinguished. In general instrumental responses are
not reinforced or extinguished in the way that meanings appear
to be.

This leaves us saying that, if meaning is to be a response, it
must be, as Osgood suggests, a mediating implicit response.
We should suggest that this response may be classically conditioned. The value of these formulations depends upon the evidence that can be accumulated to indicate that meaning possesses the functional properties of a response.

V

The Nature of Language and the Possibility of a Stimulus-Response Theory of Language

Charles Morris in *Signs, Language and Behavior* [55] lists five characteristics of established (natural) languages. While a theory of language may begin with speech production and simple sign situations it must eventually deal with the complications listed below (adapted from Morris with some modifications and additions):

1) A language is composed of a plurality of signs.

2) Each sign in a language has a signification common to a number of interpreters. This criterion tells us that where there is a language there must also be a language community.

3) The signs are producible as well as interpretable by the members of a language community.

4) The signs of a language have a relative constancy of signification. They do not altogether change meaning from one situation to another. This requires that a language have a lexicon.

5) The signs in a language constitute a system of interconnected signs combinable in some way and not in others in order to form a variety of complex sign processes. This requires that a language have a structure—a syntax.

These criteria appear to be logically and empirically independent of one another. Early criteria in the list may be satisfied when later criteria are not. A man who keeps a kennel of dogs may have a plurality of whistles and calls which are understood by a number of canine interpreters. The interpreters, however, are unable to produce these signs and the whines and barks that they use do not lie within the competence of their master. Later criteria in the list are sometimes met when earlier criteria are not. Such insects as the bee and ant carry on elaborate communications understood by many interpreters. Their communication does not satisfy the first criterion, however, since they have no signs, in contradistinction to signals.

The insects have not learned the meanings of the communications. Apparently their effectiveness is entirely the result of maturation and suitable environmental stimulation. The comparative psychologist cannot, then, make a phylogenetic sequence of these five characteristics as they are here listed. It is possible, however, that all infra-human anticipations of languages can be usefully described with some such co-ordinates.

In the present ordering the first three characteristics offer no special problems to a conditioning theory of the acquisition of language. The fourth and fifth items raise some difficult questions. The greatest difficulty posed by the early characteristics lies in the behavioral definition of the sign process. If the definition proposed in the last section can be accepted it is easy enough to say that languages are composed of a plurality of signs. We need only invoke the *"Und-Verbindungen"* that have always proved congenial to associationism. As a second characteristic the signs of established languages have significations that are common to a number of interpreters. We have not attempted to explain the origins of language but have exclusively dealt with the problems of a child learning from his society. The theory involves a kind of "social selection" that assumes the existence of a linguistic community. The members of the linguistic community must be capable of producing as well as interpreting the signs of the language. This is guaranteed by the vocal apparatus and nervous organization characteristic of the human species.

The Lexical Requirement.—The fourth characteristic of the signs of established languages is their possession of some constancy in meaning from one situation to another. There are a number of units into which it is possible to analyze a language —the distinctive feature, the phoneme, morpheme, word, and phrase. The more molecular of these—the distinctive feature and the phoneme—do not ordinarily function as signs. The phoneme [d] in verbal isolation does not signify anything in English since it does not stand alone in that language. It occurs in such words as 'dog,' 'din,' and 'dunce.' These have no common meaning that could become attached to their common element. The phoneme [d] does function so as to cue a difference in meaning as when the word 'dog' is opposed to the word 'bog.' The distinctive feature is likewise a discriminatory mark which is otherwise semantically empty.

Consider again, an animal that has been conditioned to respond in one way to a buzzer and in another way to a bell. The tone qualities of these two sounds can be analyzed into formants or even individual constituent frequencies. Neither the individual frequencies nor the individual formants are functioning as signs. It might be that the bell and buzzer possess identical tonal spectra except for a differential emphasis on some particular formant. In that case the formant would serve to contrast the two patterns although it would not elicit any response if produced alone.

The foregoing remarks are not intended to suggest that these molecular stimuli are intrinsically incapable of serving as signs. If they can be produced and discriminated they can serve as signs. Of course, one cannot really produce a phoneme, since the phoneme is a theoretical construct, but one can produce individual phones that fall within the range of variation of a particular phoneme. Such sounds could serve as signs. One might use [d] to signify a man's political affiliation. Pure tones can also serve as signs, and have frequently done so in the psychological laboratory. In ordinary living, however, pure tones are not produced and are not given any significance. Individual phonemes or distinctive features are not ordinarily used with any designative consistency. All of these molecular units occur in patterns and sequences and it is the patterns and sequences that function as signs.

In order of increasing molarity the patterns and sequences of language are called morphemes, words, and phrases. The morpheme is reported by linguists to have some constancy of meaning. This is clear enough with such free morphemes as 'can,' 'dog,' or 'go.' The meaning of a bound morpheme like the suffix 'ful' ordinarily appears only as a common constituent of the total meaning of such complex words as 'joyful' and 'mournful.' The larger units, the word and phrase, are all "free" units that clearly possess some constancy of meaning. Beginning with the morpheme the units of linguistic analysis are all intrinsically trivial stimulus patterns that have acquired meaning. They are, in fact, signs.

The buzzer of the conditioning experiment is also a sign since it has an acquired ability to evoke some response. If the training sessions are conducted in widely varying circumstances the response evoking powers of the buzzer will become reliable and independent of situational variations. The time of day, brightness of the lights, position and movements of the experimenter will not interfere with the response. It is similarly true that those words which are used in varying contexts with a relatively invariant designation will acquire stable lexical meanings. The zoologist can formulate many sentences in many lecture halls using the word 'vertebrate' and it will possess much the same meaning in every instance. The relative constancy of signification manifested by the signs of language is also apparent in the conditioned stimuli of the psychological laboratory.

The Syntactical Requirement.—Morris observes that the signs of a language are combinable in some ways and not in others in order to form a variety of complex sign processes. From any sentence (as complex sign process) we obtain many meanings not described in the dictionary definitions of the lexical items. Words in combination yield structural meanings which are signalled by the devices of grammer. Professor Fries [56] illustrates structural meanings occurring in the sentence "The man gave the boy the money":

We are told that the 'man' performed the action, not the 'boy'; we are told that only one man and only one boy are involved; we are told that the action has already taken place, it is not something in process, not something planned for the future; the information is given to us as a statement of fact, not something that is questioned, nor something that is requested. Such meanings constitute what we shall call the *structural meanings* of the sentence.

These meanings are signalled, as Fries has shown, by the highly complex cues identifying the "form class" or "function class" of the words in a sentence.

There are, in addition, the unsystematic variations in meaning that are a function of nonverbal context. The meaning of 'this dog' or 'that building' might depend upon an actual dog or building within sensory range. 'The president' conveys a meaning that varies from nation to nation and from one year to another. These variations are not part of the linguistic meaning of a sign. They shade off into what Fries has called social cultural meanings and also into what the psychologist knows as personal meanings. There are both conscious and unconscious varieties of personal meaning.

Of course, contextual (verbal and nonverbal) variation in the significance of stimuli is not limited to language. We have already seen that the sounds to which an animal is variously conditioned may be made up of different combinations of the very same frequencies. In such a case meaningless elements are put together to produce meaningful wholes. The parallel case in language is the combination of phonemes into morphemes. However, the syntactical requirement does not refer to stimulus patterning at this level. In a language "signs are combinable so as to produce complex sign processes." Signs are units that have meaning when they occur as verbal isolates. They enter into patterns which retain something of the former meanings (the lexical requirement) but which also yield additional meaning (the structural requirement).

With a few notable exceptions American experiments on conditioning have neglected the problems of configurational conditioning which are most relevant to linguistic structure. There is, however, an extensive output from the laboratories of Pavlov, Bekhterev, Krasnogorski, and Beritov. Professor Razran [57] has summarized and contributed to this important literature. There is no doubt that some animals can be conditioned to make one response to a pattern of stimuli and another quite different response to an individual component of that pattern. The stimuli may be patterned either simultaneously or sequentially. In an experiment from Beritov's laboratory, dogs learned to go to one feeding box upon the presentation of a compound of stimuli and to another box when individual components were presented. In some early work from Pavlov's laboratory dogs learned to respond to a particular sequence of tones in a manner different from their response to any other sequence of the same tones.[58]

The distinguished American psychologist, Clark Hull, has made room for the facts of configurational conditioning in his systematically developed behavior theory. The construct of habit strength, symbolized as $_sH_R$, is fundamental in Hullian theory. It represents the magnitude of tendency for a particular stimulus to elicit a particular response. How can such a theory explain the fact that a buzzer, when sounded alone, produces a response quite unlike that obtained when the same buzzer is sounded simultaneously with other buzzers? The same stimulus is present in both cases but the response differs. The answer lies in the definition of the stimulus. In the second postulate of his theory, Hull [59] says: "All afferent neural impulses active in the nervous system at any given instant interact with each other in such a way as to change each into something partially different. . . ." Reactions are elicited by central afferent impulses—that is, by stimuli as modified by neural interaction. In this way Hull accepts the contention of Gestalt theory that we respond to configurations of stimuli and, at the same time, retains a working model having a single response to each stimulus.

In the avoidance learning experiment that we have used in a previous section, animals learned to respond with fear to a buzzer that warned of impending shock. Suppose they then learned to avoid the shock and turn off the buzzer in a variety of ways that changed with the total situation. In one kind of experimental box a wheel would have to be turned; and in a third a hurdle would be jumped. We might conceptualize these results by saying that the buzzer is a sign possessing an invariant meaning (fear of impending shock) but that it elicits different overt responses depending upon the situation in which it is sounded. It would then be tempting to identify the constant (lexical) element in meaning with the classically conditioned mediating response and the variable (structural) aspect of meaning with the overt instrumental acts. Such a conceptualization destroys the value of the experiment as a linguistic paradigm. As one reads a page of print there are structural variations in the meanings of lexical items but there may be no instrumental acts. The implicit mediating responses must be alleged to vary with the patterning of stimuli. It would be acceptable to say that the mediating response changes somewhat whenever the total stimulus configuration changes. We might prefer to say, with Hull, that the buzzer has different central effects in each experimental box. Each of these effects is then linked by training to an appropriate instrumental act. All the mediating responses evoked by the buzzer are fear—plus something else that is evoked by the situation in which the buzzer is sounded. The fear is the common element, independent of structure, the lexical meaning of the sign. The "something else" is the addition to the lexical meaning made by the particular context in which the sign occurs.

Linguistic structure poses no problems for conditioning theory so long as it simply requires that responses be learned to complex sign processes which are different from the responses learned to the component signs. These effects have been demonstrated and conceptualized. They are learned in accordance with familiar principles of selective reinforcement and extinction. The fact is, however, that linguistic syntax is more than simple contextual variation or stimulus patterning. Syntax possesses certain regularities; it is systematic. Systematic stimulus patterning can be illustrated with a study of Karl Lashley's called *Conditional Reactions in the Rat*.[60] The term 'conditional reaction' is, incidentally, to be preferred to 'conditioned reaction' in discussing linguistic learning, since the former term suggests that contextual dependency which is of the essence of language. Rats were presented with two cards and required to jump to one or the other. On the one card there was printed an upright triangle and on the other, the identical triangle was inverted. In the first stage of this experiment the animals learned to discriminate the cards (position was, of course, randomly varied) and jump to the upright triangle which was a sign of food. Twenty errorless trials were

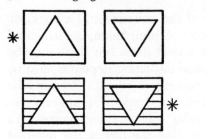

* indicates reinforced choice

required as a criterion of learning and the criterion was quickly reached.

In the second stage of the experiment the same figures were presented on a horizontally striped background. In the first twenty trials with this background the animals consistently jumped to the upright triangle, demonstrating the equivalence of the triangle on the new background to the training triangle. They were now trained to select the inverted triangle and avoid the upright, a reversal of the prior training. This required many more trials than the original task, but was eventually accomplished.

In a third stage the rats were sometimes exposed to the first pair of cards and sometimes to the second. They learned to respond appropriately in each case. To make a linguistic analogy that overlooks many differences [61] this performance is something like that involved in reacting to the commands "Come here" and "Don't come here." The approach reaction evoked by the first command is inhibited by the addition of the word 'don't.' In Lashley's experiment the upright triangle is approached when it appears on a plain background, but this approach is inhibited by the addition of a striped ground. Some question may be raised as to whether or not this is really a case of a sign showing contextual variations in the response it elicits. The words 'come here' are still identifiable units in the expression "Don't come here," but is the triangle recognized on the striped ground? May not the animals have simply learned to prefer one striped pattern to another and also to prefer one simple figure to another? The evidence that the triangle is not perceptually imbedded in the striped background is the manifestation of sensory generalization at the beginning of the second stage in training. Unless the triangle or some aspect of it was recognized on the striped ground it would be difficult to see why the rats began the reversed training with a consistent preference for the upright figure.

Linguistic structure makes possible great economy in the learning of language because of its systematic character. When we have grasped the significance of adding the word 'don't' to several different commands it will not be necessary to learn laboriously the effect of this word on every command in the language. We can generalize our learning and are, thus, able to understand immediately what is meant when the word 'don't' is added to any command with which we are familiar. When we have learned the significance of the plural ending '–s' or of the verb ending '–ed' we are able to understand what is meant when these elements are appended for the first time to familiar words. When we learn that a word belongs to Form Class I (the noun as functionally redefined by Fries) we know a great deal about the ways in which it can be combined with other words. Artificial languages like Ido and Esperanto maximize this economy by regularizing structure—plurals can all be formed in the same way, there need be no irregular conjugations, and form classes can even be identified with some common cue.

Lashley made a structural economy available to his rat subjects. He trained them on a series of problems in all of which cue values were reversed when presented on a striped back-

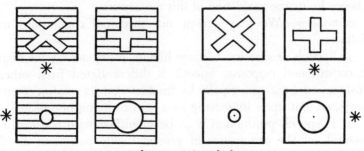

✳ indicates reinforced choice

ground. Had his animals learned this structural principle they would have been able to respond correctly on the very first trial after the background was changed. That they did not learn it was evidenced by the fact that a large number of trials was always required in the second stage of training before the response was appropriately changed. Apparently, this problem was too much for the rats. The experiments of Harlow [62] suggest, however, that chimpanzees are able to utilize an economy of a related sort.[63]

The structure of a language makes it possible for us to understand statements that we have never heard before and to say things we have never said before. This is a problem in the transfer of learning. It is not a matter of simple sensory generalization, of responding to a new sentence as we have responded to some equivalent sentence in the past. The response configuration, the total meaning, may never have occurred before. Presumably the stimulus interactions produced by the new sentence are reminiscent of a number of different past experiences and responses are transferred from these and somehow integrated with one another. As yet, however, we have no laws of afferent neural interaction, only the recognition that such interaction must occur. Sensory generalization follows continua of similarity that usually cannot be antecedently identified (which is one reason why problems of metaphor, physiognomic characters, and iconicity in general are so difficult). There is the possibility of describing linguistic structure within stimulus-response theory, but the incompleteness of all such theory limits the usefulness of this description.

Summary.—We may review our principal conclusions as follows:

1. Speech production is more like an instrumental act than a conditioned response. Speech is differentiated from other instrumental acts principally by the fact that its reinforcement is dependent upon its serving as a sign to living organisms.

2. If speech production is to be identified with the instrumental act the occurrence of grammatically patterned novel combinations of semantic forms remains to be explained.

3. The sign function or meaning is more like a classically conditioned response than an instrumental act.

4. If the sign function is to be identified with a conditioned response that response must be implicit.

5. If the sign function is to be identified with a conditioned response it remains to be explained how that response varies systematically with changes in stimulus patterning.

Chapter 4

ARTIFICIAL LANGUAGES

1. *Two Approaches to Formalized Languages.*—The essential property of a language or symbolic *system*, which serves to distinguish it from a mere collection of names, is that the meanings of combinations of symbols are determined by the meanings of their constituent symbols and their mode of combination. The significant and valuable feature of a language is that one who knows its vocabulary and syntax can understand sentences which he has never encountered before.

The artificial symbolic languages studied by logicians, mathematicians, and philosophers, which can be called 'formalized languages,' [1] must be distinguished from semiartificial languages,[2] like Esperanto, which have been proposed as international media of communication on nontechnical matters. They must further be distinguished from the result of adding abbreviational devices and specially coined scientific terms as appendages to natural language. However, an understanding of the importance of such specialized technical vocabularies will help us to understand the motivation for constructing wholly new symbolic or formalized languages. The words of ordinary language are notoriously vague and ambiguous, so the sciences achieve greater precision of expression by the introduction of special terms defined to have a single exact meaning. Moreover, the emotive suggestions or connotations of familiar words are often disturbing to persons interested only in their literal or cognitive meanings. The introduction of new terms whose usage is confined exclusively to the cognitive enterprise will free the scientific investigator from the distraction of emotional associations acquired by words in other contexts. A third advantage has to do with economy of expression. The scientist economizes on the space and time required for writing out his reports and theories by adopting special symbols to express ideas which would otherwise require long sequences of familiar words to formulate. More important, he reduces the amount of attention or mental energy required, for when a sentence or equation grows too long its sense cannot easily be "taken in." A good illustration of this type of economy is provided by the mathematical symbol for exponentiation. What is now written quite briefly as $A^{13} = B^9$ could previously have been expressed only as

$$AxAxAxAxAxAxAxAxAxAxAxAxA = BxBxBxBxBxBxBxBxB$$

or by a sentence of ordinary language instead of a mathematical equation. Similar advantages have been achieved by the introduction of graphic formulas in organic chemistry. Many scientific advances are marked by this type of symbolic innovation. But no matter how many special symbols are added to a natural language, the result is simply an *enlarged* or *supplemented* natural language, not an artificial or formalized language of the sort we wish to discuss here.

Perhaps the nature of these artificial symbolic languages may be explained most clearly after an explanation of how they came to be constructed. Two paths have led to the study of formalized languages, one by way of logic, the other by way of mathematics proper. Let us consider the logician's approach first.

Aristotle, the founder of logic, declared that ". . . its subject is demonstration . . . ," [3] and this view of the nature of logic has prevailed down to the present day. C. S. Peirce, one of the important founders of modern symbolic logic, wrote that ". . . its central problem is the classification of arguments, so that all those that are bad are thrown into one division, and those which are good into another . . ." [4] Alonzo Church, one of the most distinguished of contemporary logicians, has characterized logic by saying that it "investigates the structure of propositions and of deductive reasoning." [5] There is no disagreement among competent logicians about the nature of their subject. Granted that the aim of logic is to distinguish valid arguments from invalid ones, how has this purpose led logicians to investigate artificial symbolic languages? After all, propositions are not linguistic entities: since the same proposition can be formulated or expressed in various *different* languages, it is not peculiar to any of them. And an argument is usually defined as a collection of propositions of which one (the conclusion) is claimed to follow from the others (the premises), which are regarded as supplying evidence for the truth of that one. Arguments are not peculiar to particular languages either, for the same argument can be expounded in many different languages, and its validity or invalidity will be independent of the language in which it happens to be enunciated.

However, the *communication* of propositions and arguments requires the use of language, and this complicates the logician's task. An argument formulated in English, or any other natural language, may be difficult to appraise or evaluate because of the vague and equivocal nature of the words in which its propositions are phrased, the amphiboly of their constructions, the misleading idioms involved and, possibly, the exciting but deceptive metaphorical style. These are difficulties, but their resolution is not the central problem for the logician, for even when they are resolved, the problem of deciding the validity or invalidity of the argument remains. To avoid these irrelevant or peripheral difficulties, it is convenient to set up an artificial symbolic language, free of these defects, into which statements and arguments from natural languages can be translated. It must be admitted that in using an artificial symbolic language for the sake of appraising an argument formulated in a natural language, all these problems of interpretation must be resolved in the course of its translation. On the other hand, if a formalized language could be used for actual communication, with arguments stated in it directly rather than first being put in a natural language and then translated, problems of interpretation would simply not arise. The question of whether or not a formalized language *could* be used in actual communication will be discussed in a subsequent section of this chapter.

Formalized languages have been developed *by way of* the addition of special symbols to natural languages. The first steps in this direction were taken by Aristotle himself, who realized that validity is a *formal* property. To say that validity is a formal property is to say that if an argument is valid, every other argument having the same *form* must be valid also. For example, the syllogism

> All humans are mortal;
> All Athenians are humans;
> Therefore, all Athenians are mortal

is valid, and so is any argument which has the same *form*, such as:

> All reptiles are scaly;
> All snakes are reptiles;
> Therefore, all snakes are scaly.

Their common *form* may itself be represented by using letters or other special symbols, as, for example:

> All B's are C's;
> All A's are B's;
> Therefore, all A's are C's.

Hence it is economical and fruitful for the logician to deal with *argument forms* rather than to confine his attention to particular arguments. The use of letters for the sake of expressing the forms of propositions and arguments originated with Aristotle.[6] Modern symbolic logic has grown by the introduction and use of many more specialized symbols and abbreviational devices.

The formal nature of validity suggests a further value of the special symbolism. If a symbolism can be devised of such a sort that there will be a sensible difference (in shape or sound) between the formulations of valid arguments on the one hand and formulations of invalid arguments on the other, that symbolism will be of greatest utility to the logician. For it will relieve him of the need to *think* about the actual propositions involved in distinguishing between valid and invalid arguments, since he can differentiate between them on the basis of differences in their *formulations,* which are open to direct visual or auditory inspection. A concomitant utility attends the actual drawing of inferences, for an appropriate notation can be supremely useful in this connection. This sort of advantage is illustrated by the superiority enjoyed by Arabic numerals over the older Roman notation. Any schoolboy can multiply 148 by 47, while it is much more difficult to compute the product of CXLVIII and XLVII. As Alfred North Whitehead, one of the great contributors to the advance of symbolic logic, has remarked: "By the aid of symbolism, we can make transitions in reasoning almost mechanically by the eye, which otherwise would call into play the higher faculties of the brain." [7] For these advantages to be enjoyed, there must be certain rules according to which some expressions will be derivable from other expressions in virtue of their forms or structures or shapes, without any attention having to be paid to their meanings. These rules are not arbitrary, of course, or the project would be idle. What are desired are rules for manipulating symbols in such a way that an expression will be certified to follow by the rules as conclusion from certain other expressions taken as premises, if and only if the proposition symbolized by the one expression follows by a valid argument from the propositions symbolized by the other expressions. These "transformation rules" for expressions, as they have been called by Carnap and others, are formal or syntactical analogues of principles of valid inference.

It must be noted that there are no valid transformation rules which can be applied mechanically to natural languages. In English, for example, the obviously valid argument

> Men are mortal;
> Socrates is a man;
> Therefore Socrates is mortal

is aped by and structurally indistinguishable from the ludicrously invalid argument

> Men are widely distributed over
> the earth;
> Socrates is a man;
> Therefore Socrates is widely
> distributed over the earth.

Logicians have therefore separated their special symbolic apparatus from the natural languages of which it was first merely an extension, in order that it should constitute a "language" for which purely syntactical transformation rules would suffice to permit all valid and only valid inferences. Before giving a more precise characterization of the artificial symbolic languages which have resulted from this process, let us examine the somewhat different path by which mathematicians have been led to the same end result.

The *systematic* study of mathematics may be said to have begun with the Greeks. Before them the truths of geometry had merely the status of glorified rules of thumb for surveying and construction work. Euclid, whose *Elements* marks a high point in this development, systematized both the terms and the propositions of geometry. The terms were systematized by definitions; the propositions, by taking a small number of them as axioms and postulates, and deriving all the rest as theorems. It was formerly believed that the postulates were self-evident, necessary truths, and that the theorems, since they followed logically from the postulates, were necessary truths also, though perhaps not self-evident. But with the development of non-Euclidean geometries, it became clear that the truth or falsehood of the postulates and theorems was a matter of empirical fact rather than logical or mathematical necessity. The *mathematical* aspect was the systematization of those propositions in the form of a *deductive system*. The mathematician asserts neither the postulates nor the theorems; he asserts only that the theorems follow logically from the postulates, so that *if* the postulates are true, *then* the theorems must be true also.

The development of mathematics has seen a rise in the standards of rigor demanded for proofs or demonstrations. Euclid's own proofs do not measure up to present-day standards of rigor; indeed, an error can be found in his very first proof. The flaw in his proof, paradoxically enough, was the result of his knowing too much about his subject, so that his conclusions did not depend upon his premises alone, but upon what might be called his geometrical intuition.[8] Where a chain of argument involves familiar notions, there is always the danger of assuming more than the explicitly stated premises warrant. This is particularly serious in the development of a deductive system, for any attempted systematization which introduces new and unacknowledged hypotheses in the demonstrations of its theorems thereby *fails* to achieve its aim. In a deductive system the theorems must be derived or deduced *rigorously* from the original postulates. If they are not, however true they may be, the result is not a system but a mere collection or catalogue of propositions.

Lapses from rigor are most often occasioned by too great familiarity with the subject matter being discussed. To achieve greater rigor, then, mathematicians have found it helpful to minimize or eliminate that familiarity. In the case of geometries, this is accomplished by abstracting from the meanings of such geometrical words as 'point,' 'line,' and 'plane,' and developing the theorems as purely formal consequences of the postulates. The familiar geometrical words, with all their associations and suggestiveness, are replaced by arbitrary symbols. Instead of deductive systems explicitly and avowedly concerned with geometrical entities, mathematicians today develop *formal* deductive systems whose primitive or undefined terms are arbitrary, uninterpreted symbols, usually letters of the Greek or Latin alphabets. Since the undefined terms of a *formal* deductive system are arbitrary symbols without any interpretation or literal significance, the postulates are not statements or propositions at all, but mere *formulas*. As has already been remarked in our reference to the valid argument form

> All B's are C's;
> All A's are B's;
> Therefore all A's are C's

it is possible to deduce some formulas as theorems from other formulas assumed as postulates. Since 'A' and 'B' are without the connotations of 'point' and 'line,' the investigator is freed from the temptation to follow his intuition and assume more about his terms than the postulate formulas assert.

More than rigor is gained by the formal development of deductive systems. Since the symbols of a deductive system are uninterpreted, it may be possible to give them different, alternative interpretations. And since the theorems are formal consequences of the postulates, any interpretation of the arbitrary symbols which makes the postulates true will of necessity make the theorems true also. The additional advantage of *generality* is thus gained. An example may help to make this clear. Given some knowledge about astronomy, it might be desirable to set up a deductive system for the subject. To avoid the errors into which familiarity with the subject matter may lead in deducing theorems from the postulates chosen, the system may be developed *formally*. Instead of taking, say 'stars' and 'planets' among the undefined terms, one may take 'A' and 'B.' The postulates and theorems will contain these symbols, and when the system is developed, all its formulas may be interpreted by letting all occurrences of the symbol 'A' designate stars, and all the occurrences of the symbol 'B' designate planets. Now, if the postulates are *true* when so interpreted, the theorems will be true also, and the formal system with this interpretation will constitute a science or deductive system of astronomy. But it may be possible to find a *different* interpretation of the symbols 'A' and 'B' which also makes the postulates true and hence the theorems also. The formulas of the system might be made into different, but equally true statements by letting all the occurrences of the symbol 'A' designate atomic nuclei, and all the occurrences of the symbol 'B' designate electrons. Could this be done (and at one stage in the recent history of atomic physics it seemed highly plausible), the original formal system with this second interpretation would constitute a science or deductive system of atomic physics. Hence developing a deductive system formally, i.e., not interpreting its undefined terms until after its theorems have been derived, not only helps achieve rigor in its development, but also achieves greater generality through the possibility of finding alternative interpretations for it. This advantage is often realized in pure mathematics. For example, the same deductive system suffices to characterize both the points of the linear continuum and the real number system, and this is the theoretical foundation of that branch of mathematics called analytical geometry.

From the mathematician's point of view, apart from freedom from contradiction, rigor is the essential characteristic of a deductive system. It is for the sake of rigor that arbitrary rather than familiar symbols are taken as undefined or primitive terms, and the system developed *formally*. Listing all the undefined terms clearly, and stating all the postulates used as premises for the theorems explicitly, will help to specify which formulas are to be esteemed as theorems and which are not. With the increased emphasis on rigor that characterizes the modern period, however, critical mathematicians have seen that this is not enough. To achieve complete rigor, more is required.

A system is rigorous only when its theorems are derived logically from its postulates. It has now been realized that however clearly its postulates are stated, a formal system will lack rigor unless the notion of *logical proof* or *logical derivation* is specified precisely also. All formal deductive systems which contain logical terms such as 'all,' 'some,' 'if,' and the like, in addition to their own particular uninterpreted symbols, depend upon "ordinary logic" for their development. They *assume* logic, in the sense that their theorems are supposed to follow *logically* from their postulates. But they do not specify what this "logic" is. Hence all deductive systems, whether of geometry or physics or psychology, contain concealed assumptions which are not explicitly stated as postulates. These hidden presuppositions are the rules or principles of logic appealed to in constructing proofs or derivations of theorems. This means that all such deductive systems fall short of complete rigor, for not all their presuppositions are acknowledged. Their developments are not entirely rigorous, but more or less loose. The question naturally arises: how can this looseness be eliminated, and greater rigor achieved? The answer is obvious enough: a deductive system will be developed more rigorously by specifying not only what postulates are assumed as premises in deriving theorems, but also what principles of inference can be used in the derivations. The postulates must be supplemented by a list of valid argument forms, or principles of valid inference. It would be unsystematic—and probably impossible—simply to list or catalog *all* required rules of logic or valid modes of inference. A deductive system of logic itself must be set up. Such a deductive system will have deduction itself as its subject matter. A system of this type must differ from the ordinary, less formal, variety in several important respects. Since its subject matter is deduction itself, the logical terms 'if,' 'and,' 'or,' 'not,' and so on, cannot occur in it with their ordinary meanings simply assumed. In their stead must be uninterpreted symbols. And the logical principles or rules of inference that are assumed for these symbols should be few in number, so that they may be explicitly stated.

Thus, by different paths, both logicians and mathematicians have been led to the construction of artificial symbolic languages, or "logistic systems," as they have been called. A logistic system will contain no words of ordinary language, but will contain a basic vocabulary of symbols of different categories (which must be distinguishable formally or syntactically, i.e., without regard to their intended interpretations). Certain combinations of these symbols are characterized (again syntactically) as being "well-formed" formulas: these are formulas which on the intended interpretations of their constituent symbols will be (or are expected to be) meaningful or significant, i.e., they will assert propositions. The syntactical characterization of "well-formed formula" is given by means of *formation rules*. In addition, certain *transformation rules* are stated by which some well-formed formulas can be inferred, in a completely formal fashion, as conclusions from other well-formed formulas taken as premises. These transformation rules are selected so that on the intended interpretation every "syntactical inference" drawn by their means will be a valid inference, that is, when the well-formed formulas are made true or false by their being interpreted, no false conclusion will be alleged to follow from true premises by the transformation rules of the logistic system. Finally, of course, some of the well-formed formulas of the system will be singled out as postulates, and all well-formed formulas which can be derived from the postulates by the transformation rules will be called theorems.[9]

2. *The Philosopher's Interest in Formalized Languages.*—
The primary purpose for which formalized languages have been constructed is to aid in the codification and study of the principles of valid inference. There are, however, other purposes for which philosophers have recommended the construction and study of formalized languages. Ordinary language, that is, natural language, has been criticized by many philosophers on the grounds that it is very misleading, so that its uncritical use leads to philosophical as well as other kinds of errors. On the whole, this attitude is more characteristic of modern philosophers than classical or medieval thinkers. Thus the founder of modern philosophy, Descartes, complained in his second Meditation: "Words often impede me and I am almost deceived by the terms of ordinary language." And Berkeley's opinion was that "most parts of knowledge have been so strongly perplexed and darkened by the abuse of words, and general ways of speech wherein they are delivered, that it may almost be made a question whether language has contributed more to the hindrance or advancement of the sciences." [10] One contemporary writer has formulated the same view by saying that "the English language, as now used by philosophers, offends by provoking erroneous metaphysical beliefs." [11] The implication is fairly clear. If philosophers are to escape what have been called "the blandishments of grammatical analogy" of natural language [12] they must do their philosophizing either in, or with reference to, an artificial symbolic language which shall be less misleading than natural languages are.

Perhaps the strongest evidence that can be marshalled for this view is provided by the logical paradoxes. In natural languages, at least those which are standard average European, explicit contradictions can be derived by apparently unobjectionable inference from apparently unobjectionable premises.[13] Apparently unavoidable in ordinary language, the logical paradoxes cannot be derived in any of the various formalized languages which are currently employed, even those in which the whole of the theory of sets (or classes) can be established. There is no single method by which all current formalized languages avoid these paradoxes, but there are many different methods, some of which involve restrictions on *formation* rules, others restrictions on *transformation* rules. Obviously then, natural languages have important defects from which artificial languages are free.

Other errors can be attributed to peculiar morphological features of natural languages. In English, the true statements 'men are fallible,' and 'men are numerous,' have exactly the same structure. There is a temptation to infer that the facts asserted by them have the same structure also, and to believe that they can play analogous roles in argumentation. From the first and the additional premise 'Socrates is a man,' the conclusion 'Socrates is fallible' follows validly. But from the second, and the same additional premise, the analogous but ridiculous 'Socrates is numerous,' does not follow at all. In the usual type of formalized language, the two original propositions would be symbolized respectively as 'M $\subset$ F' (the class of men is a subclass of the class of fallible beings) and 'M ϵ N' (the class of men is a member of the class of numerous classes). The two expressions in a formalized language have quite different structures, and there is no temptation to draw invalid inferences of the type suggested above.

Philosophers have been quick to accuse each other of being misled by the vagaries of ordinary or natural language. Russell even coined a special term for this kind of mistake, calling it the ". . . fallacy of verbalism . . . the fallacy that consists in mistaking the properties of words for the properties of things." [14] Ramsey argues "that nearly all philosophers, including Mr. Russell himself, have been misled by language." [15] It might be urged that philosophers ought to know better than to be misled by the accidental characteristics of the language they speak. But it has been suggested that "almost all thinking that purports to be philosophical or logical consists in attributing to the world the properties of language." [16] Along this same line Peirce has quoted with approval Sayce's remark that "had Aristotle been a Mexican, his system of logic would have assumed a wholly different form." [17] Peirce adds that "it is lucky that Aristotle's only language was one that led him into as few errors as did the Greek." [18] If we agree that language and philosophy are so intimately related that the use of defective language leads to the formulation of an erroneous philosophy, then it seems reasonable to suppose that using an 'ideal' or 'logically perfect' language will lead to the construction of a philosophy which shall be free from error. This has been seriously proposed by some contemporary writers.

3. *Artificial Languages and Philosophical Issues.*—Around the beginning of this century, Russell wrote that "the study of grammar, in my opinion, is capable of throwing far more light on philosophical questions than is commonly supposed by philosophers." [19] And more recently he asserted: "For my part, I believe that, partly by means of the study of syntax, we can arrive at considerable knowledge concerning the structure of the world." [20] The path by which a study of language is supposed to yield knowledge about the rest of the universe is charted by what Russell regarded as "perhaps the most fundamental thesis" of Wittgenstein's *Tractatus Logico-Philosophicus*. Wittgenstein had written that if a certain sentence is to assert a certain fact, there must, however the language be constructed, be something in common between the structure of the sentence and the structure of the fact.[21] The linguistic program for metaphysical inquiry may be described as follows. Every fact has a certain ontological form or structure. For a given sentence to assert a particular fact, the sentence must have a grammatical structure which has something in common with the ontological structure of the fact. Hence, on the reasonable expectation that sentences are easier to investigate than the facts they assert, the examination of sentences will reveal metaphysical truths about the world.

There are, however, difficulties. Natural languages have misleading structures, and very different ones. Ordinary languages have many "accidental" features: the same fact may be asserted by sentences with widely different structures. Recognizing the sometimes pernicious influence of language, and at the same time persuaded that language analysis can be a valuable tool in philosophical inquiry, Russell was led to conclude that "common language is not sufficiently logical . . . We must first construct an artificial logical language before we can properly investigate our problem." [22] Wittgenstein too was concerned with this problem, writing: "In order to avoid these errors, we must employ a symbolism which excludes them, . . . A symbolism, that is to say, which obeys the rules of *logical* grammar —of *logical* syntax." [23] Russell explains that Wittgenstein was here "concerned with the conditions which would have to be fulfilled by a logically perfect language." [24] The relevance of constructing an artificial symbolic language which shall be "ideal" or "logically perfect" to the program for investigating metaphysics by way of grammar is clear. If we have a "logically perfect" language, then its structure will have something in common with the structure of the world, and by examining the one we shall come to understand the other. Thus an "ideal" language is a sufficient tool for this technique of philosophical inquiry. But it is also a *necessary* tool, for an imperfect language will have a misleading structure which will render unsound any inference drawn from *its* structure to the structure of the world.

The nature of such an "ideal" language has never been completely specified. But some clues have been given, such that its vocabulary must be neither vague nor ambiguous. More emphasis, however, has been given to morphology than to lexicon: an "ideal" language must be *logical*. Russell wrote: "A logically perfect language has rules of syntax which prevent nonsense . . ." [25] Wittgenstein pointed to the ideal of "language itself preventing every logical mistake," [26] and suggested that then current formalized languages constituted steps in the right direction, saying parenthetically that "the logical symbolism of Frege and Russell is such a language, which, however, does still not exclude all errors." [27] The essential feature of an "ideal" language is that its structure must "correspond to" or "mirror," in some sense, the ontological and logical structure of reality.

However, even if an "ideal" or "logically perfect" language could be devised, the proposed program for investigating the logical or ontological structure of reality by means of investigating the syntactical structure of an "ideal" language is impossible of fulfillment. For the project must have the following sequence: *first,* an "ideal" language must be set up, and *then,* through it, the metaphysical structure of the world is to be discovered. On this view, the construction of a "logically perfect" language is not an end in itself, but a *means* to the end of more general philosophical inquiry. But this program cannot possibly be realized, because the only way to tell of a given language that it is "ideal" is by comparing its structure with that of reality. For this comparison to be significant, we must have prior and independent knowledge of the structure of reality. A "logically perfect" language cannot be utilized as a *means* to philosophical inquiry, because no language could possibly be known to be "ideal," in the sense indicated, until after the completion of such a philosophical investigation. Surely no device can seriously be proposed as a *means* to an end, if the end must already have been attained before the device can be certified as the desired means. The proposed program involves a vicious circle and must therefore be rejected.

There is a quite different philosophical utility which has been claimed for artificial symbolic languages. As has been discussed in Chapter 1, there is a close connection between languages and philosophies, despite the fact that widely divergent philosophical systems can be expressed and argued in one and the same language. It has been suggested that a given philosophical doctrine can best be expounded by constructing a special formalized language which shall in some sense embody that doctrine. Then the adequacy of the doctrine can be shown by establishing that the language which embodies it is adequate to the formulation of all the truths which are known (especially scientific truths). There are two directions which this project takes, one pertaining more to lexical items, the other more to syntactical.

Two competing metaphysical doctrines which have some currency today are phenomenalism and materialism. In an older terminology, phenomenalism is the view that so-called material things, physical objects, are nothing but congeries of sensations; and materialism is the view that only physical objects exist, and that so-called mental phenomena are completely explicable and describable in terms of matter in motion. Contemporary discussions about these opposing doctrines tend to concern themselves with the languages which would most appropriately fit in with them. The phenomenalist claims that a language in whose lexicon *no* physical-object words occur would be completely adequate to describe the world, to formulate physics as well as psychology. On the other hand, the materialist claims that a language in whose lexicon *only* physical-object words occur (along with whatever logical symbols are needed) would be adequate to psychology as well as to physics. It seems clear that if either party could construct its promised langauge and establish its adequacy, this would establish—in some sense—the tenability of the philosophical doctrine espoused. But of course it would not establish the falsehood of the opposing theory. If one such language were established as adequate, but not the other, this would tend to settle the dispute, although not decisively. Unfortunately, however, both remain programmatic: neither party has as yet succeeded in constructing the artificial symbolic language whose adequacy would show the tenability of the metaphysical doctrine involved. It must be remarked, of course, that simply constructing the language is not enough. The problem is to show that the language, once it is available, is really adequate to describe the world. And to settle this question might very well require some prior agreement about the nature of the facts to which the language is supposed to be adequate. Of course this alleged difficulty might be evaded by an agreement such as considering only those facts which are scientifically established. This would beg no philosophical question.

The preceding example concerned languages whose connections with particular philosophical views are *necessary*, that is, logical rather than psychological. Not all connections between language and doctrines are of the logically necessary sort. A very interesting kind of connection is that which is merely psychological. We may say that there is a psychological connection between a language and a philosophical doctrine when users of the language are strongly tempted, or even predisposed, to accept that doctrine because of the structure of their language, even though they are not logically compelled to do so. Thus it has been claimed that standard average European languages, because of their subject-predicate grammar, lead their users to accept a substance-attribute ontology. The leading, of course, is psychological rather than logical, because process philosophies, as opposed to substance ones, have been formulated in Greek, German, French, and English (by Heraclitus, Hegel, Bergson, and Whitehead). Those who adopt a philosophical position which is different from the one psychologically implied by the language they speak may be motivated to construct an artificial symbolic language which shall be more congenial to their own philosophies.

As a modest illustration of this latter point, we may consider the philosophical problem of the "reality" of relations, not the problem of their Platonic existence as abstract entities, but rather the question as to whether any objects are or could possibly be related to each other. The denial of relations was one of the main pillars of the philosophy of F. H. Bradley. His argument against their reality can be paraphrased as follows. To say that one thing, a, is related to another thing, b, implies that there is a relation R between them. But for R to be between a and b means that a must be related to b, by relation R_2 say. But now there must be a relation R_3 between a and R_1, another relation R_4 between R_1 and R, and so on. Thus since the very notion of relation leads to an infinite regress, Bradley charged, relations cannot be real. Many objections may be made to this line of argument, but we wish to focus on the particular one raised by Bertrand Russell. He felt that Bradley was being psychologically influenced by English syntax to accept a false philosophical doctrine. Russell suggested that the trouble with Bradley's line of reasoning was that he conceived of relations in the same way he conceived of individual objects, and that he was led to this mistake by the fact that "words which mean relations are not themselves relations, but just as substantial or unsubstantial as other words." [28] Russell asserted further "that this single fact is at the bottom of the hopeless muddle which has prevailed in *all* schools of philosophy as to the nature of relations." [29] This peculiarity of standard average European languages is shared by all current formalized languages, and seems, in fact, to be a necessary property of every language whose complex expression are *linear* sequences of their simple symbols. In the usual logistic system, that a has the relation R to b is symbolized either as 'aRb' or '$R(a,b)$.'

Wittgenstein discussed the nature and representation of relations with great penetration, writing: "We must not say, 'The complex sign 'aRb' says 'a stands in relation R to b' "; but we must say, " 'That 'a' stands in a certain relation to 'b' says *that aRb*.' " [30] The suggestion is that the relation between a and b should not be represented by placing a term between their names, but rather by a *relationship of* their names 'a' and 'b.' Russell wrote that "in this respect a map, for instance, is superior to language, since the fact that one place is to the west of another is represented by the fact that the corresponding place on the map is to the left of the other; that is to say, a relation is represented by a relation." [31] Just as standard average European languages symbolize both individual objects and relations by the same type of symbol and thus suggest the Bradlean regression, so we may devise an artificial language which represents them differently and thus suggests the Russell-Wittgenstein view that relations do not involve any regression. Such a language must have a nonlinear syntax, of course. Consider a language in which proper names of individual objects are lengths of rope, distinguished by differences in color, or texture, or design, or length, or any one of the many different ways that suggest themselves. Since there are infinitely many different knots, both symmetrical and asymmetrical, which can be used to tie ropes together, we can use these knots to symbolize relations. Thus where rope$_1$ represents Socrates and rope$_2$ represents Plato, we can assert that Socrates was a teacher of Plato by tying rope$_1$ to rope$_2$ with, say, a sheet bend, which is an asymmetrical knot. Or we can assert that Socrates and Plato were contemporaries by tying rope$_1$ to rope$_2$ together by, say, a reef knot, which is a symmetrical knot. In such a rope language we should be able to express relations between things by means of relations between their names, as in a map, though without the restriction to geographical relations. In ordinary language there may be a temptation to wonder, with Bradley, what relates a relation to the objects related by it. But with respect to our rope language, there should be no temptation to wonder what connects a knot to the ropes in which it is tied. It seems plausible to suppose that there would have been less of what Russell called "muddle" about relations if philosophers like Bradley had used a rope language. To the extent that it is more conducive psychologically to the acceptance of relations as real, it would presumably be preferred by those who agree with the Russell-Wittgenstein doctrine. A question might be raised as to whether or not such a rope language could be developed to the extent that it would be adequate to the expression of more complicated propositions, but a discussion of this point would take us too far afield.

As has been suggested by the comparative study of American Indian languages and those characterized as standard average European, sufficiently different natural languages embody different views of the world.[32] The preceding examples of proposed artificial symbolic languages suggest that regardless of whether or not the Whorf thesis is true of natural languages, it certainly is true of artificial symbolic ones. The construction of a particular formalized language, then, cannot decide a philosophical issue: it is rather the case that one's prior acceptance of this or that philosophical position will determine what artificial symbolic language he will be led to construct and find congenial.

4. *Formalized and Natural Languages.*—There is a further application suggested for the construction and investigation of

artificial symbolic languages—the proposal to use them in the study of natural languages. This proposal which could prove to be of importance at least in theoretical linguistics has been very clearly stated by Alonzo Church, and we cannot do better than to begin by quoting his remarks in this connection:

Let us take it as our purpose to provide an abstract theory of the actual use of language for human communication—not a factual or historical report of what has been observed to take place, but a norm to which we may regard every-day linguistic behavior as an imprecise approximation, in the same way that e.g. elementary (applied) geometry is a norm to which we may regard as imprecise approximations the practical activity of the land-surveyor in laying out a plot of ground, or of the construction foreman in seeing that building plans are followed. We must demand of such a theory that it have a place for all observably informative kinds of communication—including such notoriously troublesome cases as belief statements, modal statements, conditions contrary to fact—or at least that it provide a (theoretically) workable substitute for them. And solutions must be available for any puzzles about meaning which may arise . . .[33]

The use of artificial symbolic languages as models for natural languages that Church proposes should not be confused with the use of the axiomatic method for the description or analysis of natural languages themselves, as attempted by Leonard Bloomfield in "A Set of Postulates for the Science of Language"[34] and more recently by Bernard Bloch in "A Set of Postulates for Phonemic Analysis."[35] Attempts to axiomatize nonmathematical areas are not uncommon: Spinoza's *Ethics* is a case in point. Too often, however, the attempts are made prematurely. Only those fields can fruitfully be arranged in the form of a deductive system in which considerable knowledge has already been obtained. The axiomatic method is primarily a method for introducing *order* into an already developed field. Euclid's own axiomatization of geometry was only possible on the basis of a highly developed body of geometrical knowledge and theory, going back through two or three centuries of geometers, certainly to Pythagoras, perhaps even to Thales. Where there is an insufficient body of knowledge to be ordered, the powerful but complicated machinery of the postulational-deductive method cannot profitably be employed, and the less formal, more ordinary scientific method of hypothesis and confirmation will be more useful. Examples of premature axiomatizations are those of Hull[36] and Woodger.[37] The writer's impression is that the general field of linguistics, and even restricted but still broad divisions within that field, e.g., phonemics, are not yet ready for axiomatization. Nothing is accomplished by simply listing all known results as axioms (or, as is sometimes erroneously done, as definitions) with but few if any theorems alleged to follow from them. The result is still a catalogue, whose items have been provided with mistaken and misleading labels. But to devise an artificial symbolic language as a model for this or that particular natural language is a much more modest and more promising activity.

An even more ambitious program can be envisaged, which will not confine attention, as Church proposes, to "informative kinds of communication." It is well known that language is used for other purposes besides the communication of information. Among the most important of these other, noncognitive functions of language are the expressing and evoking of emotions and the issuing of commands or requests, and semantical rules for these can be laid down. More generally, it may be possible to construct, as a model, an artificial symbolic language which shall be adequate to *any* function, cognitive or noncognitive, normally served by natural language.

Questions immediately arise with respect to this more ambitious program of using formalized languages as models in theoretical linguistics. One has to do with the possible utility for the science of linguistics of such a program. No certain answer can be given, of course, until after a serious attempt has been made. But the extent to which progress has attended the use of models in other areas of scientific inquiry suggests that their application in the field of linguistics can be similarly fruitful. Idealized models such as Carnot's engine in physics and molecular models in chemistry have had the highest utility in those sciences, and more recently the study of artificially organized and structured social groups has proved of value in social psychology. By analogy, the construction and investigation of artificial symbolic languages as models for natural languages can be hoped to yield valuable results in linguistics.

The feasibility of such a project may be questioned, however. It must certainly be admitted that linguists have little or no interest in those properties of formalized languages which have been most extensively studied up to now, such as consistency, completeness, and availability of decision procedures. But there are other properties which are possessed, to a greater or less degree, by natural and artificial symbolic languages alike. One of these is expressive power; another is that in any language only some combinations of symbols are admissible as significant or "well-formed." With respect to this last characteristic, the chief difference between natural and artificial symbolic languages is that for the latter, as now conceived, the rules which determine which sequences of symbols are well-formed and which are not are laid down in advance, once for all, while there are no such definitive rules for natural languages. An artificial symbolic language is constructed all at once, and the makers of such languages, being keenly aware that the admission of ill-formed expressions can lead to contradictions (as in the case of the logical paradoxes), insist upon having rules which, in a mechanical fashion, prevent such modes of speech as have led to difficulties in the past. As little as possible is left to the judgment of those who use the language. The situation is quite different for natural languages, which are governed by no antecedent rules, but are matters of traditional usage with occasional innovations to be expected. A great deal is left to the judgment of the users of a natural language, and any rules which may be formulated are merely descriptive of past usage, not prescriptive for the future. But this difference between them does not preclude the possibility of using a formalized language as a model in the study of natural languages. After all, the highly idealized models in the physical sciences are quite different from the actual phenomena which they are used to investigate: Carnot's engine, a closed system without friction, is invaluable in the science of real engines, none of which are closed systems and all of which are subject to friction.

The most salient differences between natural languages and those artificial symbolic languages which have been studied so far can be expressed as follows. Every formalized language is static, determined once and for all by the rules which define it. But a natural language is really a series or family of more or less different languages. There is a temporal series of languages all indifferently called "English." The earlier languages of the series have different lexicons than the later ones. Some words of the older member languages have become obsolete, such as the Old English *loppestre* for jumper.[38] Some words of the newer member languages have been borrowings, like 'toboggan,' borrowed from the American Indian, and some have been derived from proper names, either of actual persons like Captain Boycott, or of fictional characters like Chaucer's Pandarus. Modern English also contains recently *coined* terms like 'kodak,' 'chortle,' and 'blurb.' Some modern English words are derived from words of the older member languages, by one process or another, e.g., "Old English *bryd-guma* ['bry:d-, guma] 'bride-man' was replaced by *bride-groom,* thanks to the obsolescence of *guma* 'man.' "[39] Even where the same form occurs both earlier and later, there may be differences in meaning, as in the case of the word 'meat,' which earlier meant food generally, but which now has the narrower meaning of edible flesh.[40] The differences between the earlier and later languages of the series called English are not merely lexical. There are morphological differences as well. The older languages were more highly inflected, e.g., "in early modern English one still said *my friend: mine enemy.*"[41] And the methods of plural formation vary with time also, as in the older *eyen* and *shoon* for eyes and shoes.[42]

A natural language is not just a temporal series of different languages, for at any given time a single natural language may be a whole family of dialects, each of which is significantly different from the others both in lexicon and morphology. Bloomfield has remarked that "Dutch and German actually form only one speech-community, in the sense that there is no break between local speech-forms, but the extreme types are mutually unintelligible . . ." [43] The various definite languages which comprise a single natural language at a given time are determined not only geographically, but by the other factors as well. In discussing the latter, for the United States, Bloomfield writes:

> The most striking line of cleavage in our speech is one of social class. Children who are born into homes of privilege, in the way of wealth, tradition, or education become native speakers of what is popularly known as "good" English; the linguist prefers to give it the non-committal name of *standard* English. Less fortunate children become native speakers of "bad" or "vulgar" or, as the linguist prefers to call it, *non-standard* English. [44]

Thus, we see that a single natural language is in reality a whole family of distinct definite languages which differ from each other both temporally and spatially. Natural languages are dynamic, growing by gradual changes in their lexicons and by innovations in their morphological features. But even the dynamic aspects of natural languages can be studied by using formalized languages as models if we are willing to enlarge our concept of the latter. There is no reason why even the extension of vocabulary by way of metaphor cannot be permitted and actually prescribed for an artificial symbolic language. The crude rules of thumb for the construction of metaphors suggested by Aristotle in his *Poetics* [45] are susceptible of the same sort of extension and improvement as the discussion of inference presented in his *Organon*. This is merely a program for research, of course, but there seems to be no reason to suppose either that it could not be carried out or that it would not be of value in the study of language.

We may summarize our remarks in this chapter as follows. Artificial symbolic languages made their first appearance in the course of logical and mathematical investigations. Their value in such research has been established beyond question.

Some philosophers have urged their use in place of natural languages for purposes of philosophical inquiry. This suggestion was partly motivated by the realization that natural languages contain certain defects of a logical sort, as attested by the logical paradoxes which are derivable within them. Another motivation was the fact that some natural languages seem to lend themselves better to the formulation of one kind of metaphysic than another, so that those who use a given natural language are thereby predisposed to take a specific stand with respect to philosophical issues. Examination of formalized languages may point up more vividly the fact that some philosophical doctrines are more awkward, or psychologically more difficult to express in one language than in another, but this is equally well revealed in the comparative study of non-Indo-European natural languages. As for the alleged value of replacing philosophical disputes over metaphysical doctrines by disputes over which of two proposed languages is "better," this would seem to be a mere complication, since deciding between the alternative languages—if really relevant to the original problem—would seem to require exactly the same type of consideration, with no gain anywhere along the line. It is worth stressing again that "improved" languages which avoid this or that logical or metaphysical blunder are not a *means* to increased philosophical insight, but rather can only be constructed as a result of prior insight. Finally, not despite, but because of the striking differences between them, artificial symbolic languages might fruitfully be used by logically trained linguists as models in their study of natural languages.

Chapter 5

SOME ASPECTS OF LANGUAGE

I.

Most recent writers on the philosophy or psychology of language have attacked what they call the traditional theory of language, which they state in various ways, all generally resembling one another, and which they usually regard as going back from Wundt to Aristotle. Some have attacked this theory as mentalistic or nonnaturalistic or as involving metaphysical dualism. Others have attacked it on the lines indicated by Benjamin Whorf.[1] But another line of criticism, which is partly interwoven with these, may be described as arguing that the traditional theory represented too cognitive, too intellectual, too theoretical a conception of the nature and function of language. Sometimes it did recognize that language is used to express feeling, but on the whole it stressed the fact that language is used to communicate thought and information. Its entire semiotic, to borrow Morris' term, reflected this emphasis. Attention was concentrated on the conceptual content of language, and on the indicative or declarative sentence. There was little recognition of emotive content, of other kinds of sentences, or of noncognitive uses of language. As against this, recent authors—anthropologists, literary critics, linguists, psychologists, and philosophers alike—have been insisting that language is not primarily an instrument for the communication of thought or for the expression of belief, and they have put forward a putatively very different and more adequate semiotic.

The drift of this recent discussion may be indicated as follows. Back in 1927, Mrs. DeLaguna quoted Wundt, Sweet,

Whitney, Paul, Tylor, Wissler, Russell, and Sapir as examples of the traditional theory.[2] Today it would be much harder to find important examples. The movement of thought can be illustrated by the case of Sapir. On the basis of *Language* (1921) he could be regarded, with some, but not with complete, justice, as a proponent of the traditional theory.[3] But in his subsequent papers, besides anticipating Whorf, he emphasized the *expressive* as against the *referential* aspect or function of language and even suggested that the former is psychologically and genetically primary.[4]

There have been, roughly speaking, two stages in the development of the more recent theory. In the first stage, which was dominated by Ogden and Richard's *The Meaning of Meaning* (1923) and supported by logical positivism, people recognized various species of meaning or use of language, but put them under two general headings: (1) the scientific, descriptive, representative, referential, denotive, cognitive, etc., kind of meaning or use, and (2) the emotive, expressive, noncognitive, etc., kind of meaning or use. Since this theory centers in the notion that language has two sharply distinct sorts of meaning or function, we may call it "linguistic dualism."[5] It was characteristic of most of its proponents to put poetic, ethical, metaphysical, and religious utterances under the emotive use of language, thereby disposing of them for all cognitive purposes. In the second stage, not sharply divided chronologically from the first, but on the whole more recent, this "dualism" has been subjected to criticism or at least modification. Sometimes the change has been in the direction of a kind of "linguistic monism," though not one along traditional lines; sometimes in the direction of a kind of "pluralism"—by Dewey, Morris, Kaplan, Black, Empson, Segerstedt, Toulmin and Baier, Urban, and others. Some of these critics have been impelled simply by an interest in a more adequate semiotic theory; others by a concern for aesthetics and the arts, or for ethics, or for metaphysics, which the "dualists" seemed to be relegating to limbo.

It is our purpose to discuss this topic of the cognitive and noncognitive aspects of language somewhat independently, but taking full account of the literature just mentioned. We shall first distinguish a number of aspects or features of linguistic utterances which seem relevant to this topic, and then, in another chapter, ask which of them are cognitive and which noncognitive. In our discussion we shall avoid as much as possible using the ambiguous and vague word 'meaning,' even though it does indicate the subject-matter we shall be dealing with better than any other term. We shall not consider "prelinguistic" cries, etc., but only properly linguistic utterances, including conventional expressions like 'ouch!' and sentence-words like 'Fire!' And, since the sentence, if we include the sentence-word, is generally agreed to be the unit of linguistic utterance, we shall concern ourselves with sentence-utterances primarily. Sometimes, however, we shall also deal with word-utterances, because the meaning and use of a sentence are linked with the meaning and use of its constituent words. It will not always be convenient or necessary to distinguish between words and sentences, even though, as we shall see, some points hold for the one that do not hold for the other (a fact which is too often neglected, e.g., by Empson, and sometimes overplayed, e.g., by Russell and Segerstedt).[6]

In considering linguistic utterances, it must be constantly remembered that they occur in a context, with a certain intonation, and that this context and intonation are essential to their analysis or interpretation. Thus, whenever in the following paragraphs a linguistic utterance is taken as an example, one must always supply imaginatively some appropriate context and tone of voice in which it might occur, else the discussion is certain to go awry.

II.

With this preface, consider such sentences as the following:

(a) The janitor is coming.

(b) Thy judgments are a mighty deep.

Taking them as uttered in some normal context, and remembering that two parties are involved, a speaker and a hearer, we may say a number of things which are relevant to our present topic.

1) First, each has a *primary conceptual content,* which it is taken to symbolize by both speaker and hearer, namely the thought of the janitor's coming or of the profundity of God's judgments. By 'primary conceptual content' here is meant the complex of concepts, ideas, or images, which is in some way essential to an English-speaking person's understanding of the sentence in question in its context. By saying that it is symbolized by the sentence is meant only that it is referred to by the sentence. In other words, the speaker formulates and presents the content in the sentence, and it is evoked in the hearer by the sentence if communication is successful.[7] It happens that in (a) and (b) the content is also asserted to be true, but this is a further point, as we shall see. We must distinguish between the mere presentation of conceptual content and its assertion. All that is necessary for a sentence to be referential, or to have a sense, or to have symbolic reference, is that it have or present a conceptual content, whether it is assertive or not—a point well made by Black but neglected by Ogden and Richards and others.[8]

The conceptual content symbolized by a sentence such as (a) has been called a proposition, an objective, a descriptum, a possibility, a conceptual complex, and the like. Calling it a proposition brings in the notion of assertion and a claim to be true, which we wish to avoid just now, and on the whole the phrase 'conceptual content' seems least objectionable for our purposes.[9]

The conceptual content of a sentence, it should be noted, is partly a function of the lexical meanings of the words composing it taken separately, as is clearly the case in (a). But it is not entirely a function of these; it also depends on the structure of the sentence, so far at least as the structure is not used to distinguish asserting from commanding, and the like. The conceptual content of 'The noble hound hath slain the wolf' is different from that of 'The wolf hath slain the noble hound,' even though it is impossible to tell which is presented by Scott's line:

The noble hound the wolf hath slain,

when taken out of context. But the conceptual meaning of a sentence is dependent also on what Richards calls "the inter-animation of words." As he puts it:

> When Octavius Caesar is gazing down at Cleopatra dead, he says,
> She looks like sleep,
> As she would catch another Antony
> In her strong toil of grace.

'Her strong toil of grace.' Where, in terms of what entries in what possible dictionary, do the meanings here of *toil* and *grace* come to rest?' [10]

Intonation, stress, and the like, are also important in the presentation and understanding of the conceptual content of a sentence. Suppose that A, hearing footsteps in the hall but not looking, says, "The janitor is coming," and that B, looking into the hall, sees the president of the university coming. Then B's reply might well be, "The *janitor* is coming?" with a guffaw, and A would take this to mean that someone who was definitely *not* a janitor was approaching. This illustration shows that, even in a nonmetaphorical utterance, the primary conceptual content is not always the dictionary meaning, since a set of words may have different primary conceptual contents in different occurrences when the dictionary records no corresponding ambiguity in any of the words involved.

But while the conceptual content does depend in part on the structure and intonation of the utterance, it does not vary with grammatical mood. Take the following sentences:

(c) The janitor is coming!

(d) Is the janitor coming? The janitor is coming?

(e) Come, janitor!

(f) Would that the janitor would come!

These sentences, and (a), all present the same conceptual content, viz. that involved in the thought of the janitor's coming. As R. M. Hare has put it, they all have the same *descriptive* meaning and involve the same *descriptor,* but differ in *dictive* meaning and involve different *dictors.*[11] This, however, brings us to another topic.

2) To consider a second aspect, besides presenting their

conceptual contents, our sentences (a) and (b) also assert these contents to be true, as we have already noticed. So does (c). But sentences (d)–(f) do not. They do not merely present their conceptual contents, but neither do they assert their truth or express a belief in their truth. They do something else; they ask if the conceptual content is true, or wish that it were or something of the sort. The point is that a sentence ordinarily presents a conceptual content and at the same time expresses some attitude or state of mind with respect to this content— belief, interrogation, wonder, desire, or the like—"propositional attitudes" they have sometimes been called. Thus, we have the various kinds of sentence recognized by grammar: indicative or declarative, interrogative, imperative, optative, vocative.

Something about a sentence, then, serves as a clue to its character and shows that it is assertive, interrogative, or whatever the case may be. This is what Hare calls the dictive element or dictor. It may be a word—what Fries calls a "function word" [12]—or other lexical item, but it may also be a structural element, or the intonation, or simply the context, which serves as such a clue. Compare, for example, (a) and the two sentences under (d). It is important, in any case, to note that mere grammatical form does not suffice to tell us what the real character of a sentence is. A rhetorical question such as 'Who cares?' is really an assertion that no one cares. A sentence like 'The janitor is coming,' depending on the situation and the tone of voice, may be indicative, interrogative, imperative, or optative. According to Carnap, the sentence 'Killing is wrong,' is a command; according to Russell, it is a wish; according to Ayer, it is an exclamation or interjection; for none of them is it an assertion, as it is grammatically.[13] They may be mistaken, but this cannot be shown by an appeal to grammatical form alone.

Of course, our sentences not only express the propositional attitudes of the speaker, but tend to evoke such attitudes in their auditors.

3) So far we have seen that a sentence-utterance may present (and evoke) a certain primary conceptual content and express

(and evoke) a certain *propositional* attitude with respect to it. But they also may, and frequently, if not always, do, present and evoke a *secondary conceptual content* or *Nebensinn*, consisting of concepts, images, and thoughts which are no strict part of the meaning of the sentence to a user of standard English, or whatever the language involved may be, but which have become associated with the words used or with the sentence itself. This *Nebensinn* is part of what some writers call "connotation," though it does not belong to what Mill and other logicians refer to by this term, which is closer to our primary conceptual content.

For example, sentence (a) may be accompanied by images of the janitor of the first apartment house one lived in, (b) by memories of looking down from the deck of an ocean liner, or of the contents of a recent nonfiction best-seller, or by the thought of a "briny deep," etc. It is clear that such associated conceptual contents will vary greatly from person to person, but a certain association may be more or less standard among members of a culture, e.g., most of us would think of a janitor as being relatively poor and not very well-dressed, although it is not part of the definition of a janitor. It is such standard associations in which we are now primarily interested.

Here, I should think, is where we may put most, if not all, of what Empson refers to as the "Implications" of a "complex word." [14] For he says that "the usual as well as the logically necessary properties of the referent will tend to appear among the implications of the word," so that we "can treat 'quadripedal' as an Implication of the word cow." A "merely private fancy," he adds, "would be called an *Association* of the word," and, of course, comes under our present heading. Where to put "the logically necessary properties of the referent," which for him are Implications, is not so clear. Empson thinks that "quadriangular" is an Implication of the word quadrilateral and not a part of its Sense, apparently because, although a quadrilateral necessarily has four angles, we need not attend to this while mentioning one. In our terms, should this kind of an Implication be included in the primary conceptual content of an utterance or in its secondary conceptual content? Perhaps the answer is that it depends on what one is doing, logic or rhetoric. It may also be that we need a third category.

The question of metaphor is interesting here. Contrast, for instance, sentence (b) with sentence (a). One may say that in (a) there is a primary conceptual content (the janitor's coming) which is directly or literally symbolized, but that in (b) there is a primary conceptual content (God's judgments being profound) which is symbolized indirectly or metaphorically. This account, however, is somewhat incomplete. For in (b) there are two conceptual contents: the "thing-said" or "vehicle" (God's judgments being an ocean), and the "thing-meant" or "tenor" (God's judgments being profound, etc.). Now the latter is clearly a primary conceptual content of (b), and one may think that the former is a secondary one. But the two are not related as primary and secondary contents are usually related, since the first in this case symbolizes the second. We must say then that there are in (b) two primary conceptual contents, one being the vehicle symbolized by the words and the other being the tenor symbolized by the vehicle. There may also, of course, be secondary conceptual content; "the mighty deep" may suggest saltiness and storms.

In the case of other metaphors, such as "All the world's a stage," while one may distinguish vehicle and tenor, it is virtually impossible and perhaps pedantic to distinguish primary and secondary conceptual content, since many interpretations are possible, all poetically relevant. In so-called "dead" metaphors, on the other hand, the tenor has become the sole primary conceptual content and the vehicle has disappeared or become secondary content; for example, if in talking of the hood of one's car one thinks of an article of clothing at all, this will be simply as association.

4) This secondary conceptual content, or part of it, may also be asserted in a declarative utterance like (a) or (b). In propaganda, e.g., it is often asserted or at least suggested. In Empson's terms the assertion of the Sense of an utterance is or may be accompanied by the assertion of its Implications.

As he says, "many uses of *honest* imply 'brave' because honesty often requires courage," and presumably, in these uses, when we say that a man is honest, we are also saying that he is brave.[15]

What Empson says about the ways "in which a word can carry a doctrine" is also relevant here.[16] According to him, a word may contain an *existence assertion,* "which says that what the word names is really there and worth naming," e.g., the word 'God.' Thus, "if you go on talking about astrology without positive disclaimers people will begin to say 'He talks as if he really believed in it.'" The other ways in which a word can carry a doctrine involve an implicit assertion of an *equation* between different senses, or between a sense and an implication, of a word. Empson gives as an illustration the case of a Victorian matron saying, "You can't take Amelia for long walks, Mr. Jones; she's *delicate.*" Here, he says, 'delicate' has two senses, "refined" and "sickly," and the matron is implicitly asserting an equation between them, viz., "Refined girls are sickly."

It appears that primary and secondary conceptual contents may be distinguished in terms of the ways in which they are asserted, when they are asserted. Take the case just cited. The matron is not committed to "Refined girls are sickly," as deeply as she is to "Amelia is delicate," not because the former is only implict and the latter explicit, but because she will give up the one sooner than the other. It may be that there is always this sort of difference in the degree of commitment as between our two kinds of conceptual content, if there is assertion at all, and that they may be distinguished in this way.

Questions, commands, and other nondeclarative sentences may, of course, contain such implicit assertions too. Thus, sentences may express and evoke beliefs involving the secondary as well as the primary content presented by them. But presumably they may also express and evoke other "propositional attitudes" with respect to their secondary content, namely interrogation, wish, etc., just as in the case of their primary content.

Such sentences as (a) and (b), then, *present* a primary and a secondary conceptual content, and *express* some propositional attitude or other toward them. And it is necessary to note that what is presented and what is expressed by an utterance are not the same. There is, as G. E. Moore was one of the first to point out, "an important distinction, which is not always observed, between what a man *means* by a given assertion and what he *expresses* by it." [17] Moore's way of labeling the distinction here is marred by the ambiguity of the phrase 'what a man means.' Suppose B asserts sentence (a), and someone asks, "what do you mean?" B may answer, "I mean that the caretaker is coming" *or* "I mean that I think the janitor is coming" *or* "I mean that the meeting is over." All of these answers are proper and in the sense in which 'mean' is used in the second, there is no distinction between what a man *means* and what he *expresses* by an assertion. But Moore's point is correct, if we put it in our terms. What (a) presents is the conceptual complex "that-the-janitor-is-coming"; what it expresses is B's state of believing that this complex is true. It also asserts or states that the janitor is coming. But it does not assert or state that B believes he is coming; that B believes he is coming is only expressed, not asserted. In being expressed it may also be revealed to the hearer, as we shall see, but even so it is not part of what is stated, since it is not a part of the conceptual content of B's utterance.

In general, then, we must distinguish between what is presented, asserted, commanded, wished, etc., in a sentence-utterance from what is expressed. And we must distinguish sentences like (a), (c), (d), and (e) respectively, from sentences like

(g) I believe the janitor is coming.
(h) I am asking whether the janitor is coming or not.
(i) I command the janitor to come!
(j) I wish the janitor would come!

For the latter can be true (or false) when the former are false (or true) or neither true nor false. But we must not take this point without a grain of salt. For we do often, perhaps usually, use sentences of the latter sorts as substitutes for sentences of the former sorts. Thus "I wish the janitor would come!" may be simply a way of saying "Would that the janitor would come!", and an emphatic "I believe the janitor is coming" may be simply a way of saying "The janitor *is* coming." In such cases what has been said does not hold.

5) Besides expressing the speaker's beliefs, sentences (a) and (b) may also, and will ordinarily, *express* his *feelings* and *conative attitudes* toward the things talked about, the audience, etc. Thus Empson speaks of the "Moods of a word," which he describes as "a mixed class giving the hints of the speaker about his own relations to the person addressed, or the person described, or persons normally in the situation described." [18] In the same connection Richards talks about the "tone" of an utterance, by which he means its expressiveness of the speaker's feelings and attitudes toward his audience, his referent, or the world.[19]

It is obvious that the intonation of an utterance has a great deal to do with its expressiveness in this respect. 'Go to hell!' may express anger, disgust, hate, and even affection, depending on the tone of voice. Context and accompanying gestures are likewise important. This is also the place to mention euphemisms, pronouns of address like 'tu,' 'du,' 'vous,' 'Sie,' and other linguistic conventions by which a speaker indicates his attitudes, social class, and the like.

Here, again, we must remark that a sentence does not assert that the speaker has the feelings or attitudes in question, any more than it asserts that he believes what he says; it only expresses them.[20]

6) In addition to expressing emotions, utterances like (a) and (b) may be said to have an *emotional tone,* or value, consisting of emotions which have become associated with the words 'janitor,' 'mighty,' etc. Thus many writers have spoken of "emotive meaning," "emotional connotation," "*Gefühlswert,*" etc. Empson, for example, having found Senses, Implications, and Moods in words, goes on to find Emotions. The Emotions in a word are what is left in the way of "feelings" when Senses,

Implications, and Moods "have been cut out," and they are not simply the feelings expressed by the speaker. "The emotion in a word . . . is an extremely public object, practically as much so as the Sense; there is a presumption that anybody would feel it under the circumstances, rather than that the speaker feels it." [21] Of course, some of the emotions in words vary from person to person because of their divergent experiences, and are not thus public. But many words do carry the relatively standard emotions Empson speaks of—the emotional difference between 'murdered' and 'killed,' for instance, is relatively standard—and it is primarily these more public emotions which are referred to as the emotional tone of such words.

In (5) it was the speaker who was involved; here it is the hearer. In fact, we may describe the emotion in a word or its emotional tone in terms of the emotions which it tends to, or is disposed to, evoke in its hearers. But it should be observed that when a word has acquired this disposition or power to evoke emotion in its auditor, it may also be used to express emotion by the speaker.

7) We have seen that sentence-utterances express the state of mind of the speaker, his beliefs, attitudes, etc. This fact has a converse side, namely, that his utterances may *reveal* his beliefs, feelings, and attitudes to the hearer, intentionally or unintentionally. One can learn a great deal about a man from what he says, the fact that he says it, and the way he says it. If B says, "The janitor is coming," we infer that B believes the janitor is coming. He does not state that he believes this, but his utterance reveals that he does. If he says "God's judgments are a mighty deep," we learn that he is religious, though he did not assert that he was. In this way suspects may reveal very important information to detectives, patients to psychoanalysts, politicians to their opponents, and poets to readers.

Again, however, notice that none of the information thus gained about a speaker and his culture belongs to the conceptual content of his assertions, questions, etc. In their present capacity utterances act not as *symbols,* but as *signals;* they are not signs of the speaker's attitudes, nor do they mean them, in the way in which the word 'Rain!' is a sign of, or means, rain, but rather in the way in which dark clouds are signs of, or mean, rain, or a frown is a sign of concentration or disapproval.[22]

As in the case of conceptual content, primary or secondary, and of emotional tone, we must distinguish between what is private and what is relatively standard. An utterance of A's may reveal something to a friend who sees much of him which it does not reveal to another. Such special revelatorinesses are not linguistically important. But a certain utterance with a certain kind of structure and intonation in a certain kind of context may have a certain standard revelatoriness, that is, a disposition to reveal something definite to the average hearer in the community. Thus the indicative grammatical form is revelatory in this standard way—it tends to reveal a state of belief in the speaker. Another kind of intonation tends to mean (that is, reveal) a feeling of disgust.

The difference between what is expressed and revealed, on the one hand, and what is presented and asserted as secondary conceptual content, on the other, is not always noticed, and must be emphasized. Both may be described as what is "suggested" though not "stated," but there is an important difference. What is expressed and revealed is always some statement about the speaker, and this is only signaled by his utterance; it is not symbolized or asserted. What is presented and asserted as secondary content, however, is symbolized and asserted, not merely signaled, and it is not about the speaker but about the things talked about. Take Empson's case of the matron again. "Refined girls are sickly" is symbolized and asserted in a secondary way, not just signaled or expressed, and it is not about the matron but about girls like Amelia. What is expressed and revealed, however, is not that such girls are sickly, but that the matron believes they are and enjoys telling Mr. Jones that he can't take Amelia for long walks.

8) We may regard expression, evocation, and revelation as kinds of effect which an utterance may have on speaker or

hearer. But, of course, a linguistic utterance may have *other kinds of effect* too. It may even break glass by producing vibrations in the air. In any case it provides its hearers, including the speaker, with sensations of sounds or letters. If it is sudden and loud it may cause fear, and if it is sustained and monotonous it may produce sleep. It may also give pleasure aesthetically simply as being the pattern of sound that it is.

Effects of these additional kinds may be intentional or not, and must be noted here, but since they are effects which noises produced by the inorganic world may also have, are not important for our purposes.

Another, and more important, sort of effect which an utterance may have must be classified here. If A tells B that the janitor is coming, B may perhaps swear in irritation, or perhaps go to the door to meet him. Here the utterance, intentionally or unintentionally, has certain effects on B's feelings and actions solely by virtue of the information it communicates, given the situation and B's interests. Its having these effects, thus, presupposes its having conceptual content and revelatoriness (of belief), and is not of the same order as its expressiveness, revelatoriness, conceptual content, or emotional tone. Moreover, the effects are entirely relative to the situation and the interests of the hearer; there is nothing standard about them, as there is about an utterance's conceptual content, emotional tone, etc. With the same emotional tone, conceptual content, etc., the utterance might have a quite different effect on another hearer, for example, one who was having heating difficulties and wanted the janitor to come.

9) A sentence-utterance is on the speaker's part an act, a piece of behavior, a response to a situation. As such it has a purpose, use, point, function, or intention. This may be deliberate or impulsive, conscious or unconscious, express or ulterior, but at any rate, as Pepper has said: "A verbal judgment is a little purposive act of its own." [23] The purpose may be to communicate information, but it need not be, and recent writers on language have agreed in attacking the older view which

seemed to them to assume that language was primarily "the means of expressing or communicating ideas." This view, they hold, is sterile and mistaken, or at least inadequate. Speech, they insist, "is an essential activity of human life, fulfilling an indispensable function in the economy of life." "Speech is the great medium through which human cooperation is brought about . . . Men do not speak simply to relieve their feelings or to air their views, but to awaken a response in their fellows and to influence their attitudes and acts. It is further the means by which men are brought into a new and momentous relationship with the external world." [24] DeLaguna, Ogden and Richards, Gardiner, Malinowski, Dewey, Bloomfield, Morris, Segerstedt, Britton, M. M. Lewis, and many others have all written to this effect. To quote but one more expression of this newer philosophy of language:

> . . . it is agreed that language has many other purposes and many other effects besides that of making statements, such as expressing the speaker's feelings and emotions; arousing feelings and emotions in others and in himself; making others act in certain ways; enabling the slight awkwardness of strangers' meeting to pass smoothly into easeful social communion. . . ; being a beautiful or pleasant sound; and so forth. In most cases these other functions are vastly more important. It is a naivete to assume that language is primarily a device for making statements and that its other functions are mere minor concomitants; and much misunderstanding has in the past been created in philosophy and logical theory by that innocence.[25]

There are some points here which we shall want to discuss later, but in general the newer view seems well-taken, and is here accepted. But just now it is sufficient to remark that on any view, linguistic utterances will still have a purpose, even if it is only that of communicating information. And an utterance *has* or *serves* this purpose, it does not *present* it; i.e., its having this purpose is not part of what it says. It may *express* and *reveal* this purpose, but it need not. Having a purpose is not the same as expressing or revealing one. But, of course, the purpose of an utterance may be to present, express or reveal the purpose or purposes of the speaker or his society, as when I say, "I always aim to please" or "You talk too much!"

A note on our use of terms is perhaps desirable here. We are employing the words 'purpose,' 'use,' 'function,' 'point,' and 'intention' as synonymous, very much as Morris does.[26] There is a second use of 'function' with which ours must not be confused, namely, that of linguists like Bloomfield, according to which the positions in which a form appears are its functions, so that the form 'the man,' for instance, has the functions "actor, goal, predicate noun," etc.[27] Yet another usage of the terms 'function' and 'use' occurs in Ogden and Richards [28] and many other writers, when they speak of the referential or symbolic *use* or *function* of language. And, of course, we do in a sense employ a sound like 'table' to stand for, symbolize, or refer to, tables or the property of being a table. To do this, however, is to use a sound, not a word. Sounds are not words or language until they are given, or have acquired, some such employment, or, rather, some one of the powers or modes of efficacy to be described below. That is, to be a word a sound must be expressive, or have a conceptual content, etc.; and to use a word is to use for some purpose a sound which already has "meaning," conceptual, expressive, emotive, or revelatory.

The fact that the phrases 'having a use' and 'having a purpose' may mean either "has a purpose" or "has a 'meaning' or sense" seems to have led many writers to confuse having a purpose and having a conceptual content. The word 'meaning' may lead to the same confusion, for it may refer to the conceptual content of an utterance or to its function (or to what it expresses, etc.). Something of this confusion appears in the following discussion of the question, "Got a flat?": "Your question does not really mean that you are puzzled and are seeking to understand what is going on. The intent of the question is to establish a friendly relation between you and the driver of the other car. What meaning the question has is almost entirely a matter of tone." [29] It seems necessary therefore to do something here to establish the distinction between "meaning" in the sense of conceptual content and "meaning" in the sense of purpose or point.

The main consideration, probably, is that sentences with the same conceptual content can be used for different purposes. This is obvious if we are right in saying that sentences (a), (c), (d), and (e) all have the same conceptual content, for it is certain that these sentences may serve different functions. But, even if this is not so, it remains true that the sentence 'The janitor is coming' may serve different purposes without change in conceptual content. If one says it in one tone of voice it merely communicates information, for others to do with as they wish. If one says, "The janitor is coming!" it may serve to break up the meeting. It would of course be good English to say that it then "means" that the meeting should be broken up, but then we must still distinguish between its meaning in this sense, (i.e., its purpose) and its conceptual content.

Another consideration supporting the distinction in question is the fact that meaning (in the sense of conceptual content) precedes point. We may and do call linguistic utterances pointed or pointless, referring to their function. It seems clear that whether or not an utterance has a point in its context *depends on* its meaning (conceptual content), and that having a point and having a conceptual content are not the same thing. Suppose that A, who lives in an ordinary family house, says to his wife, as he walks out of his study for a glass of water, "The janitor is coming." She will be surprised or at least puzzled, but only because she first takes his sentence to have its ordinary conceptual content and purpose, and then realizes that it cannot very well have its usual purpose in the context, if it has its usual conceptual content. She may then say, "What a pointless remark!" Or she may infer that his point is simply to see what she will say, or to show her that he is still alive. Either way she is assuming that his meaning (conceptual content) is the customary one.

Of course, instead of saying, "What a pointless remark!" she may say, "What a meaningless (or nonsensical) remark!" and be speaking acceptable English. But then again we must separate meaning in the sense of purpose from meaning in the sense of conceptual content.

The fact that the pointed utterance of a sentence in a certain situation is a clue, and sometimes the only clue, to its meaning (conceptual content) is illustrated by the case of 'Business is business.' If we assume this to have a point or function in a discussion (besides just ending it) we must read into it a meaning other than the literal one, which is a tautology. For example, we may take it to say that business has its own autonomous code of behavior.

To summarize the discussion thus far, in the case of certain sorts of indicative, interrogative, imperative, and optative sentence-utterances (i.e., those of the sorts illustrated), it seems possible to distinguish a number of factors, each of which may be and has been referred to as the meaning or part of the meaning of the utterance. These are:

1) The primary conceptual content symbolized, i.e., presented and evoked.
2) The propositional attitude (with regard to this) expressed and evoked.
3) The secondary conceptual content presented and evoked.
4) The propositional attitudes (regarding this) expressed and evoked.
5) The emotions and conative attitudes expressed.
6) The emotional tone.
7) The emotions and attitudes revealed.
8) Other kinds of effects.
9) The purpose.

Mrs. Langer has maintained that we have in art, especially in music, symbols which do not merely express emotion in the "speaker" or evoke it in the "hearer" or reveal to the latter that the former is feeling it, which rather articulate emotion and present it to the "hearer" for his contemplation very much as an ordinary sentence-utterance articulates and presents conceptual content for contemplation.[30] This is an interesting and controversial view and will be discussed elsewhere in this volume,[31] but we may note here that, if it is true, we must extend our notion of language to include music and must add another aspect of language—and a cognitive one—to our list namely, the emotions presented.

Will the account we have given hold of all sentence-utterances? What of interjections and exclamations? Some such utterances are really prelinguistic, e.g., involuntary cries, ejaculations, shouts, and babbling. Even these are like linguistic utterances in that they *express* and *reveal* a state of the speaker's mind or organism, and may serve as "signals" to a hearer. But they are neither "symbolical" in meaning nor conventionalized in form and so may be disregarded here. Conventionalized forms like 'Ah!,' 'Oh!,' 'Hurrah!,' 'Booh!,' 'Damn!,' 'Hello!' are, however, properly linguistic; and here, it is true, one can hardly speak of some of the factors we have listed—primary conceptual content, and propositional attitude, for example. One can, however, still find expression, revelation, purpose, and effects. In some cases, such as the four-letter expletives which are better left unmentioned, we may also find emotional coloring and conceptual content. But some exclamations are more elaborate, for instance, (c) above or 'How white that wall is!' and here all nine of our factors are present again.

The same is true of sentence-words like 'Fire!' and of sentences in poetry and fiction; there is a question about the sense in which the latter involve assertion, but some kind of propositional attitude does seem to be present, if only a "willing suspension of disbelief." It would seem, then, that we are justified in holding that all kinds of sentence-utterances, with the relatively trivial exceptions just noted, involve the nine factors we have distinguished.

As for single *words* like 'janitor' and 'deep,' when they occur not as sentences ('Janitor!,' 'Deep!') but as parts of sentences, as they do in (a) and (b)—it is hard to see that they, by themselves, express propositional attitudes like belief and wish. Empson holds, indeed, that "words may carry doctrines," but it does not appear that he ever shows that single words by themselves do so. His existence assertions and equations always seem to depend on more than a single word—in fact to depend on the whole sentence. At any rate, he does nothing to show that single words always express propositional attitudes. The other seven features, however, do seem to belong to words as well as to sentences—e.g., conceptual content, emotional aura, function, etc. But words like 'janitor' have another feature which we do not ascribe to sentences—*denotation*. Here 'denotation' is used in its logical sense, following Mill. In this usage the denotation or extension of a term consists of the individuals, if any, which have the properties which form its primary conceptual content (connotation or intension). There is also a loose use of 'denotation,' according to which denotation covers *both* or *indifferently* intension and extension.[32]

We do not mean, in likening words and sentences, as much as we have, to deny Russell's distinction between the *meaning* of a word and the *significance* of a sentence, insofar as this is intended to stress the difference between what Fries calls the lexical meaning of a word and the structural meaning of a sentence, or the other differences between words and sentences which have just been noted. But Russell, and Segerstedt who follows him, also says that while words and sentences both have meaning (sic!), only sentences have purpose or intention. This is plausible, since the sentence is the unit of complete utterance, but neglects the fact that each word is in a sense selected as the sentence is formed, and so may be said to have a function.[33]

With some exceptions, then, we find that linguistic utterances, especially sentences, have, or at least may have, nine distinct aspects or features, of which eight are relevant to our topic. It would be desirable to have more rigorous definitions of them, and more adequate criteria for distinguishing them, than have been given above. But we cannot here present an entire system of semiotic, and can only hope that enough has been done to show that our nine factors must be recognized and dealt with in such a system, and in particular any discussion of "the uses of language" or of its "cognitive and noncognitive aspects." We may, however, give a brief systematic indication of the relations between our nine factors as follows.

As we have seen, a sentence-utterance may have effects of eight different sorts. But in each case, if the utterance is to have these effects, the sentence involved must first possess the power or disposition or tendency to produce such effects when uttered, e.g., to cause sleep, to express feeling, or to evoke thoughts, an utterance must respectively be monotonous, or expressive, or have a conceptual content. Thus we may say, on the one hand, that a given utterance may have effects of eight different sorts, or, on the other, that it may have eight different powers, dispositions, or modes of efficacy. Of these powers, some are possessed by an utterance simply in virtue of its own physical or sensible character, e.g., its monotony or its aesthetic quality. These come under (8). The others it has in virtue, not of its own nature, but of convention, usage, and past history. Those described in (1)–(7) are of this acquired kind. Symbolizing primary or secondary conceptual content and expressing belief, for example, are capacities which an utterance has, not *qua* sound, but as a result of its previous life or that of the words, structures, and intonations involved.

We may, then, regard our first eight aspects of language as modes of efficacy or powers of producing effects of certain kinds. Possessed of these powers linguistic utterances are like other actions or processes, human or nonhuman. They do something; they are among the powers of nature which an organism or group may employ, as is implied by the title of Segerstedt's recent book, *Die Macht des Wortes.* That words have a remarkable efficacy is the basis of the magical use of words by so-called primitive peoples, as has often been pointed out.

But also because sentences have the powers we have described in (1)–(8), their utterance in a certain context may have a use or function, that is, they may be uttered with the purpose, conscious or unconscious, of producing the effects they are disposed to produce. Having a function presupposes having or being thought to have some mode of causal efficacy— expressiveness, revelatoriness, emotive force, etc. The uses to which an utterance may be put are legion, but the purpose is always to produce an effect of some sort—to express one's attitudes, to convey information, to cause sleep, etc. The effect may be desired either for its own sake or for the sake of something ulterior. For example, the aim of an utterance may be to evoke belief or emotion for its own sake or in order to produce action.

Thus we see the relation of purpose to the other eight aspects of language. Taking them as powers, it presupposes one or more of them, and taking them as kinds of effects, it seeks to produce one or more of them. It should be noticed, however, that, like any other action, a verbal utterance may have effects which are not intended or fail to have effects which are intended. When Rip van Winkle, having slept through the Revolution, said, "I am a loyal subject of the king, God bless him!" his words had an effect not all of which was intended.

Segerstedt makes it a main thesis of this book not only that *Funktion* and *Bedeutung* are to be distinguished, as we also have argued, but that *Funktion* presupposes action, or serves to release feeling, or both. "This, however, presupposes that the words . . . have a meaning. Meaning is always a presupposition of function." [34] This dictum seems to mean that having a function always presupposes having conceptual content, primary or secondary. This is not true of some exclamations and interjections. These may perhaps be regarded as irrelevant because pre- or non-linguistic. But even in the case of conventional expressions like 'Alas!' and 'Oh, no!' it will be true only on the cognitive field theory to be discussed in Chapter 6. Function presupposes conceptual content only if the possession of each of the other modes of efficacy presupposes the possession of conceptual content, and this Segerstedt does not establish. What is true is that, when its function is not merely to produce effects of the sort listed under (8), a linguistic utterance can have and accomplish its function only if through convention and usage it has acquired at least one of the powers under (1)–(7). And sometimes this is all that Segerstedt seems to be asserting. This does not mean that there must always be some conventional usage which the utterance is simply following—else we should not have metaphor or irony. But even in

metaphor, for example, the vehicle must be symbolized in accordance with usage, even though it in turn symbolizes the
tenor in accordance, not with any convention, but with some
perceived similarity.[35]

III.

So far we have distinguished nine features of sentence-utterances, and said something about their relations to one
another. What we have done is partly based on, partly a
modification of, what has been said by a large number of
authors, of whom some have been mentioned. Therefore, it
seems appropriate now to make a few remarks, not at all exhaustive, about the views of some of these writers, in addition
to those already made. Since their views cannot well be summarized here, these comments must be somewhat cryptic.
Further discussion of some points will appear in the next section.

Most recent writers have recognized several of our nine
aspects of linguistic utterances, e.g., (1), (2), (3), and (6).
One of the most interesting discussions of (1), (3) and (6)
is by K. O. Erdmann.[36] Many have recognized and even dwelt
on the distinction between having conceptual content or reference and expressing states of the speaker's mind, and so have
spoken of the double nature of linguistic utterances, e.g., Ayer,
Russell, Marty, Sapir, Ogden, and Richards.[37] The most complete failure to notice this distinction is in Mill's *Logic*,[38] but
the difference is not explicitly observed even now by all writers
and is minimized by some who are aware of it.

Many authors, however, fail to distinguish at all clearly or
consistently between meaning (in the sense of conceptual content), function, and effects. This is true of Ogden and Richards.
True, they speak of five "uses" or "functions" of language—
symbolic reference, expression of speaker's attitude to his audience, expression of his attitudes to the things referred to,
promotion of intended effects, and support of the reference—
and these five contain several of our nine aspects. But they are
all indifferently called meanings, uses, functions, or effects. In

fact, the "dualistic" theory of language is usually represented by Ogden and Richards and their followers as holding that there are two sorts of meaning or use of words, without its being made clear whether this means two sorts of content, two sorts of function, or two sorts of effect. Even in Richards' later views he does not clearly enough make the necessary distinctions. Neither do Sapir or Malinowski in their otherwise very stimulating essays, nor, for that matter, Marty or Erdmann. Fries nicely differentiates between "linguistic meaning" (which includes "lexical" and "structural meaning") and "socio-cultural meaning." [39] But it would seem that the latter covers a number of different kinds of things which ought to be discriminated in any complete theory (though perhaps not for his purposes)— secondary conceptual content, emotional connotations, what is expressed, what is revealed, purpose, and incidental effects.

We have used Empson's very helpful "bits of machinery"— distinction between Senses, Implication, Moods, and Emotions, and his notion of "doctrines in words." But Empson does not take use or function as one of his bits of machinery, though it seems relevant to his general theme. In fact, he minimizes Morris' distinction between modes of signifying and uses of language, which roughly corresponds to ours between modes of efficacy and functions, on the ground that it is simply a recognition of the difference between the viewpoint of the speaker and that of the hearer. [40] Here he seems to be confused. The purpose of an utterance indeed falls on the side of the speaker, but the other factors do not all fall on that of the hearer. Thus his analysis is not adequate for our purposes, even if it suffices for his.

The most adequate discussions are those of Russell, Morris, and Segerstedt. [41] Of these we can only say something about Morris' *Signs, Language, and Behavior*. He recognizes nearly all of the features of language which we have discussed. Thus, he distinguishes denotation, signification, expression, function, psychological and physiological accompaniments, and effects. He is particularly emphatic about the need to distinguish the uses or functions of signs from their other aspects. But he labels the other aspects with which he deals "modes of signifying," and it is difficult to know what to include in or exclude from that heading. He includes five modes: the identificative, designative, appraisive, prescriptive, and formative. But he excludes expression and revelation (which he fails to distinguish), as well as emotional tone, which on our scheme can be regarded as co-ordinate with designation. His method of arriving at his five modes, moreover, is rather *a priori*, assuming among other things that evaluational and moral judgments are not designative. This may be true, but it needs discussion. It is in any case not easy to see what "mode of signification" appraisals and prescriptions have, if this is not designation (conceptual content), expression, revelation, or emotive force. One cannot help but wonder about Morris' conception of signification; it seems both too broad and too narrow. Morris then goes on to discover that for each of these modes, except the first, there is a use or function (information, valuation, incitement, and systematization), and this is just too fortunate a coincidence to be convincing. At any rate, one may regard his modes as hypostatized uses, and hence our account has taken somewhat different lines, substituting the notion of modes of efficacy for that of modes of signification. The treatment of evaluational and moral utterances is left for another occasion, on the assumption that they can be dealt with entirely in terms of the machinery here provided and do not require any special "modes" for their analysis, as Morris seems to think.

Chapter 6

'COGNITIVE' AND 'NONCOGNITIVE'

In the years which have passed since the publication of *The Meaning of Meaning*, semioticians have in various ways felt the need of refining the distinction between referential and emotive types of discourse and of disentangling the various features lumped together under the term 'emotive.' But until the foundations of semiotic were better laid, so that the modes of signifying and the various uses of signs could be isolated, little basic advance in the analysis of types of discourse was possible. Writings such as Ernst Cassirer's *Philosophie der symbolischen Formen* and *An Essay on Man*, and Wilbur Urban's *Language and Reality* show great sensitivity to a wide range of symbolic phenomena, and so act as valuable correctives to oversimplified versions of semiotic; but their failure to deal adequately with the core problem as to the nature of sign-processes makes their work at the wider circumference more suggestive than scientific.[1]

In the spirit of these remarks by Charles Morris we may now, on the basis of what was done in Chapter 5, address ourselves to the topic of the cognitive and noncognitive aspects of language. We shall proceed by considering each of the features of language isolated there with the exception of (8) which had to do with nonlinguistic effects of speech and also effects induced in particular contexts. In the case of each such aspect we shall see in what way, if at all, one can reasonably make the distinction between cognitive and noncognitive uses of language.

See p.124 1) *Primary conceptual content.*—One of the things that people have had in mind in calling some sentences cognitive and others not is the presence or absence of a primary conceptual content. Thus, they have often spoken of the "referential"

use of language as identical with the scientific or descriptive use, and language is surely referential if it has a primary conceptual content, as we saw in Chapter 5. In this sense of 'cognitive,' presenting a primary conceptual content is both a necessary and a sufficient condition of being cognitive. But then it is clear that many kinds of sentences are cognitive. Indicative sentences are cognitive in this sense, but so are questions, commands, exclamations, and wishes. Sentence-words like "Fire!" and "Look!" are cognitive. Metaphorical sentences are cognitive as well as literal ones; and most of the sentences of poetry and fiction are cognitive.

The case of "How are you?" is interesting in this connection. When "How are you?" is meant as an enquiry concerning health it may be said to be cognitive, both in having primary conceptual content and, as we shall see, in function. But when it is used as a passing greeting one is tempted to say that it means simply "Hello!" and is noncognitive. It might be claimed, however, that in the latter use it has a conceptual content, and indeed the same conceptual content that it has in the former use, but that it serves an entirely different *purpose*. Then, even in the latter use it is cognitive in the present sense, although noncognitive in function. The same would be true of many other utterances.

Some critics of "dualism" have emphasized this presentative character of poetry and other allegedly "emotive" utterances, and with justice. For, even if we do not take presentation of a primary sense as a sufficient condition of being cognitive, it must still be admitted that insofar as an utterance presents a conceptual content it has an intellectual aspect and is not purely emotive. "The purpose of this insistence upon the presented content of a work of art," M. Black writes, "is to emphasize the importance of intellectual *understanding* as a factor in aesthetic appreciation." [2] Miss Wodehouse makes much the same point against Carnap's claim that "a lyrical poem has no assertional sense, no theoretical sense, it does not contain knowledge." "I reply," she says, "that the poet may be using metaphorical language . . . and that what he puts before us may be partly his own invention . . . but that the statement is still presentative, and emotive by being presentative." [3]

Miss Wodehouse goes on to claim that *all* use of language is presentative, and so cognitive in the present sense, but she does not really show this. "We put something before our hearer," she argues, "meaning to move him to respond." [4] But do we in all of our utterances put something before our hearer in the sense of presenting a primary conceptual content? This, we have seen, is doubtful in the case of many ejaculations, exclamations, etc., though true in the case of some, and even Empson admits that there are purely emotive uses of words (e.g., swear words, intensifiers such as 'frightfully,' etc.), arguing only that "such uses are ordinarily felt to be trivial and separate from the straightforward uses of language." [5] We may, of course, in these instances, be putting before our hearer some feeling or attitude of ours, but we do so by *expressing* it, not by talking about it, and so this point is not relevant here.

Thus, we have here a respect in which utterances of most sorts are cognitive and some noncognitive. This point does incorporate part of what critics of dualism have contended, but it must be noted that it does nothing to show that all, or most, utterances are cognitive in any *other* respect, e.g. in any of the respects discussed below. In particular, it does nothing to show that poetical utterances, commands, etc., are cognitive in the sense of making true or false assertions—the sense with which Carnap and so many others are primarily concerned.

It may be suggested, as a qualification of what has been said, that to be cognitive an utterance must not only present a conceptual content, but one which is capable of being true or false, one which may be, even if it is not, the content of an assertion. Then many locutions which are cognitive in the above sense become noncognitive, e.g., such expressions as 'sixth the of notion decimal in virtue place the.' These expressions present a conceptual content, but not one which can be true or false. Perhaps some poetical passages will be similarly noncognitive. But many will be cognitive since they present, literally or metaphorically, a primary sense which may be true or false even if they are not concerned to assert it to be either. Wishes and commands will also be cognitive, for the content they present may be the content of a true or false assertion. What are we to say of religious and metaphysical utterances, literal or metaphorical? This depends on our theory of meaning (or rather of conceptual content). If, according to our theory of meaning, such terms as 'God' and the other terms of theology and metaphysics have conceptual content, then we may say that the sentences in question are cognitive, otherwise not. Ordinarily, they would no doubt be said to have a conceptual content, which may be true, but this assumption has been challenged by many recent writers, particularly by pragmatists and positivists, and cannot now be made without being supported by a plausible theory of meaning. But since we cannot here discuss the whole topic of conceptual meaning, we shall have to leave the question open.

We may also ask about ethical sentences like "Killing is wrong!" and aesthetic sentences like "This painting is beautiful!" which are often put down as noncognitive. They are cognitive in the wider of the above senses, since they present some primary conceptual content, viz., that presented by the words 'killing' and 'painting.' But are they cognitive in the narrower sense just described? This seems to be denied by those who regard ethical and aesthetic judgments as disguised interjections, wishes, or commands. We have noticed, however, that an imperative or optative sentence is not necessarily noncognitive in this sense, and that, even if ethical and aesthetic statements are disguised wishes or commands, they need not be noncognitive. And, in fact, as a minimum, the primary conceptual content presented by "Killing is wrong!" whether it is taken as an interjection, wish, or what have you, is the thought of someone's killing someone, and this may be the content of a statement which is true or false. In this respect, then, "Killing is wrong!" is cognitive even in the stricter sense already distinguished.

This reasoning, however, does not show that "Killing is wrong!" is cognitive with respect to the term 'wrong,' that is, it does not show that part of the conceptual content it presents as the whole is conveyed by the word "wrong." This is the question at issue; but it can only be answered by a discussion of the meaning of ethical terms, and so again must be left open here.

2) *Expression and evocation of propositional attitudes with regard to primary conceptual content.*—In what is a still stricter sense of the term, an utterance may be called cognitive if and only if, besides presenting a primary conceptual content, it expresses and seeks to evoke a belief that this content is true, i.e., makes an assertion which is true or false. This meaning of 'cognitive' has been particularly prominent in the literature. Thus Carnap speaks of having "assertional sense" as equivalent to "containing knowledge." And Ogden and Richards write: "The best test of whether our use of words is essentially symbolic or emotive is the question—'Is this true or false in the ordinary strict scientific sense?'" [6] Now in this sense, only sentences which really make assertions that are true or false are cognitive, and sentences which are really interrogative, imperative, etc., are not, even though they may present a conceptual content. It is, however, not always easy to tell whether an utterance is cognitive or not in this sense. Grammatical form, as we have seen, is not a sure criterion. The case of metaphysical and ethical sentences must also be mentioned again, but the remarks made above apply here too.

Thus far we have found three senses in which an utterance may be cognitive, each narrower than the preceding one. It seems clear that dualists have generally meant to call a sentence cognitive (or scientific, descriptive, representative, etc.) if and only if it is cognitive in all three of these ways, stressing sometimes one way and sometimes another, but without distinguishing them. As a result, they have dubbed "emotive" all utterances which are noncognitive in any of these three senses, as if there were no important differences among them, thus somewhat unnecessarily rousing the ire of literary critics like Empson, as well as other opponents. But some of their opponents have also failed to distinguish these ways in which a

sentence may be cognitive or noncognitive, and so have sometimes proved less than they attempted.

A fourth sense in which a sentence may be cognitive can
now be described. A sentence which is not cognitive in the
third of our previous senses may still be cognitive in the sense
of being cognitively grounded, i.e., in the sense of being rooted
in beliefs or cognitions which might be expressed in sentences
which are cognitive in our third sense. Thus, Morris contends
that evaluations or appraisive utterances, which he regards as
not in themselves designative or "scientific," are nevertheless
susceptible of control by the methods of science, since they
may be made after a utilization of reliable knowledge, as well
as carelessly.[7] But, not to assume that ethical sentences are
noncognitive in our third sense, as he does, let us take another
example. Suppose I say "Be careful!" in an appropriate context and tone of voice. Then my utterance will be cognitive in
our first two senses, but not in the third. But it will also be
cognitively grounded, since it depends on an apprehension that
some danger is threatening, and apprehension of a truth or
falsity, although my utterance does not state it.

To say an utterance is cognitively grounded is to say that it
expresses a state of mind which is rooted in belief. There are,
however, two ways in which a state of mind may be rooted in
belief. It may be based on a belief in the sense that a belief is
one of its main causes, or in the sense that it will be altered by
a change in the person's belief. Presumably, the concern expressed in "Be careful!" is cognitively grounded in both of these
senses. But the two senses should not be confused. In one the
reference is to the past, in the other it is to the future, and it
may be that a state of mind has a belief among its causes without being alterable by a change in belief, or vice versa.[8]

3) *Secondary conceptual content.*—Ordinarily, a sentence
which has a secondary conceptual content will be cognitive
at least in the first of the above senses, and perhaps also in the
second and third, since it will ordinarily have a primary conceptual content too. That it *must* have a primary conceptual
content, however, seems doubtful. Even if 'good' and 'beauti-

ful' have no symbolic reference or primary sense, as Ogden and Richards hold, they may still have associated with them a complex of ideas and images. In any case, however, our question is whether or not an utterance is in any way cognitive *in virtue of* having a secondary conceptual content. Dualists have tended to disregard secondary content, except as a nuisance, and thus seem to have denied it any cognitive value. Ogden and Richards, for instance, insist that 'good' and 'beautiful' are "purely emotive" terms, apparently in spite of any ideational associations they may have. The positivists, too, have often condemned certain utterances as cognitively meaningless, even though they are accompanied by such ideational associations.

But this position seems unduly restrictive, as critics like Empson have argued. If we regard the presentation of primary conceptual content as cognitive, we must also so regard the presentation of secondary conceptual content, since both are ideational and so far nonemotive in the same ways. What Empson calls "Implications" are as intellectual as what he calls "Senses."

4) *Propositional attitudes with respect to secondary conceptual content.*—We have seen, following Empson, that utterances may make assertions involving secondary content. When they do, we may properly call them cognitive in the third of the above senses, even if no primary content is present. When they do not, they will be noncognitive (in this sense), so far at least as their secondary contents are concerned.

Thus, the account of secondary conceptual content parallels that of primary, and brings in no new senses of 'cognitive.'

5) *Expression of speaker's emotions and conative attitudes.*—The fact that utterances express the speaker's state of mind in one way or another has often been put on the emotive side of the ledger, as it was by Ogden and Richards. This does not mean that expressive utterances are to be called noncognitive, and nonexpressive ones cognitive. For all linguistic utterances presumably express the speaker's state of mind or attitude in some fashion, if they are not merely mechanical and parroting.

Even the most neutral statements of science express at least a conviction on the part of the scientist. No one wishes to call the utterances which are not expressive in any way, if there are any, cognitive as such. To classify expressiveness as emotive or noncognitive is not so much to distinguish expressive utterances from another class of utterances, as to distinguish one aspect of utterances from others which the same utterances may have. It is to say that utterances have or may have an aspect in which they do not symbolize conceptual content or convey information, but do something different.

Now, of course, expressiveness *is* different from presentativeness, which we have already dealt with, and from revelatoriness, which we shall take up next. Both of the latter are properly called "cognitive" aspects of language, and so it is appropriate to refer to expressiveness as a noncognitive aspect, which all types of utterance may have. But, if we then go on to say that all types of utterance are noncognitive, with this aspect in mind, we should hasten to add that they may, nevertheless, also be cognitive in the various other senses here identified, including even the third.

This way of speaking puts expressions of states of knowing and believing in the same class with expressions of anger, but a somewhat different usage, compatible with that just indicated, is also possible. Believing, knowing, doubting, etc., are generally regarded as cognitive states in a way which loving, being angry, feeling humble, etc., are not. It is reasonable, therefore, to call the expression of the former states of mind cognitive, and that of the latter, noncognitive. It must be noticed, however, that a given utterance may be both cognitive and noncognitive in this sense, e.g., the line, "For he's a jolly good fellow!" which presumably expresses both belief and liking.

In either way of speaking, of course, the expression of emotion and conative attitude by the speaker—our present topic— would be called noncognitive. The expression of belief, on the other hand, which we labeled "cognitive" under (2), will be cognitive in the latter way of speaking, noncognitive in the former. But the expression of an interrogatory state of mind, which was noncognitive in the sense discussed in (2), will also be cognitive in the second sense brought out here, and noncognitive in the first.

6) *Emotional content or tone.*—That linguistic utterances have or may have various effects on the emotions and conative attitudes of their hearers (among whom is the speaker) is generally recognized, and often decried. This tendency of at least some words and sentences to evoke emotion, desire, etc., has been called their "emotive meaning" by some writers.[9] Other writers have questioned the propriety of speaking of it as a kind of "meaning" at all, and have suggested different labels: "emotive influences," "emotive content," "emotional force," etc.[10] But the tendency itself seems to be denied by no one, and, in fact, most writers make a point of insisting on its existence.

Nor has anyone directly maintained that this emotional influence of words and sentences is in itself cognitive. We may therefore quite reasonably take it to be a noncognitive aspect of language, as it has so often been taken by dualists.

It does not follow, however, that we may say without qualification that any locution which is emotionally charged is noncognitive, for it may have this emotive force and yet be cognitive in all of the above senses; in fact, this is normally the case, as dualists have always recognized; that is, utterances may be both cognitive and noncognitive in this respect; they do not fall into two mutually exclusive groups as they do with respect to the features previously discussed. In fact, it has been claimed that all linguistic utterances are both cognitive and emotive, and that none are wholly one or the other.[11] But those who have made this claim have usually not sufficiently distinguished the various items which are relevant to the discussion; for example, they have not always distinguished presenting and asserting, expressing and evoking, or expressing and revealing. With such distinctions in mind, we have seen that utterances may be cognitive or noncognitive in several different ways, and that in many of these ways a sentence cannot be both cognitive and noncognitive. Of course, as we have insisted, it may be cognitive in one way and noncognitive in another. But, at any rate, it is misleading to say, *simpliciter,* that all sentences are both cognitive and noncognitive.

It would be plausible to argue that all nonparroting utterances are noncognitive in the sense of expressive, and cognitive in the sense of revelatory. But this is not to the point in the present connection. Here the question is whether or not all utterances have both an emotive and a conceptual content, and the point is that those who have contended that they are both "presentative and emotive," for example, have not clearly answered *this* question.

Indeed, the critics of linguistic dualism have usually admitted that some expressions are purely emotive.[12] Interjections, and the like, are often listed as examples, and have been taken above as perhaps not presenting any conceptual content. They may, of course, be revelatory, as Brandt has pointed out,[13] and then they are cognitive in that sense. This does not mean, however, that they present any conceptual content, and even Brandt, who is arguing for a "Cognitive Field theory" of emotive meaning, does not claim that they do. He only goes on to assert that the emotive effect of interjections like 'Ouch!' is both small and diffuse.

Whether or not any conventional expressions are wholly without emotive influence (except for their aesthetic effects simply as sounds, etc.) has not been so much discussed, perhaps, although those who have decried the use of emotive language have certainly regarded some words as at least virtually "neutral." Perhaps, as Erdmann suggests,[14] such words as 'table' and 'pen' do not arouse any *"Begleitfühlung"*—at least not when uttered in certain contexts or tones of voice. Or perhaps they do so, but in normal cases, without affecting perceptibly the flow of our emotional lives. The technical terms conventional among scientists are presumably as neutral as can be, but, then, they are used in a somewhat artificial atmosphere, and even so frequently acquire an aura for those who use them or even for those who only hear them.

But, however this may be, we have at least seen that utterances may have a noncognitive dimension, not previously listed here, namely, an influence on the emotions of the hearer, though they may have a cognitive dimension in addition. And the question whether or not they all have both dimensions is not so interesting for our purposes as another; viz., whether or not the emotive influence (apart from its direct aesthetic effects on others such as the fear caused by its loudness) of an utterance is dependent on its cognitive aspects. Stevenson and Robinson, in putting forward an emotive theory of ethics, have contended that "emotive" may be independent of "descriptive" meaning.[15] Some of their critics, on the other hand, have argued that in all—or in all except trivial cases (among which ethical and poetic sentences cannot be included)—the emotive impact of an utterance is dependent on the concepts and beliefs which it communicates.[16] If the latter position, which Brandt calls the cognitive field theory, is correct, then we may call emotive meaning noncognitive in itself, but we must admit that it is *cognitively grounded,* and in *this* sense may be called cognitive. At least, we must then take a more intellectualistic view of the situation than dualists usually espouse.

Let us consider this question, asking whether the emotive tone of an utterance is always wholly or partially dependent on its own cognitive aspects. Now it is certainly true that the impact made by an utterance on the hearer's emotions is often due to what it says in the sense of the *primary* content it presents and asserts to be true, e.g., when one receives a message saying simply that a certain close friend has been killed in an accident. Of course, in such cases, one's emotions will also depend partly on one's already existing conative dispositions—they will be roughly a function of the bearing of the information received on those dispositions. In other words, they will be determined only partly by the cognition involved. But, at any rate, given the existing conative dispositions, one's emotions in the instance cited will depend largely on the primary content asserted.

However, the fact that the primary information communicated by an utterance has an effect on the hearer's emotions is not what is referred to by 'emotional tone' and like phrases, as we have seen. For a sentence composed entirely of "neutral" words, if there are any, might convey heartbreaking information. Hence, the above fact does not show that the emotional tone of words is dependent on their primary conceptual content. But Erdmann thinks it is largely thus dependent. "It goes without saying that the value of the accompanying feeling depends primarily on the conceptual content" by which he means what we have called primary conceptual content.[17] He gives as an example the emotionally charged word 'murder.' It is not easy to be sure just what the primary conceptual content of "He was murdered" is, but suppose that it is something like "He was killed in violation of the law." Then it does seem clear that the emotional tone of "He was murdered" reflects in part the feelings we are disposed to have toward illegal killing of human beings, and so to depend on its primary conceptual content. But it is not clear that this emotional tone is wholly dependent on this content.

It is not maintained by Erdmann, however, or even by Brandt, that emotional tone is always wholly dependent on primary conceptual content. There is also secondary or associated conceptual content, and it may be argued that the emotive force of words rests on this as well as on their primary content. Thus, Hospers writes in a slightly different connection: "I daresay that what poetic value the word 'sea' has for us is due not to the sound but to the notion of the sea itself—the concept, not the word, is poetic (the calm sea, the stormy sea, the tropical sea, etc., suggesting all sorts of words and imaginative situations)."[18] In fact Stevenson himself recognizes that emotive meaning may be thus dependent on "pictorial meaning" and "suggestion," and speaks of it as being then "quasi-dependent."[19]

However, the cognitive field theory does not involve saying that emotive force is entirely dependent on either primary or secondary content. It allows that some of the influence of discourse on feelings or attitudes derives, not from *what* is said, but "from the hearer's impression of the type, intensity, and determination of the attitudes of the speaker—especially if the speaker is a person held in awe or admiration by the hearer." Brandt argues, for instance, that a speaker's "Ouch!" influences the hearer's emotions at least partly because it affects his cognitive field "by conveying to him the impression that the speaker is probably in pain"; that is, he makes use of what an utterance *reveals,* as well as what it presents or asserts, to explain its emotive powers.[20]

It is clear that, if all of the previously distinguished cognitive aspects of an utterance are brought in, it is at any rate plausible that its emotive force is partly, or even wholly, explicable in terms of its own cognitive features. What may be said against this view?

R. H. Thouless (like many others, especially in popular discussions of semantics) claims that two words or sentences may have the same "objective meaning," but different "emotional meanings," e.g., 'casement' and 'window.' By saying they have the same objective meaning he seems to mean, however, that they have the same *extension.* And this is compatible with their having different *intensions* or primary conceptual contents, and therefore his contention, if true (and it may be questioned in the instance mentioned), would not even show that emotional meaning may be independent of primary conceptual meaning. It certainly would not show that it is independent of secondary conceptual meaning; in fact, Thouless himself stresses the fact that 'casement' has "romantic associations" which 'window' does not have.[21]

A claim similar to that of Thouless, but not confusing intension and extension, is used by Stevenson: "The independence of emotive meaning can be roughly tested by comparing descriptive synonyms which are not emotive synonyms. Thus to whatever extent the laudatory strength of "democracy" exceeds that of 'government where rule is by popular vote,' the emotive meaning of the former will be independent." [22] Now it is not clear that "government where rule is by popular vote" exhausts the primary conceptual content of 'democracy,' but suppose that it does. One may still argue that it does not have the same secondary conceptual content—the same conceptual and imaginative associations—and that the difference in emotive meaning is due to this difference in associations.[23]

Erdmann, in discussing the relation of *Gefühlswert, Neben-sinn,* and *begrifflichen Inhalt,*[24] argues that two words, like *'Leu'* and *'Löwe'* or *'Hose'* and *'Beinkleid,'* may have the same primary conceptual content but different total meanings, since they may differ in associated content and feeling. These associated meanings usually depend on the primary conceptual content, but not always. The feeling tone, he then goes on to hold, is intimately bound up with the associated content, and is usually a direct effect of it. Thus the words *'Weib,' 'Gattin,' 'Frau,'* and *'Gemahlin'* have different feeling tones, but also have different associated contents. *'Gemahlin,'* e.g., involves the thought of belonging to a higher social class. Then he says that the feeling tone of a word cannot always be explained, and that sheer accident often plays a part. This suggests the possibility of independent emotive meaning. But Erdmann does not show that these accidental determinants of emotional tone are anything nonconceptual or noncognitive. He mentions the sound of the word as one such accident, but this, of course, is not to the point, since it is admitted by Brandt that words have certain psychological effects simply as sensory presences.[25]

Erdmann also claims that certain expressions possess only feeling-tone, or rather, that their conceptual content has been wholly transmuted into feeling-value, and cites *Schimpfwörter* as examples, claiming that in some cases we have no idea what they mean (*Sinn*).[26] But even here he does not show that their impact is not due to secondary associations and suggestions, or to what their use reveals about the attitudes of the speaker.

Stevenson has urged the case of the unmentionable "four-letter words" in favor of the independent emotive meaning:

All of them are emotive to the point of being forbidden, yet each has a cognitive synonym that takes its innocent place in any text on physiology. Only a part of their emotive meaning, then, is dependent. A perhaps larger part is quasi-dependent, since the four-letter terms have cognitive suggestions that their physiological counterparts do not. But the rest, it seems to me, is independent.[27]

But is there a "rest" to be independent? Stevenson argues that there is:

> . . . take the physiological terms and add other nonprofane adjectives to them until they have as elaborate a cognitive function as you please. Their emotive meaning will still fall far short of equaling that of their four-letter counterparts.[28]

This may be admitted, but it does not seem conclusively to establish the independence of emotive meaning. (a) The difference in one's emotions at hearing the four-letter words and the technical expressions may be due to the fact that one *believes* the use of the former to be forbidden by society, insulting and offensive to its hearers, or revelatory of social depravity, disrespect for religion, and the like, whereas one believes the use of the technical terms to be respectable and respectful. (b) No matter how one proliferates the nonprofane terms in one's substitute expression one must fail to present the same secondary conceptual content as is presented by the four-letter term, for the nonprofane words will have their own associated imagery, which will be different. This may explain the difference in emotional tone. To use an example from Erdmann, the emotional force of the phrase "the bare seat" is unlike that of its shorter alternative, because it calls to mind the more innocent image of *sitting*.[29] (c) Besides, the shorter term makes its impact all at once, while the elaborated expression does so in a piecemeal way, so that even if their respective emotive influences are due wholly to the alterations they introduce into our cognitive fields, these influences may still be very different.[30]

To the first of these arguments Stevenson replies that it only throws us back on the problem of explaining why [the four-letter] terms are forbidden, offensive, etc.[31] This is true, but it is not immediately clear that they are forbidden and offensive, because they have an independent emotive meaning, or that their being forbidden or insulting can be explained only on the hypothesis that they have one. Studies of the origin of taboo words and of the way in which innocent words become derogatory are certainly not conclusive on this point. And we do know that among certain primitive peoples the use of a man's name is taboo because they believe that he who controls the name controls the man and is able to do him harm.

Another argument used by Stevenson is that words may change their descriptive meaning without altering their emotional tone, and vice versa.[32] And it does seem plain that *primary* conceptual content and emotive content are thus independently variable. In the phrase 'the sins of society' the word 'sins' has a religious aura which does not belong to the word 'misdeeds' which might be substituted without change of primary conceptual content. But this means, no doubt, that it has a secondary conceptual content as well as a feeling tone different from that of 'misdeeds,' and it may be that the feeling tone depends on the secondary conceptual content.[33]

The "brilliant Dutch writer, Jac van Ginneken," as Sapir has called him,[34] argued in 1905 that feeling tone is an independent kind of meaning because a patient suffering from aphasia may have words to express and evoke feeling, even when he has forgotten the words to describe what he perceives. For example, when shown a piece of candy or a slice of spoiled cheese, he may not be able to say what it is, but only "Good!" or "It stinks!" [35] It is not easy to analyze his evidence, but, even *if* it shows that emotive meaning is independent of primary conceptual content, it does not prove that it is independent of associated imagery.

E. McGinnies in some experiments has found (1) that taboo or critical words require longer tachistoscopic exposure before being reported correctly than do neutral words, (2) that galvanic skin response after exposures which precede correct report is greater when the exposed but not yet reported word is taboo than when it is neutral. As a result he speaks of "prerecognition emotionality," and of "perceptual defense" against becoming aware of objects which have an unpleasant emotional significance. His results and interpretation have been questioned, and cannot be taken as conclusive, but they seem interesting in the present connection. For one may take them to mean, if correct, that the emotive meaning of a word is grasped somehow before the conceptual meaning. Actually, however, they would only show that we somehow "discriminate" a word before we become sufficiently "aware" of it to make a correct report. They would not show that the emotive and cognitive contents are not discriminated at the same time.[36]

So far we have been discussing whether the emotive force of an utterance is due to its cognitive factors, i.e., to the concepts and information which it explicitly or implicitly, primarily or secondarily, literally or metaphorically presents, asserts, or reveals. And we have seen that it is not easy to find clear empirical evidence that this is not the case. On the other hand, there seems to be no decisive evidence that it is the case, and the belief in independent emotional tone does have a certain plausibility. As Stevenson says:

. . . we know that most psychological phenomena are functions of many variables; and we know that many of them are subject to conditioning—that they arise from stimuli that at first were inessential to them, even in the absence of causes that were first essential. It is not easy to believe, then, that *attitudes* are anomalous in these respects. It is not easy to believe that they are dependent on the *one* variable of cognition, and that they cannot become conditioned responses to a stimulus, such as a word, in any way that frees them from this dependence. Thus one can extrapolate, so long as only moderate probabilities are in question, from the cases that have been studied accurately to those that cannot (or have not) been studied accurately.[37]

The whole matter would seem to require further empirical study, aided if possible "by fully controlled experiments, which have not yet been made."[38]

Whatever may be the outcome of such further study, it seems certain already that the emotive force of language is very largely dependent or quasi-dependent, or at any rate cognitively grounded, as Sapir, earlier, and Empson, more recently, have insisted.[39] If it should turn out that the cognitive field theory is confirmed, we shall be able to assert that even the emotive power of words is wholly cognitive in its basis, if not in its own nature. But this must not be misunderstood. The cognitive field theory does not imply that human beings are pure intellects, or that *all* of our emotions and attitudes originate in conception and belief. What it does hold is that given "what dispositions [to react] the hearer happens to have," then "the [substantial] emotive effects of a term will all be produced by alterations which the hearing of the term introduces into [his] cognitive field."[40] This does not mean that he is readily amenable to reason, for instance, for his given dispositions to react may not be very reasonable—*they* may not even be rooted in belief—and besides, the operations of secondary conceptual content, so prominent among the alterations which the hearing of a term introduces into one's cognitive field, may be quite unreasonable.[41]

7) *Revelation of facts about the speaker*, etc.—In reply to emotive theories of ethics and aesthetics it is sometimes argued that ethical and aesthetic sentences—in fact all utterances—make known to others the speaker's thoughts, feelings, attitudes, culture and the like, and that therefore they convey information or insight and are cognitive, especially when this revelation is part of the speaker's intention, as it may be. And, indeed, it is true that any kind of utterance may be in this way cognitive in its effects, and that many utterances are so in function. For example, "You're late!" reveals the speaker's impatience. But this is a new sense in which sentences may be cognitive. In this sense an utterance is cognitive, not in virtue of the conceptual content which it presents or asserts, i.e., not in its capacity as *symbol*, but in virtue of its being uttered, i.e., in its capacity as *signal*. The propositions conveyed are not included in the conceptual content of the utterance itself; the informative character of the utterance is extrinsic or pragmatic, not intrinsic, i.e., syntactic or semantic. It remains extrinsic in this way even if the utterance is intended to convey that information, as when a young man sends a girl a poem about the

moon in the hope that she will take it as a sign that he loves her.[42]

The point is that, for every utterance I make, there is a corresponding utterance which, if made, is cognitive in all of the above senses. To A's "Today is Thursday" there corresponds B's "A believes today is Thursday," to A's "Hurrah!" B's "A is pleased about something," to A's "Killing is wrong!" B's "A disapproves of killing." B's utterances here would be cognitive in all the above senses. But this does not prove that A's utterances are cognitive in any of those senses (though they may be), as the case of "Hurrah!" seems to show. It only proves that they are or may be cognitive in *another* sense, namely revelatory.

One special case of this revelatory aspect of linguistic utterances deserves mention here.[43] One point made in the more recent philosophies of language against the traditional is that we do not always have experience first and only later formulate in words, but that the two usually, or at least often, go together. The experience, it is claimed, is created and molded in the very process of expression. And, surely, anyone who tries to write a poem or even to say what he is feeling or thinking can verify this claim. Our linguistic utterances, then, and perhaps also our works of art, reveal us, not only to others, but to ourselves; they are stages on the way to self-knowledge. This is true even though we have learned from the psychoanalysts that we cannot take such self-revelations at their face value.

It seems clear, then, that even if an expression is "purely emotive," it may still be cognitive in at least one important respect—it may have "revelatory significance."[44]

8) *Other kinds of effect.*—Omitted here.

9) *Purpose or function.*—As we have seen, if words have conceptual content, expressiveness, etc., then they can be used in social communication, consciously or unconsciously, in order to present this content, to express, etc. Some of these uses may have no ulterior motive, no end beyond themselves. On a prelinguistic level this occurs, perhaps, in the babbling of a child, as Mrs. DeLaguna, M. M. Lewis, and Segerstedt hold.[45] On a

linguistic level we find it again in word-play, conversation, literature, and science, as these same authors recognize and as Mrs. Langer has stressed.[46] We may call such uses of language *intrinsic*, and their existence must be admitted, even if it be held, with DeLaguna, Malinowski, Segerstedt, and others that the development of language has been determined on the whole by its more ulterior or extrinsic uses. These intrinsic uses are:

(a) To present or evoke conceptual content for its own sake.

(b) To express or evoke belief or some other cognitive attitude for its own sake, e.g., to convey information for its own sake.

(c) To express or evoke emotion for its own sake.

(d) To reveal facts about the speaker for their own sake.

It will be noticed that we have included the "descriptive" or "scientific" use of language as such among intrinsic uses. This is generally regarded as a cognitive use and it is one of the characteristic theses of the recent view of language that it is relatively rare in its pure form and quite secondary among the functions of language. Thus, Malinowski contends "that language in its primitive function and original form has an essentially pragmatic character; that it is a mode of behavior, an indispensable element of concerted human action." He recognizes that "in its developed literary and scientific functions, [language] is an instrument of thought and of the communication of thought," but insists that "to regard it as a means for the embodiment or expression of thought is to take a one-sided view of one of its most derivate and specialized functions." [47] Against this view, as espoused by John Holloway in *Language and Intelligence*, J. N. Findlay has recently argued that "no one who has listened in on some conversation on a bus can doubt that the descriptive and narrative function bulks overwhelmingly in human discourse." [48] But, to meet just such an argument, Malinowski contends:

. . . . narrative speech is derived in its function, and it refers to action only indirectly, but the way in which it acquires its meaning can only be understood from the direct function of speech in action . . . . the referential function of a narrative is subordinate to its social and emotive function . . .

and again:

There can be no doubt that we have here a new type of linguistic use—*phatic communion* I am tempted to call it, actuated by the demon of terminological invention—a type of speech in which ties of union are created by a mere exchange of words. Let us look at it from the special point of view with which we are here concerned: let us ask what light it throws on the function or nature of language. Are words in Phatic Communion used primarily to convey meaning, the meaning which is symbolically theirs? Certainly not! They fulfill a social function and that is their principal aim, but they are neither the result of intellectual reflection, nor do they necessarily arouse reflection in the listener. Once again we may say that language does not function here as a means of transmission of thought.[49]

But we need not quarrel with this semipragmatic theory of language, since its wiser proponents do admit the existence of intrinsic uses of words.[50] We have seen that the purely "scientific" use of language, even if found on a bus, is a cognitive one. But in line with what was said earlier, we may also reasonably claim that among the intrinsic uses of language given on pages 123 and 125, (a), (b), and (d) are cognitive, and that only use (c) is noncognitive. Among intrinsic uses of language, then, cognitive ones are predominant. But, of course, they will not all be cognitive in the same sense. And (b) is also noncognitive in the sense in which all expression is "emotive."

We come now to extrinsic or ulterior uses of language. These certainly do exist, and according to the prevailing semipragmatism, they are in some sense or other predominant. In fact, there seems to be no doubt that purely intrinsic uses are relatively rare, and that presentation, expression, etc., usually occur as *means* to further ends, e.g. action, or at least as *parts* of a larger process which has such other ends. Even in (d) the expressive use of words serves as such a means or part, and in (b) and (c) the presentative use generally does. And revelation and evocation likewise probably occur usually as means to or parts of something larger. What are these larger ends? They may be various—specific or generic, near or remote, individual or social, etc. Recent theorists have tried to describe them in general terms. Mrs. DeLaguna [51] notes, "the primary function of speech in the coordination of the behavior of the individual members of the social group . . . Its fundamental and primary value . . . lies in its social function of associating individuals," and, in general, her view is typical. Malinowski in the quotations given above takes the same position, and Segerstedt identifies as the main functions of language the production of action, the isolation of one group from another, and the development of a *"Zusammengehörigkeitsgefühl"* within the group.[52]

Our question is whether these larger uses of language are cognitive or noncognitive. Perhaps we must in general describe them as noncognitive, since their goal is presumably not usually to promote knowledge, belief, or doubt, but to obtain money, pleasure, co-operation, and the like. Even in saying this we are neglecting the ancient and long prominent view that the real end of life, the good for human beings, is contemplation or knowledge, but perhaps we may be forgiven for doing so here. Some of the larger uses of language, however, do have knowledge as their goal, at least in part, e.g., the use of language to promote a scientific society or a research project interested in knowledge for its own sake. These larger uses will then be cognitive.

There is an important point here, however, which is not sufficiently observed by Malinowski and other semipragmatists, though it does not invalidate their general position. Take the example, "There is a table behind you." One might say this just for the sake of passing on a bit of information. Then his purpose is intrinsic and cognitive. But he is not likely to say it for this reason. More likely his aim is to produce some appropriate action such as keeping him from backing into it. Then his purpose is extrinsic and noncognitive. In saying all this the semipragmatists are correct. But in the latter kind of case one is still communicating information and is doing so intentionally, even if his motive is to prevent someone's hurting himself or breaking a vase. One is seeking to communicate information in order to prevent another's bumping the table, or to prevent his bumping the table by communicating information. We have here, then, a twofold use of language, and must distinguish within it a more proximate and a more ultimate goal. The more ultimate goal may correctly be described as a noncognitive one, but the more proximate goal is nevertheless cognitive. In this sense the cognitive use of language plays a much more important role in ordinary, and even in so-called primitive, speech than it is explicitly accorded by many recent accounts. Neglect of this fact is perhaps due to the fact that we identify *the* function of an utterance with its more remote purpose, which is ordinarily harmless enough, but misleading in such discussions as this.

Even a "purely emotive" purpose may be served by the presentation of conceptual content, or by the communication of information, as when one tells another a true story in order to amuse him. In "nonsense" utterances and jingles and in poetry the function seems often to be the communication of emotion through the presentation of images, concepts, and at least quasi-beliefs. If one calls these uses of language purely emotive, then, one must remember that they are emotive only in function, and are cognitive in other respects.

A somewhat similar case is the sentence, "I love you!" uttered by a young man whose fancy has been more than lightly turned in spring. According to D. H. Parker,[53] this is not a proposition at all, but a volitional expression; it seeks "to share a desire or satisfaction, or to make a desire prevail. . . . the lover's love . . . is a force there trying to kindle a like warmth in the beloved . . ." Here Parker is stressing the function of the young man's utterance, which is certainly to express and evoke love, and therefore noncognitive. But the utterance is just as certainly cognitive in content. It has the same conceptual content and even makes the same assertion, true or false, that it would if the youth were simply relating his autobiography to a young lady; only its function is not descriptive but dynamic.

It must also be remarked that the situation may be reversed. A may send B to the mailbox, knowing that if B goes he will see a new kind of bird. Then A's more proximate goal is noncognitive, and it is the more remote one which is cognitive. In this way the function of sentences which are in themselves

SENSE	MEANING OF 'COGNITIVE'	MEANING OF 'NONCOGNITIVE'	DISCUSSED ABOVE UNDER
1	Has a conceptual content, primary or secondary	Does not have a conceptual content	(1), (3)
2	Has a conceptual content which is capable of being true or false	Does not have a conceptual content capable of being true or false	(1), (3)
3	Makes an assertion, true or false, i.e., expresses and evokes belief, with respect to its primary or secondary conceptual content	Does not make an assertion	(2), (4)
4	Is cognitively grounded	Is not cognitively grounded	(2)
5	Has a cognitive power, i.e., has conceptual content or is revelatory	Is expressive of some feeling, belief, or attitude of the speaker	(5)
6	Expresses and evokes a cognitive attitude: belief, doubt, question, etc.	Expresses an emotion or noncognitive attitude: anger, desire, etc.	(5)
7	Has a cognitive power, i.e., has conceptual content or is revelatory	Is emotive or has emotion tone, i.e., tends to evoke emotions and conative attitudes of certain sorts	(6)
8	Reveals feelings, beliefs or attitudes of the speaker	Is nonrevelatory	(7)
9	Is cognitive in function	Is noncognitive in function	(9)

noncognitive (in our third sense at least)—questions, impera-
tives, etc.—may be cognitive. In fact, the speech of science is
full of such sentences, which seek to release action in order
to produce knowledge. It becomes apparent then that all sorts
of sentences, noncognitive as they may be in other senses, may
be cognitive in *use*, as Toulmin and Baier, as well as Morris,
have cogently pointed out [54]—a fact which is entirely obscured
by the usual dualist way of speaking.

The preceding table will indicate the various senses of 'cognitive' and 'noncognitive' which have been distinguished in our
discussion.

Some notes seem desirable here, even if they involve repetition. It will be clear that an utterance may be cognitive in one
of these senses and noncognitive in others, and vice versa. It
will also be seen that in senses (1), (2), (3), and (8) "cognitive" and "noncognitive" are mutually exclusive, but that in
senses (5), (6), and (7) they are not, so that in the latter
senses an utterance may be both cognitive and noncognitive.
In sense (9), too, an utterance can be both, since it may serve
a cognitive and a noncognitive function at the same time. And,
if the cognitive field theory is true, even emotional tone will be
cognitive in sense (4) at least. All this we have already observed, but this table also makes it apparent that some of the
senses of cognitive overlap. (1) includes (2) but is wider, and
(2) includes (3) but is wider. Similarly (6) includes (3), and
(5) includes (1) and (8), and coincides with (7).

Before we close, there is a matter that needs some consideration. We have been making a distinction between certain
attitudes, such as believing, knowing, and doubting, which
were called cognitive, and other attitudes, such as loving,
being angry, or feeling disgust, which were called noncognitive, even though they may be cognitively grounded.
This distinction seems justified on a rough common sense
basis, but perhaps something should be said in defense of
it. One is tempted to argue at once that belief is an attitude
taken toward propositions, while desiring and the like are attitudes taken toward things. But Russell and others have held

that desire is as much a "propositional attitude" as belief on the ground that "I desire A" means "I desire *that* A be mine, be realized, etc.," and so is like "I believe *that* the janitor is coming." [55] Suppose this to be true. It is not clear that a similar account can be given of anger and other attitudes which we have been calling noncognitive, but in any case this account does not show that "desiring that. . . ." and "believing that. . . ." are attitudes of the same kind; even if they are both propositional they may be specifically different. Thus one may still be able to distinguish between cognitive and noncognitive propositional attitudes. One may contend, for example, that belief nevertheless differs from other attitudes "in the object toward which it is directed . . . Beliefs are *interested* in matters of truth and falsity; other attitudes are not." [56] This quotation is perhaps too strong, since other attitudes may be cognitively grounded. But one may fairly claim, it would seem, that beliefs are directly and essentially interested in truth and falsity, while other attitudes are interested in them only indirectly and incidentally.

Even if belief and desire are both propositional attitudes, then, they may well be quite differently conditioned. This, however, has been questioned. It is pointed out that our beliefs influence our conative attitudes, and that these influence our beliefs, and that disagreements in belief and disagreements in conative attitude are very parallel in structure.[57] But it does not follow that believing and taking a conative attitude are one and the same thing, or even the same specific kind of thing. Until this is shown it seems reasonable to proceed as we have, distinguishing cognitive and noncognitive attitudes. For even if all *changes* in our attitudes are due to changes in our cognitive field, as the cognitive field theory affirms, it may be that our basic needs and drives are themselves not cognitive either in source or in goal.

II

To conclude, we have found that there is no simple duality of "meaning" or "use"—no single pair of kinds of "meaning" or "use," of which an utterance must have one and may have both. Utterances have several distinct, if related, aspects, and in consequence there are several different ways in which an utterance may be cognitive or noncognitive, and an utterance may be cognitive in some of these senses and noncognitive in others. The distinctions cut across one another, and, in particular, that between being cognitive and noncognitive in *use or function* does not coincide with any of the others. As Toulmin and Baier have put it, there is no one Great Divide in the linguistic terrain, there are many small divides, not all running in the same direction.[58] But in each case there is a division between cognitive and noncognitive, a point which they neglect.

It follows that one cannot call any utterance cognitive or noncognitive, scientific or emotive, without explanation. Either one must give up talking in terms of any single pair of words, or if one continues to use a single pair of words, as we have here, one must give each of them nine different senses.

What of "dualism" then? In a way, like Morris, we have but moved "further in the direction which [Ogden and Richards] have seen to be desirable," [59] since we have kept the distinction between cognitive and noncognitive. But we have refined it in the direction of a kind of pluralism. And, on the other hand, we have moved in the direction of a kind of monism in admitting that the cognitive field theory may be true.

Chapter 7

METAPHOR

I.

There is little new to be said on the subject of metaphor. It has been discussed from ancient times to the present and on the whole there has been a rough agreement. The excuse for the present chapter is not that it sets forth new truths concerning metaphor, but that it attemps to fit the old ones into a more general theory of symbolism by characterizing metaphor semantically and by showing its semantic functions. Two such functions shall engage us principally, the use to extend language to meet new situations and the poetic use to give language color and nuance.

Because of the continuity in the discussions of metaphor, we may develop a characterization of it by beginning with and modifying Aristotle's explanation. He says: "Metaphor consists in giving the thing a name that belongs to something else; the transference being either from genus to species, or from species to genus, or from species to species, or on grounds of analogy." [1]

With reservations to be indicated shortly, we may follow this account which emphasizes two aspects of metaphor: a shift of nomenclature—from 'something else' to what is being named, and a specification of the property in virtue of which the transfer takes place. Each of these may be considered briefly.

It is apparent that the terms 'thing' and 'name' in Aristotle's account must be construed very broadly—'thing' referring not merely to physical objects but also to any topic of thought. Similarly, 'name' must be used not in the restricted sense of proper or common names but must be taken as any sign whatever. Thus, what we are left with is the notion that some object of thought is referred to by means of the sign for some other

such object. This will do well enough, but it is a little more convenient to say essentially the same thing from the side of the
sign rather than from the object signified. Thus we may say
that in a metaphor a sign having a conventional sense is used in
a different sense. Though too broad in some respects and incomplete in others this may serve as the basis for an account.
Thus when Milton says of Belial:

> through his tongue
> Dropt Manna, and could make the worse appear
> The better reason . . .[2]

clearly he does not intend us to conclude that Belial exuded
food; rather, 'tongue,' 'dropt' and 'manna' are used in an unusual
sense to suggest that he spoke soothingly and persuasively.
Each of these words appears in a double role—first in its conventional sense such as it might have in other contexts and
second in a sense characteristic of this metaphor. This is what
is central in Aristotle's statement.

This duality of sense is characteristic of metaphor and some
terminology will make reference to it easier. By the *literal sense*
of a word we may mean the sense which a word has in other
contexts and apart from such metaphoric uses. By *figurative
sense* we may mean that special sense on which the metaphor
hinges. Thus, in Milton's figure quoted above, the literal sense
of 'manna' is a food which appeared miraculously to the Israel-
ites in the desert: its figurative sense is, approximately, delight-
ful language. This duality of sense is referred to by other writers
on the subject. Thus our two senses correspond generally,
but not always, to I. A. Richards' use of 'vehicle' and 'tenor.'[3]
Our literal sense also corresponds closely to what Empson[4] calls
the "head meaning" of a word. In any case, the literal sense
most often would be the meaning of a term given by a dictionary or, if there is more than one dictionary meaning, the meaning which is appropriate in context. There may be cases, however, in which an author gives terms a special sense, either
implicitly or by explicit convention, and this may serve as the
literal sense.

It may happen that the figurative sense of a term in a meta-phor is identical with the literal sense of some other term. If this does not occur, there would at least always be a literal sense which is as close to the figurative sense as any literal sense can come. This literal sense we shall call the *paraphrase* of the metaphor. By introduction of this term we do not wish to prejudge the issue as to whether metaphors have equivalent literal senses, we have merely provided the terminology for discussing it. The question may now be phrased in what re-spects may the paraphrase of a metaphor be adequate; this is a question which we shall take up later.

One other bit of terminology will be required. 'Literal sense' and 'figurative sense' both refer to meanings of terms. We shall want some way of referring to the relationship between a word and its various meanings. This may be accomplished by saying that a word is an *immediate sign* of its literal sense and a *medi-ate sign* of its figurative sense. These terms are appropriate since it is only through the literal sense that one arrives at the figurative.

In the definition quoted, Aristotle speaks of the basis of the transference of names or—in our terminology—of the bases for the shift from literal to figurative sense. He enumerates a num-ber of these—substitution of genus for species, of species for genus, of one species for another, or shifts by analogy. A later tradition used the generic term 'trope' to cover all of these and some others, and restricted the term 'metaphor' to cases where analogy was the ground of the shift in sense. While the most recent tendency is to use 'metaphor' in Aristotle's generic sense, there are important differences between metaphor and the other tropes, so we shall observe the finer distinction.

Traditionally, the transitions from literal to figurative sense by way of substitution of genus for species or species for genus, as well as similar substitutions of whole for part and part for whole, go by name of *synecdoche*. In the figure quoted from Milton, the use of 'tongue' to mean organs of speech would be a case in point. Again looser connections by way of some rela-tion felt to be important, as when one speaks of reading an

author instead of his works, go by name of *metonymy*. In *irony*
the connection between literal and figurative sense is by way of
negation. These together with metaphor complete the standard
catalogue of tropes. Whether metonymy is elastic enough to
include deliberate and transparent overstatement is not clear;
if not, this is a separate trope.

We may take from Aristotle then a general definition of trope
of which metaphor is one species. In all tropes at least one term
signifies mediately, thus acquiring a figurative meaning. Every
figurative meaning has a literal paraphrase—though how adequate remains to be seen. To get at what is typical of metaphor,
however, we must consider analogy which characterizes it as
the means of transition from literal to figurative sense.

It must be noticed at the beginning that there is no one sort
of analogy or parallel which is characteristic of all metaphors.
In some two distinct situations are indicated and the one understood in terms of the other; in other metaphors however
there is a mere qualitative similarity between two characteristics of the same thing. Still others are intermediate. We may
begin with a few examples. When, in one of his early verses,
Keats writes:

> When by my solitary hearth I sit,
>   And hateful thoughts enwrap my soul in gloom [5]

there are two distinct situations evoked by the second line,
the one of someone or something enveloping a person in something. It may be a cloak or a blanket or something of the sort.
It may be a net in which the person is caught or it may even
be a monstrous web, but, at any rate, it is something concrete.[6]
The other situation is that of hateful thoughts making one
gloomy. The second is presented in terms of the first and this
metaphor is developed in terms of quite distinct situations. On
the other extreme, we have such a metaphor as is involved in
calling a sly person an old fox. Here the parallel does not involve sets of things in relation but is limited to the common
characteristic of the two. Intermediate between these examples
is such a metaphor as the following: "An obliging thrush

hopped across the lawn; a coil of pinkish rubber twisted in its beak." [7] Here the contorted worm is described in terms of another situation, but the bird which holds it is not. Thus the extent of the parallelism may vary, but, in some degree, it is always present.

II.

In terms of this parallelism, it is possible to explain metaphor as a type of symbolism and to assimilate it to a more general theory of symbolism. This is most easily done by recourse to the distinctions made by C. S. Peirce between symbolic and iconic modes of signification. [8] A sign is a *symbol* insofar as it signifies according to an arbitrary rule, insofar as it is a conventional sign. A sign is an *icon* to the extent that it signifies in virtue of similarity. Thus, ordinary words are symbols, but onomatapoeic words contain an iconic element as well. Such a sign as a map is primarily iconic although, in such details as having special designations for county seats, there is also a conventional, and so symbolic, element.

Given this distinction, there is clearly an iconic element in metaphor. We have just seen that a metaphor, as distinguished from other tropes, depends on analogy, and in this analogy one side is used to present the other. Thus, envelopment in a cloak is used to present the notion of gloom; the character of a man is presented through its likeness to a fox, and the appearance of a worm through its likeness to a bit of rubber. In each case we are led to think of something by a consideration of something like it, and this is what constitutes the iconic mode of signifying.

But if there is an iconic element in metaphor, it is equally clear that the icon is not presented, but is merely described. In the sentence from Virginia Woolf, we are not given a coil of rubber—a piece of rubber could not be part of a sentence—rather we are given a description of such a coil. It is as if information concerning a country were given not by showing its map, but by describing the map, by saying, as for example one might of Chile, that it looks long and skinny on the map. This situation regarding the icon may be stated in a number of ways. We may say that we are given not the icon, but a description of what would be an icon. Alternatively, one might say that not the icon, but its essence is brought before the reader. Again, to say approximately the same thing more safely, one may claim that what is presented is a formula for the construction of icons. Thus Virginia Woolf may be understood as saying something like: "Take any coil of pinkish rubber of a size to be carried by a thrush and you have an icon of what I mean."

Metaphor, then, is analyzable into a double sort of semantic relationship. First, using symbols in Peirce's sense, directions are given for finding an object or situation. Thus, use of language is quite ordinary. Second, it is implied that any object or situation fitting the direction may serve as an icon of what one wishes to describe. The icon is never actually present; rather, through the rule, one understands what it must be and, through this understanding, what it signifies.

There is, of course, an advantage in not having the icon actually present. Confronted with a thrush carrying a coil of rubber, one would most likely mistake it for a worm and so lose the comparison. The rubbery aspect of the worm would escape attention completely. Or, to take a case where such confusion is impossible, if a person wrapped in a cloak were exhibited as indicating the character of gloom, so many other aspects of the person's appearance and demeanor would be prominent that the intended relationship might never be noticed. Thus, the double symbolism of metaphor allows calling attention to aspects of an icon which might not be prominent in the presentation of the icon itself.

Given the general role of icons in metaphor, we may notice their various types a little more closely. Peirce shows two ways, *prima facie* different, in which icons may signify, and both are relevant to metaphor. In the one, there is a direct qualitative similarity between sign and thing signified, as when a colored square on a chart represents a given shade of color. It exemplifies the color and so is directly similar. A more involved type of icon occurs when sign and thing signified have little or no direct similarity, but rather the two have a similar structure. In this sense a map of Michigan is an icon of Michigan even though the map is small, smooth, and easily folded, while Michigan itself is large, relatively rough, and comparatively resistant to folding. The structure of the two is the same, however, and, for example, the angle between two roads in Michigan is the same as the angle between their resprestentation on the map. In this type of sign-relationship, not merely does one complex structure represent another, but elements of one structure represent elements of the other in virtue of holding analogous positions. Thus, one dot on the map of Michigan represents Ann Arbor not because the two look alike—Ann Arbor does not look round—nor because they have the same structure —Ann Arbor is not homogeneous—but because they occupy corresponding places in similar structures.

Although the alternatives of qualitative and structural similarity leave open a vast number of possibilities, it must not be thought that anything may be an icon of any other thing. While it may be that any two things are similar in some respect, this, by itself, is not sufficient to make one an icon of the other unless someone is led to consider one by its similarity to the other. The similarity must be noticed and used as a means of signifying. This would require at the very least that the similarity between an icon and what it signifies should not be shared by a great many other things as well. Thus, while the number seventeen is similar to an elephant in that they share the characteristics of being different from the moon, this is an insufficient basis for iconicity. Some special or striking similarity is required. We have just seen that, by describing an icon rather than presenting it, a metaphor may call attention to similarities which might otherwise pass unnoticed; but even here there are limits to similarities which may be used without simply leaving the reader blank or making him think that the similarity is trivial.

Icons involving both qualitative and structural similarities enter into metaphor. In the metaphor of the fox there is the same sort of relationship between the fox and the characteristic of being sly that there is between the color card and the shade it embodies. In the metaphor in which thoughts enwrap the soul the relationship between the two situations set up is closer to that involving the map. It is not precisely the same as the relation of the map to the territory mapped, however, because this relationship can be expressed entirely in formal, mathematical terms. In the metaphor, it is not merely that there are parallel situations—the same elements in the same arrangement, but also that there is a felt similarity between corresponding components. Thus, gloom in some way or other is thought as something amorphous and enveloping, capable of surrounding in the same way a cloak or blanket does. A cloak or blanket is preferable to a coat because there are no analogues of sleeves in gloom. For similar reasons it would not have done to speak of hateful thoughts entrapping the soul in gloom although it would have left the metre unchanged. However multifarious the forms of traps they are all sharp, with definite edges, and this spoils the correspondence with gloom.

If one asks why only certain objects are felt appropriate to represent gloom the reply would be in terms of the characteristics of gloom itself. Gloom is a pervasive affair in that it influences one's entire mental outlook. It need not have consciously felt causes or itself be the object of direct awareness but rather it tinges all other mental activities. In these respects it is like a wrapping which covers the whole of an object and which allows its form to show through, though modified by the covering. Thus the aptness of metaphor depends on the capability of elaborating it—of extending the parallel structure. In this respect the parallelism is like that of the map and what is mapped, though to a lesser degree and without the rigid similarity.

It is this capability of extension which justifies the differentiation of metaphor from the other tropes. In a figure where the species stands for the genus, one apprehends the relationship, one gains a flavor of concreteness, one perhaps attributes to the entire genus something of the feeling toward the species, and that is all. No further development of the synecdoche is possible. Metaphor, on the other hand, can be spun out, following a line of analogy or even several lines at once, carrying it quite far. For poetry, this is of primary importance; hence the separation of metaphor from the other tropes.

So far metaphor has been described in semantic terms but not yet defined. The characterization given is too broad and includes other things besides metaphor. Thus, we have paraphrased Virginia Woolf's figure as by the phrase "Take any coil of pinkish rubber of a size to be carried by a thrush and you have an icon of what I mean." This phrase itself symbolizes an icon but it is not a metaphor. For some purposes its differences from metaphor are unimportant, and we may use the terms 'metaphoric statement' and 'metaphoric thought' in any case in which there is a reference to anything or any situation by symbolizing its icon. Metaphor then becomes a particular kind of metaphoric statement whose differentia is the following: In a metaphor some terms symbolize the icon and others symbolize what is iconized. This may be said, though less succinctly, in other terms. We have noticed that a metaphor is developed by suggesting parallel situations. In a metaphor some terms refer literally to one situation and figuratively to the second while other terms refer literally only and refer to the second situation only. Thus, in Keats's line 'enwrap' refers literally to the situation of a person with a cloak and figuratively to that of the melancholy person. 'Soul' however has no figurative use and refers only to the melancholy person.

Since we have a semantic characterization of metaphor, this is a convenient point to distinguish it from two related forms—simile and allegory. Simile is differentiated in that it contains no terms with figurative senses. It is true that a simile makes a comparison, often elaborate, which provides a situation parallel to one under discussion, but both sides of the comparison are overtly stated instead of one being symbolized through the other. The similarity between two situations is explicitly mentioned rather than being used symbolically. Everything is on the surface instead of having different semantic levels. Nevertheless, because of the parallel, one side could be used as an icon of the other so a simile may be an invitation to metaphoric thought. Perhaps this is what J. Middleton Murry has in mind in claiming that metaphor is compressed simile.[9] That it is compressed no one will doubt, but, more than this, it is the materials of a simile used to create a new symbolism.

If none of the terms of a simile signify mediately, all those of an allegory do—or at least all the important terms. Thus, an allegory may be considered merely on its literal level and presents a complete account, but there is a deeper meaning, never presented but to be inferred by its parallel to the more superficial meaning. In contrast to this, a metaphor contains some terms which have both literal and figurative meaning (e.g., 'enwrap' in Keats's line) and others which have a literal sense only (e.g., 'soul' and 'gloom' in the same line). Or, to put the point in other words, we have said that there are parallel situations contemplated in a metaphor. Some of the words, taken in their literal sense, refer to one of the situations and some to the other. It is this mixture of literal references to different situations which at once differentiates metaphor from allegory and gives it the impact which psychologically is its distinctive feature.

III.

Besides being discussed from the point of view of the symbolism involved, metaphor may be considered from the point of view of the listener. Here its outstanding characteristic is the sort of shock which it produces. Ordinarily one takes words in their literal sense and this is impossible in a metaphor. This impossibility in fact is what drives one on to seek a figurative sense. When Homer makes the shade of Agamemnon lament:

Upon my son Clytemnestra gave me no time to feed my eyes,[10]

it is absurd to think of eyes literally being fed, so one looks for a figurative sense. Occasionally, a metaphor occurs in which the literal sense is not absurd but merely conveys the wrong meaning. Thus Shakespeare begins his description of Cleopatra's meeting with Anthony as follows:

> The barge she sat in, like a burnish'd throne
> Burn'd on the water [11]

Here 'Burn'd' would make literal sense in the description of a conflagration, but since the context clearly rules this out, a further meaning must be sought. Whether taking all terms in their literal sense produces an absurdity or merely something incongruous the clash of literal meanings must be felt. If it is not, one of two situations must obtain—either the passage is taken literally without encountering any difficulty and no suspicion of a metaphor arises, or else the figurative meaning is so usual that the reader goes to it immediately. In this case one has an idiom or a "dead metaphor" which, properly, is no metaphor at all.

Where the clash of literal senses is felt, however, the problem is to discover which terms cannot be taken in a literal sense and what figurative sense may be attributed to them. That a well-constructed metaphor provides clues for deciding these problems may be seen from a consideration of the metaphor in the following lines:

> Romira stay
> And run not thus like a young Roe away
> No enemie
> Pursues thee (foolish girle) tis onely I
> I'll keep off harms
> If thou'l be pleased to garrison mine arms; [12]

the metaphor in question is that in the last line quoted. Here there is a sort of pun on 'arms' in the sense of upper limbs and also in the sense of weapons. The latter gives an air of paradox with 'garrison' since arms might be used in garrisoning but would not themselves be garrisoned. Since, however, it is the other sense which is intended, this aspect of the line may be neglected, though it unquestionably adds to the effect.

Coming directly to the analysis of the figure, the phrase 'garrison mine arms' contains a clash and cannot be an immediate sign of an attribute of Romira—or of anyone else for that matter. Taken in their literal sense these terms are either meaningless or at best apply to nothing. On the general principle that people try to talk sense and to make statements which are at least possibly true, the passage must be construed as containing a figurative sense. The next question is, what is literal and what is figurative? This question may be answered by noticing that the phrase is applied to Romira, so 'garrison' must be used in a figurative sense. It would be unusual to speak of one person garrisoning anything and, if one did, it must be a redoubtable hero, not a fleeing maiden. Granted this, 'arms' must be taken in a literal sense, for the clash can be resolved only by taking one term of the phrase literally and the other figuratively; and it must be 'arms' in the sense of appendages, not weapons, for there is presumably nothing which Romira could do with a sword or pistol which would make it worthwhile chasing her. Thus far we know that Romira is being instructed to do something mediately signified by 'garrison' to his arms. What she is to do may be discovered by following out the literal sense of 'garrison.' Ordinarily, the only people who garrison anything are soldiers and what they garrison is a fort or citadel or something of the sort. Thus, Romira is to have the same relation to his arms that soldiers have to a fort in garrisoning it. Soldiers defend forts and this may contribute an overtone but it cannot be the basis for a parallel between the situations. The arms are in no need of defense; they seem, rather, bent on aggression. Soldiers also occupy forts and this gives something like the desired sense.

It would be silly to suggest that the term 'occupy' exhausts the meaning of the metaphor; it is merely a first approximation to it. Nor need one suggest that, in reading the lines, one goes through the explicit process set forth above. The intent was not to paraphrase the metaphor or to describe the conscious stages in the apprehension of it, but to show that there were enough clews in the passage to account for the metaphor's being understood. It might happen, moreover, in difficult metaphors that there was some such conscious process.

In simpler metaphors in which there is merely an attribute used in a figurative sense, analysis of this sort is more difficult since there are no articulated parallel structures on which to work back and forth. If one calls a man an old bear there is no relational network in which one can work out the parallel situations; 'bear' has a figurative sense—but there is no structure to delimit it. One must choose therefore some prominent characteristic of the animal as the point of similarity. Where, as in this case, the animal has a number of distinctive characteristics it is a matter of convention which is selected. Thus, the roughness and clumsiness of the bear have been chosen as the basis of the metaphor and this has become entirely standardized. Under other circumstances or in another civilization the fact that the bear is omniverous might have been more impressive and a person of catholic tastes described as a bear. Campbell in his *Philosophy of Rhetoric* remarked:

. . . let it be observed that the noun *sail* in our tongue is frequently used, and by the same trope the noun *puppis* in Latin, to denote a ship. Let these synecdoches of a part of the whole, which are so very similar, be translated and transposed, and you will immediately perceive that a man would not be said to speak Latin, who in that language should call a ship *velum;* nor would you think that he spoke better English, who in our language should call it a *poop.*

What he says of synecdoche applies equally to metaphor, and he continues:

. . . of two words even in the same language, which are synonymous or nearly so, one will be used figuratively to denote an object, which it would be insufferable to employ the other to denote, though naturally as fit for suggesting it. It hath been said, that "an excellent *vein* of satire runs through the whole of Gulliver's travels:" substitute here *artery* in the room of vein, and you will render the sentence absolutely ridiculous.[13]

Campbell's point may be stated in another way. There is a narrow sense of understanding a language in which one may be said to understand a language when he knows the grammar, the literal meanings of all the terms, and even the meaning of idioms. Such knowledge does not suffice for the understanding of the metaphors of the language. In addition one must know something of linguistic conventions—such as that governing the choice of 'vein' and 'artery' and even of minor facets of the general culture, such as what characteristics of bears are uppermost in people's minds. This aspect is especially prominent in metaphors where an evaluation is the basis of the parallel. A popular song of some years ago praised a young lady by saying to her "You're the cream in my coffee." Entirely the wrong impression would be obtained in a community which drank its coffee black. This sociological aspect of metaphors has been employed by Whorf and his students in using language as a means of analyzing culture,[14] comparing widely differing cultures, though its value with more closely related societies remains to be seen. For this purpose commonplace and more or less standard metaphors are, of course, of greater value than the more original creations of poets.

Thus far we have seen something of the semantic structure of metaphor and something of the psychological elements leading to its apprehension—the consciousness of clash of literal senses from which its starts and the clues and conventions by which it is apprehended. This is not to claim, of course, that everyone can understand every metaphor. Often, of course, metaphors are not understood; they rest on a similarity which is unfamiliar to the reader or on a convention which he does not know. Often also a metaphor is only partly understood. One develops a feeling for the kind of parallel required without quite seeing what it is.

IV.

The function of metaphor in general is to extend language, to say what cannot be said in terms of literal meanings alone. Such extension may be in either of two directions, by way of increasing the scope or breadth of language or alternatively by increasing the finesse or depth of language. Metaphor is the same in either case, it is the sort of thing we have been describing, but the use to which it is put is different and the qualifications for successful use vary accordingly. It will be advantageous, therefore, to discuss these two uses separately.

Metaphor may be used whenever something new is invented

requiring a name or whenever it seems desirable to call attention to an undesignated aspect of something already known.
In such a case there are a number of possibilities open—the
obvious one is to create an entirely new word, but this has the
disadvantage of being completely unintelligible when first
heard. A common alternative is to construct a compound word
whose sense is derivative from that of its components: 'micro-
scope' and the German 'fernsprecher' are cases in point. Alternatively a metaphor may be used. In many cases this has the
advantage of enabling the person hearing the metaphor to
identify the object even though he has never seen it before
and never heard the word in its figurative sense. Thus, the
lower shell of a turtle is called its plastron, which originally
meant a breastplate, as in a suit of armor. When applied to a
turtle this must originally have been a metaphor, yet knowing
only what then was the literal meaning of the term and seeing
a turtle there would be no doubt as to what was its plastron.
Again, when automobiles became common, a terminology became necessary to their various parts. The name given to the
part over the motor was assigned by what was originally a
metaphor, i.e., it was what stood in the same relation to a car
that a hood did to a person. It is interesting to notice, in this
connection, that the metaphor 'hood of a car' could have been
designated either of two parts—the hood or the top which is
called 'hood' in England. Here the metaphor does not uniquely
select the intended object but, by limiting the possibilities, still
serves a useful purpose.

Metaphors of this type tend to vanish, not in the sense that
they are no longer used, but in the sense that they become
literal, so that today no one would think of saying that 'plastron
of a turtle' or 'hood of a car' were metaphors. What seems to
be involved in the shift away from metaphors seems to be approximately as follows: One way of coming to understand a
term is to know how to apply it. It has been argued that this
is the only way, but this controversy need not detain us here
since, certainly, it is a way. Thus, hearing the metaphor 'hood
of a car,' when this was a metaphor, one was enabled to dis-

cover the required part by looking for something in proper relationship to the car. Having found it, however, one could notice its shape, its position on the car and its relation to other parts and so recognize it. Independent of the metaphor, one would have memories of how hoods had looked and expectations of how they should look. Then any meaning for 'hood' except these memories and expectations became unimportant and the metaphorical element dropped out. We have seen that a metaphor requires a clash of terms. When the phrase was first heard there would be such a clash—a wondering what a head-covering would do on an automobile. Once the required part was recognized, however, the clash may be forgotten and the phrase might be considered a single unit, designating something whose appearance is known. Thus the metaphor would disappear and a new literal sense would be born. As we shall notice subsequently, there is considerable discussion among literary critics as to whether metaphors may be paraphrased adequately and so reduced to literal meanings. Metaphors of the type here discussed have obviously been forgotten in such controversies since, clearly, they become literal meanings.

There are other metaphors which become literal and extend language, although not in the simple fashion noticed above. Eric Havelock has traced the development of some of the Greek philosophic concepts from the stage at the time of Homer.[15] They were not expressible in Homeric Greek, and metaphor is one of the principal means whereby they were developed. So for example, Havelock suggests that the term 'cosmos' originally referred to a pleasing sort of array such as a woman's head-dress or the trappings of a horse's harness. Later, by a metaphorical extension it was applied to the ranks of an army and then, by a further extension of the same sort, to the order of the universe as a whole. Here again the term did not remain metaphorical, but engendered a literal meaning. The process used to explain the earlier examples will not serve here, however, since there can be no recognition or identification of a cosmos in the same sense that a hood of a car can be recognized. We know of no satisfactory theory as to how such terms become literal and presumably it must wait on the working out of a general theory of meaning. In cases of this sort, however, metaphor is even more important for extended language than in those considered before. After all, the undershell of a turtle is simply there and can be pointed at if necessary to call attention to it. A world order may equally be there, but it certainly cannot be pointed at in the same way. The only means of thinking about it may be the metaphor. Perhaps the new idea is inconceivable apart from the metaphor.

There can be no doubt then that both in the development of concrete and abstract terms metaphor plays an important role, but how important has not been sufficiently worked out.

Cohen [16] gives some hint of it when he says: "Indeed whenever we speak of the mind doing anything, collecting its data, perceiving the external world, and the like, we are using the metaphor of reification, just as we use the metaphor of personification whenever we speak of bodies attracting and repelling each other." Regardless of whether or not one wishes to agree that all these terms are metaphors, at least this is how they all must have originated. While a tremendous number of etymologies attest to the scope of metaphor in linguistic change, there seem to have been no general studies of the topic. Cohen has mentioned two pervasive metaphors; are there others equally prevalent? Can they be classified in any way? Are the same general types of metaphors common to all languages? These are similar questions; all remain unanswered. The importance of metaphor in the development of abstract concepts similarly can only be guessed at and any more accurate determination must await further studies.

v.

The use of metaphor discussed in the preceding section is creative in that it adds to the range of a language, enabling it to deal with new situations. The literary or poetic use of metaphor is also creative, but in a different way, bringing out a new aspect, or showing a new way of feeling, concerning something already describable in the language. Because metaphor symbolizes one situation by means of another, there is the opportunity of infusing the symbolized situation with the feeling belonging to the one which functions as symbol. That this transfer of feeling occurs may be seen from a consideration of inverse metaphors, whose existence was already pointed out by Aristotle. He says: "As old age (D) is to life (C), so is evening (B) to the day (A). One will accordingly describe evening (B) as the 'old age *of the day*' (D + A)—or by the Empodoclean equivalent; and old age (D) as the 'evening' or 'sunset of life' (B + C)." [17]

That such inversion is possible is of course a consequence of the iconic character of metaphor. It would be possible in every metaphor but, and this is the point, the feeling tone is different in the two cases. Both Aristotle's metaphors are hackneyed by now and have lost their bite, but even so there is a pleasant and cheerful feeling in talking of the sunset of life— because the sunset itself is this sort of event—and there is something cold about the old age of the day. In a society which placed a premium on old age this might be different, but these examples indicate at least that the feeling which goes with the literal sense carries over to the figurative one.

To make the same point with less trite examples, we may recall Hall's metaphor inviting Romira to garrison his arms. It not merely suggests occupying or coming within as was claimed above but suggests a certain way of doing it—the way in which soldiers might occupy a fort. They take possession—a self-assertive act. They show, or prepare to show, courage in the forthcoming defense. Thus the suggestion is not merely that Romira come to him, but that she comes confidently, as if this were her proper place, and bravely instead of ignominiously running away. This, of course, is no more than a suggestion of the feeling indicated, but let us look at those in the converse metaphor. In the given case Romira was asked to come into his arms through being asked to garrison them. Conversely— changing grammatical subject and object—that a fort is garrisoned might be expressed by saying that the fort embraced the troops. But here the suggestion is different. Instead of merely receiving them, we now have the notion that the fort welcomed them, that there was joy in their reception. Here again in either the metaphor or its converse there is a carry-over from the feeling of the literal sense to that of the figurative.

Thus there are two similarities which may enter into a metaphor—an antecedent similarity, the aspect which makes it possible for one situation to represent another iconically which was discussed in Section II. In addition there may be an induced similarity, such as the similarity of feeling which, as we have just noticed, is transferred from symbolizing situation to situation symbolized. 'Transferred,' however, is too strong a word here—the feeling is not simply carried across from one situation to the other, rather an aura of the feeling in the one case pervades the other. We do not feel toward Romira's coming as we would to soldiers entering a fort, but the comparison has created just the suggestion of a proud or triumphal entry. This nuance of feeling may well be the reason for the employment of the figure, for in many cases there does not seem any other way of conveying just the same impression.

In the preceding chapter, various aspects of meaning, cognitive and noncognitive, were pointed out, and it was maintained that a term in a metaphor must have a double primary cognitive content—that involved in its literal sense and that involved in its figurative sense. What we are now suggesting is that there is similarly a double feeling expressed in the metaphor but that the two are not unrelated and that the feeling accompanying the figurative sense is modified by and in fact caused by the feeling accompanying the literal sense. This modification of the way of thinking of what the metaphor symbolizes indirectly may be called the *induced content* of the metaphor. The matter may be put in this way: a metaphor we have noticed has to do with two situations—that symbolized literally and that symbolized figuratively. There must be an initial similarity between them to make the metaphor possible. We are now arguing that supervening on this initial similarity there may be an additional similarity suggested or caused by the use of the metaphor. This is the induced content.

In the above discussion the only sort of induced content considered was feeling. On the other hand the definition was framed so as to avoid any such limitation. This at once raises the question as to whether there may not be induced conceptual content as well. Such contents, if they exist, are of relatively minor importance in poetic use of metaphor and so have not been discussed here. They may however be of importance in connection with the use of metaphor to extended language in cases where the metaphor vanishes. In some cases, we noticed that the metaphor acquired a literal meaning by the development of the ability to recognize what it designated; in other cases this explanation could not be given. Many philosophical terms are of this latter sort and it is difficult if not impossible to develop means of recognition for such terms as 'substance' or 'ego.' It may be in such cases that part of the meaning is given by an induced content. There must in the case of 'substance,' for example, have been a primary similarity between the characteristic of an object and the foundation of a house. In terms of this, one could metaphorically refer to something standing under the qualities, but additional properties of substance such as its permanence would seem to be induced content.

To return to the literary use of metaphor, something similar to the view suggested here has been quite differently but admirably expressed by Kenneth Burke, who writes: "Metaphor is a device for seeing something *in terms* of something else. . . . A metaphor tells us something about one character considered from the point of view of another character. And to consider A from the point of view of B is, of course, to use B as a *perspective* upon A." [18]

The use of 'perspective' here is of course itself metaphorical but it is hard to see what it would mean except that one situation is seen in terms of the feelings of another. Perhaps this also is in Murry's mind when he suggests that metaphor is "the means by which the less familiar is assimilated to the more familiar, the unknown to the known." [19] In general, the conceptual subject matter of poetry is familiar enough, but it is the way of feeling which needs explanation.

It is this aspect of metaphor which renders the question of paraphrases of metaphors difficult. In the language-building function, we have seen, a metaphor becomes its own paraphrase, but in the cases where subtlety of way of seeing and feeling are desired this is not the case and there is doubt whether a paraphrase can express anything like the exact import of the original. There are all sorts of opinion to be found on the point. Thus Hershberger has argued:

. . . that metaphor, the distinctive feature of poetry, *is* fundamentally an expository, and—in its way—economic prose usage; that in principle, through scientific study of the aesthetic experience, a metaphor is reducible to a multiplicity of integrated prose arguments; that science is admittedly inadequate at the present time, for this analysis; and that pseudo-scientific analysis has discredited such an approach by failing to be conducted by aesthetically sensitive persons.[20]

While on the other hand Cleanth Brooks in discussing the view that poetry makes an assertion says:

Let the reader try to formulate a proposition that will say what the poem "says." As his proposition approaches adequacy, he will find, not only that it has increased greatly in length, but that it has begun to fill itself up with reservations and qualifications—and most significant of all—the formulator will find that he has himself begun to fall back upon metaphors of his own in his attempt to indicate what the poem "says." In sum his proposition, as it approaches adequacy ceases to be a proposition.[21]

Clearly, for Brooks, metaphors can never give way to their paraphrases. Cohen expresses a similar view.[22]

Without going into the arguments in either side, it may be well to follow a suggestion of I. A. Richards in discussing what one wants when he attempts to express a metaphor in other terms. He says: "We can put varying sorts of limitations on 'express'; they give us different kinds of meaning—mere sense, sense and implications, feelings, the speaker's attitudes to whatever it is, to his audience, the speaker's confidence, and other things." [23] Richards then goes on to argue that while perhaps any of these senses may be paraphrased, all of them cannot be in a single paraphrase.

In one respect at least Richards is unquestionably right. There is a sense of shock about a metaphor which we have noticed before and which results from the clash of juxtaposed literal sense. It has almost an epigrammatic quality and this must be lost in any paraphrase. Unquestionably it is part of the effect of the metaphor and, if all effects be counted as part of the meaning, then no paraphrase can be adequate. Even given this limitation it seems quite probable as Richards suggests, that further sacrifices must be made in paraphrase.

For one thing, many poetic metaphors are multiple iconic— there being not merely one basic similarity on which the metaphor is based but several. Each of these may be capable of indefinite expansion, and there may be interactions between the similarities. Where one leaves open a range of possibilities, another may narrow them. Perhaps this interaction might be paraphrased if one were willing to take the similarity successively instead of almost simultaneously, but clearly there would be a tremendous loss of effect. If one is willing to sacrifice this aspect as well then there is no absurdity in holding that there should be a literal sense with the same cognitive content and emotional expression as is contained in a metaphor. Two points must be remembered however; first, that a paraphrase of this sort would not be equivalent to a metaphor in effect. It would be very long and cumbersome and would lose the interaction of the similarities. Second, while such a paraphrase is a theoretical possibility its construction would, to say the least, be very difficult and, practically speaking, impossible. Thus, as a matter of fact though not of logical necessity one must agree with Brooks' remark. This is not to say, however, that Herschberger is right in claiming the possibility of an ideal paraphrase into scientific statements. To make this claim is either to maintain that scientific statements may be more than cognitive or to claim that noncognitive aspects of meaning are reducible to cognitive. Since this problem is discussed in Chapter 5 we need here only indicate our disbelief in either alternative. There is one more aspect to the problem. We have seen that where metaphor is used to extend language, the disappearance of the primary clash of senses produces a literal sense of the term. In metaphors of the more poetic type, something of the same sort may go on, resulting in a well-established figurative sense of a term and a trite metaphor. Thus one may call a man an old goat or a poor fish with hardly any consideration of either animal, something may be nipped in the bud without much thought of flowers, and one may claim something is liquidated while hardly considering fluids. Such metaphors have been used in so wide a variety of circumstances and so often that there is a tendency to consider merely a sort of standard figurative meaning without paying attention to the literal one. Wherever this happens, a metaphor may be more easily paraphrased.

We may conclude that apart from the impact of a metaphor in presenting a conflict in so small a compass, there is no obstacle in principle to the adequate paraphrase of a metaphor though the difficulties may be very great in practice. They are least when the metaphor has become trite. Metaphors, like chemical elements, display unusual powers in a nascent state.

Chapter 8

SYMBOLISM

IN THE NONREPRESENTATIONAL ARTS

I.

There are four important ways in which those interested in the arts might hope to profit by studying the nature of symbolism. Only the fourth will be developed in this chapter, but a brief mention of the first three is needed to indicate the neighborhood, so to speak, in which the fourth is located.

In the first place, an interest in symbolism may spring from an effort to clarify and supplement the vocabulary of criticism. A critic who uses the term 'spatial rhythm,' for instance, may or may not communicate to us exactly what he means. If he attempts to define the term he takes a first step toward an interest in symbolism; and if he finds that an acceptable definition is not easily given (as he is likely to) he may be led to discuss terminological issues of a more general character. Thus, he may ask such questions as these: "Can a term like 'spatial rhythm' be helpfully defined by means of other terms, or must one point out its meaning by the use of examples?"; or "To what extent does 'spatial rhythm' become intelligible from the use of the word 'rhythm' in other contexts, such as those dealing with the rhythms of music and poetry?" This sort of interest is evident (to take only one of many possible examples) in Bernard Heyl's *New Bearings in Aesthetics and Art Criticism*,[1] where the author, a historian and critic of the spatial arts, feels hampered by the terms that are at his disposal. In trying to remedy the situation he is led to study signs more generally, with attention to the nature and function of definitions.

In the second place, the interest may spring from an effort to understand an artist's personality or his times by making a careful study of his works. Here the sign in question is not this or that term that a critic uses in discussing the arts, but is rather a work of art itself—the term 'sign,' of course, being used in an extremely broad sense. Thus Freud attempts to disclose certain of Leonardo's unconscious desires, finding signs of them in the *Mona Lisa* and other paintings—the symbolic meaning of these paintings being interpreted by much the same techniques that Freud uses in interpreting dreams.[2] We have much the same thing, on a less complex level, outside psychoanalysis. When Robert Graves, in a novel,[3] portrayed Milton as an insensitive, harsh, and altogether petty man, his critics insisted that Milton's poetry was in itself a sufficient sign (in the very broad sense of that term that we are now considering) that Graves's characterization was unjust. Or for that matter, we have a simple case when we take our radio and television programs as a sign of the prevailing level of our culture. One can make off-hand observations about these matters, of course, without any general and explicit *theory* of signs; but a theory might help to make our observations more trustworthy. Note that it would be a broad and many-sided theory, suited to this broad sense of 'sign.'

Although the work of art is considered as a sign in these cases, its sign function is not necessarily of a sort that must be grasped by those who are appreciating the work. If it should happen that the work is better appreciated after this aspect of its sign function is attended to, that would be somewhat accidental; for aesthetic interest here gives place to an interest in biography, history, and psychology.

The third sort of interest in symbolism takes us closer to peculiarly aesthetic problems. It is concerned with the arts normally classified as representational (such as literature, portrait painting, etc.) and not with the arts normally classified as nonrepresentational (such as pure music, nonobjective painting, architecture, etc.) Here the work of art has a sign function that we must presumably take into account if we are to have a full appreciation of the work. A critic helps us in our interpretation of signs, for instance, when he analyzes an obscure passage in a poem, or when he comments on the subject matter of a picture. A *general* theory of signs can obviously be important as a background for interpreting these particular signs —as is the case with Richards, Empson, Burke, Murry, Brooks, etc.,[4] though these writers frequently have the first sort of interest we have mentioned as well.

The fourth sort of interest in symbolism is simply a generalization of the third. It is based on the hope that the arts normally classified as nonrepresentational, no less than those normally classified as representational, have an important sign-function—and one that is not merely of biographical, historical, or psychological interest, like that mentioned in our second heading, but one that is of genuine aesthetic interest. Thus Schopenhauer wrote of music: "The composer reveals the inner nature of the world, and expresses the deepest wisdom in a language which his reason does not understand; as a person under the influence of mesmerism tells things of which he has no conception when he awakes." [5] And Croce speaks of all the arts, representational and nonrepresentational alike, as being a "language." [6] Views of this sort differ markedly from one another, and by many writers are rejected altogether. But whatever one may think about them, they frequently reappear in aesthetic theories of the present day—theories that appeal to the study of signs in an effort to reveal unsuspected relationships between the several arts, or to enhance our appreciation of them, or even to explain the importance of the arts in social and individual life.

These four headings do not *exhaust* the ways in which a study of symbolism is related to aesthetics. To take a passing example, none of them includes the interest in symbolism that one would have if he were trying to simplify the notation of music, or improve or standardize the notation that is used in choreography. But they will be sufficient to orient the fourth heading, which, as has been said, is the only one that the present chapter will attempt to discuss.

II.

In a very broad sense of 'sign,' and one constantly used by Charles Morris,[7] the arts commonly called nonrepresentational have *quite obviously* the status of signs. But the very obviousness of the point should warn us against taking it to be more than of passing interest. To understand this let us examine Morris's work somewhat closely, with particular attention to what he wants the word 'sign' to mean.

Morris speaks of a *sign situation* whenever any entity, S, leads us to take account of some entity, D. He goes on to say that S, when so used, is the *sign*, that the process-of-taking-account-of is the *interpretant* of the sign, and that D is the sign's *designatum* or *denotatum*. A sign has a denotatum only when the designatum actually exists (as Morris uses the terms); thus 'unicorn' has a designatum but no denotatum.

Now when 'sign' (along with its supplementary terms) is used in this way, its sense is extremely broad, since the phrase 'take account of' is ubiquitous in its applications. We have a sign situation when a dog, detecting the scent, chases a fox. We have another when, on seeing a friend, we reach out to shake his hand; for our visual experience obviously leads us to take account of something—namely, the friend himself, or if you like, merely his hand, or the experience of feeling his hand as we shake it. We have another sign situation when an astronomer takes the present state of the heavens as a sign of a coming eclipse—or for that matter, when an astrologer takes it as a calamity, for if the calamity doesn't come it will even so be the designatum of a sign that has no denotatum. It is not easy, in fact, to find a complex psychological process that *doesn't* involve the interpretation of a sign. So for this broad sense it is only to be expected that we should find many sign situations in our appreciation of the arts—including even such arts as pure music and nonobjective painting.

Morris himself gives such examples as this: in any complex work of art one part may occasion expectations that are fulfilled in another part, and since the one leads us to take account of the other it becomes a sign of it.[8] There can be no doubt that this happens in ever so many cases of aesthetic appreciation; but it is of no more than passing interest, as suggested above, simply because the observation is so elementary, and because the situation is so little illuminated by being called "symbolic" rather than something else.

Morris gives this further and more strained example: in considering whether a nonobjective work of art, such as a Greek border, can have a denotatum, he points out that "every iconic sign has its own sign vehicle among its denotata," and that "there is sometimes no denotatum other than the aesthetic sign vehicle itself." [9] This can be made a little more concrete than Morris makes it by the following observation: A man who sees a Greek border only casually may immediately become more interested in it, and take a second look. So the border, *via* the first look, may lead the man to take account of it via the second look, and may thus become a sign of itself. Moreover, since a sign becomes iconic in virtue of a similarity between itself and its designatum, we need only the principle, "Everything resembles itself," to conclude that a Greek border can be an *iconic* sign of itself. Note that the same thing can be said of anything on earth, provided only that it is perceivable and of sufficient interest to get a second look.

Morris presses these considerations still further. If a work of art can be a sign of itself, it can also be a sign of its properties —for in leading us to take account of itself it leads us to take account of its properties as well. And if its value is one of its properties, it may lead us to take account of that, becoming a sign that "designates a value"—a conclusion that Morris welcomes.[10]

There can be no doubt that signs referring to themselves have sometimes interesting examples. Thus in Pope's familiar:

And ten low words oft creep in one dull line,[11]

his words immediately lead us to take account of themselves, and so (in Morris' very broad sense) are signs of themselves. But it is hard to believe that this simple observation has far-reaching implications.

In general, when Morris remarks, "Aesthetics thus becomes in its entirety a subdivision of semiotic" [12] ('semiotic' being his name for the study of signs), it is important to realize that no one would be likely to disagree with him. If his statement at first seems surprising, that is only because it suggests that he is finding more sign situations in the arts than others are accustomed to recognize. But he is not doing that at all. He is simply calling an unusual number of processes by the name 'sign situation,' using the name in such a broad sense that its application to nonobjective painting, pure music, architecture, etc., can be taken for granted.

If anything is to come from Morris' approach, it must come not merely from an attempt to classify aesthetics as a branch of the theory of signs but rather from a detailed study showing that the problems of aesthetics, when so classified, can be discussed in a more illuminating way. In particular, it must be shown that the skills developed elsewhere in the study of signs (in linguistics, for example, and in certain parts of logic) can be transferred to parallel situations that arise in the study of the arts. And Morris has scarcely made a beginning of this. He has suggested that all the arts have their syntactical, pragmatic, and semantic rules,[13] but it is hard to see how his suggestion will help us to improve our understanding of these rules. Presumably, the syntactical rules of music are no more than the rules of harmony and counterpoint, together with those broader rules of composition that concern the form of the sonata, the fugue, etc. And it is not clear that these familiar disciplines, once they are classified as "syntax," will have enough in common with the syntax of ordinary languages, or the syntax of logic, to make the classification useful.

It is possible that Morris' programmatic suggestions will some day be worked out in detail and that his innumerable sign situations will prove, in spite of their many differences, to have similarities such that they may be profitably studied together. His own more recent work,[14] however, is disappointingly silent about this. And until more detailed work has been done, his views can have only the importance that comes from a promise, and not the importance that comes from an achievement.

III.

If we use 'sign' in a somewhat narrower sense than Morris does, ruling out the more trivial of his examples, an application of the theory of signs to the arts in general (and not merely to those normally classified as representational) becomes much harder to defend. Such arts as pure music and nonobjective painting appear to have no aesthetically relevant symbolic function at all. Mrs. Susanne Langer, however, has argued that they do in fact have such a function, and a very important one. And whatever is to be thought of her view, it is not trivial; rightly or wrongly, it ascribes a symbolic function to the arts that other writers have often denied to them. So let us summarize a part of what she says and see if it is plausible. The account that follows will be based largely on her *Philosophy in a New Key;* [15] and it will deal with her views on music, since that is the part of her work that she has subsequently generalized in dealing with the other arts.[16]

The symbolic function of music, according to Mrs. Langer, serves primarily to relate it to the *emotions*. Her conception of this relationship is so complicated, however, that we can best come to understand it by contrasting it with a simpler one that she explicitly rejects.

It is often said that music *expresses* the emotions; but 'expresses' is not necessarily a synonym of 'symbolizes' or 'designates.' So if one of the older expressionists had stated his view in contemporary terminology, he might have been inclined to make very little of the topic of symbolism, speaking in some such fashion as this: "Music is not a sign of an emotion but is rather a particularly intimate and direct cause or effect of it. If it signifies at all it signifies something that is quite distinct from an emotion. Program music may represent a storm, for instance; but although it may do this partly with the *help* of an emotion— the emotion being appropriate to the storm and thus reminding us of it—we must remember that it is the storm that it designates, and not the emotion. The emotion can at most be accessory to the *interpretant* of the musical sign; and if we should take it as the *designatum* as well we should divert 'designatum' into such a confused sense that it would be useless."

Now Mrs. Langer's way of connecting music with the emotions is definitely not this way. She sharply denies what the expressionists most wish to affirm—that music is an immediate cause or effect of an emotion. Roughly speaking, she thinks that we only suppose that we feel an emotion when we listen to music, but that we really do not. A fortiori, she denies that a felt emotion, in program music, is an accessory to the interpretant of a musical sign. Indeed, she mentions program music only in order to repudiate it.[17] And this leads her to give the emotions a place in a symbolic situation that the expressionists (or at least, those of them who subscribe to a view like the one just mentioned) do not give to it. She holds that music quite literally *designates* an emotion. It doesn't give release to the composer's emotions, and (normally) it doesn't cause emotions in the listener. Rather, it *stands for* an emotion, or *represents* it.

To those who are accustomed to the expressionist theory Mrs. Langer's repudiation of it may seem arbitrary; so let us examine this negative part of her view a little more closely.

She acknowledges, to be sure, that people *sometimes* feel emotions when they listen to music, even to the point of weeping. But this comes as an acknowledgment rather than an affirmation; and she thinks that the cases in which people feel emotions are atypical, involving a lack of psychic distance (in Bullough's sense) that most musicians are accustomed to preserve.[18] Typically, then, music is attended by no emotion; and her reasons for saying so are essentially these:

Sheer self-expression requires no artistic form. A lynching-party howling round the gallows-tree, a woman wringing her hands over a sick child, a lover who has just rescued his sweetheart in an accident and stands trembling, sweating, and perhaps laughing or crying with emotion, is giving vent to intense feelings; but such scenes are not occasions for music, least of all for composing.[19]

In the second place, she thinks that the presence of strongly felt emotions would leave us puzzled to explain how music can be performed:

If the primary purpose of music were to enable us to work off our subjective experiences it would be utterly impossible for an artist to announce a program in advance . . . or even . . . to *express himself* successively in *allegro, adagio, presto,* and *allegretto,* as the changing moods of a single sonata are apt to dictate. Such mercurial passions would be abnormal even in the notoriously capricious race of musicians! [20]

And in the third place, she feels that if we take music as providing only substitutes, as it were, for the emotions of real life, we shall be led to underestimate its importance:

Let us now explicitly abandon the problems of music as stimulus and music as emotive symptom, since neither of these functions . . . would suffice to account for the importance that we attach to it.[21]

We must consider later on whether or not these are very strong reasons for abandoning the expression theory of music. For the moment we need only note that Mrs. Langer abandons it without the slightest regret.

Like every other writer on music, however, Mrs. Langer wants to recognize some sense, and some very fundamental sense, in which we can distinguish between music that is emotionally impoverished and music that is emotionally rich. A Czerny exercise is not a Beethoven sonata, and no one could play or hear the one with the emotional insight that is appropriate to the other. So Mrs. Langer immediately proceeds to reinstate the emotions in her theory of music, though in her own way. That is the constructive part of her work to which we must now turn. Her central thesis is evident from such a remark as this:

If music has any significance, it is semantic, not symptomatic. . . . If it has any emotional content, it "has" it in the same sense that language "has" its conceptual content—symbolically.[22]

It will be observed that she here makes an implicit reference to the three elements that enter into any sign situation. The sign itself is the music; the designatum of the sign is the emotion; and the interpretant of the sign, whatever else it may be, is something generically comparable to the interpretant of a linguistic sign, being of a "conceptual" nature.

She then goes on to discuss the *particular way* in which music becomes a sign of an emotion. And here her view, though not altogether clear, is clear at least to this extent: she takes music to be what Peirce and Morris would call an *iconic* sign of the emotion that it designates. It is not strictly comparable to the iconic signs that we find in portraits, etc., since the point of resemblance between sign and designatum, in music, is more abstract. But it is nevertheless an iconic sign of a certain kind; and to understand what it is (as she conceives it) we must see what sort of resemblance it involves.

In good measure Mrs. Langer adopts a principle that has been much emphasized in contemporary psychology: that the felt resemblances between experiences extend beyond the range of any one sense-field. She holds that certain musical patterns *sound like* emotions. This is central to the view of Carroll Pratt, from whom she quotes, with approval, the following passage:

[The auditory characteristics] of music intrinsically contain certain properties which, because of their close resemblance to certain characteristics in the subjective realm, are frequently confused with emotions proper. . . . [But] these auditory characters are not emotions at all. They merely sound the way moods feel.[23]

And perhaps the point can be made in this alternative way: just as a diapason stop, on an organ, sounds more like a smooth *touch* than does a reed stop, so a soft, consonant musical phrase sounds more like a tranquil *mood* than does a loud, dissonant one.

But it is evident, throughout, that Mrs. Langer is thinking of some more complicated point of resemblance between music and emotions—some further sort of iconicity—than the above view will serve to suggest. And the clue to what she means lies in her description of music as being a "logical" [24] picture of the emotions it designates, and as having a "morphology" [25] that is similar to them. Although it is difficult to interpret these remarks, it is probable that they refer to what in logic and mathematics is referred to as an "isomorphism," in the sense previously explained in Chapter 4. Let us first examine this term, and then attempt to show its specific connection with Mrs. Langer's problem in aesthetics.

Any map is said to be isomorphic with the region it maps. For each point on the map uniquely corresponds to a point on the region mapped, and some relations between points on the map (e.g., to the left of) have corresponding relations in the region mapped (e.g., west of). More generally, when any two entities have such a correspondence between their elements, and such a correspondence between certain relations holding between these elements, then the entities are isomorphic with respect to these elements and relations.

Suppose, then (to take another, and altogether trivial example, but one that may help to illustrate the point in question) that we correlate the squares on a chess board with various musical sounds. And suppose that the sounds correlated with any given rank of squares are all of the same pitch, but grow louder and louder corresponding to a movement from left to right along the rank. And suppose that the sounds correlated with any given file of squares are all of the same loudness, but grow higher and higher in pitch, by steps of the diatonic scale, corresponding to a motion up the file. In that case the sounds in question will be isomorphic with the chessboard, since there will be a correspondence in both elements and relations. The sounds, metaphorically speaking, will be a nonspatial "map" of the chess-board. (Note that the squares covered by a bishop's move from the near left corner to the far right corner would be "mapped" by a one-octave, diatonic scale, played with a steady crescendo.)

Now the most characteristic part of Mrs. Langer's view of music (if the present interpretation of her remarks is in any way near to being correct) is that the forms of music are isomorphic with the *emotions* that the music symbolizes. So we must go on to examine the particular respects in which she thinks the isomorphism holds. One cannot easily avoid the impression, in reading this part of Mrs. Langer's work, that she has in mind a much more elaborate isomorphism than she has been able to mention in detail; but a beginning of her view is this:

In music there are passages that have a certain "tension," and others that have a certain "resolution." [26] ('Resolution' by the way, is to be understood in a rather broader sense than is current in traditional harmony.) Mrs. Langer takes these terms from von Hoeslin, but it may be mentioned, in passing, that she might equally well have taken the first of them from Hindemith, who represents the increasing and decreasing "tensions" of music by diagrams. [27] These tensions and resolutions are presumably Gestalt qualities and not reducible without remainder to this or that combination of notes; but roughly speaking, tension tends to go with dissonances, quick modulations, large melodic skips, etc., and resolutions with the opposite to these. Now in a musical composition we may consider passages with varying degrees of tension and resolution as being the *elements* which, when correlated with the elements in an emotion, begin to establish the isomorphism in question. And to see what might be considered elements in the emotion we need only remember that the emotion is not an undifferentiated feeling, but is rather a changing state of mind, some phases of it involving complex feelings and attitudes, and others relatively tranquil, simple ones. As might be expected, the intense, complex elements of the emotion are taken as correlates of the musical tensions, and the others with the musical resolutions.

This correlation of *elements* goes only part way toward establishing an isomorphism; for there must also be a correlation of certain *relations* holding between the elements. And what will these relations be? One of them, clearly, will be of a temporal nature. Whenever a musical tension occurs *before* a musical resolution, then a tense phase of the correlated emotion will occur *before* a relatively tranquil one. But the exact duration of the temporal intervals need not, presumably, be the same; for the music may "map" the emotion on either a large or a small scale. A more important relation, however, will be a *requiredness* of the sort emphasized by Wertheimer and Köhler. Whenever there is a requiredness between a musical tension and a musical resolution, there will be *some* relation between the corresponding elements in the emotion. The latter relation may also be a requiredness; but it may, alternatively, be simply a causal relation, the intense phase of the emotion bringing about physiological changes, for instance, that in turn bring about the relatively tranquil phase.

It must be understood that this is a somewhat conjectural interpretation of Mrs. Langer's view. As previously remarked, she seems to have in mind a much richer isomorphism than she is prepared to exemplify. An elaboration of her view might profitably make more of her references to Köhler, who points out that when we use musical terms to refer to the emotions of everyday life, as in expressions like "increased inner tempo," we seem to be emphasizing, by metaphor, an important analogy.[28] She finds these metaphors wholly congenial to her thesis about "morphology." But for the moment the above remarks will be sufficient to serve as a simplified model, at least, for the view that she seems to be expressing.

Mrs. Langer does not expect music, in view of the isomorphism in question, to designate highly specific emotions. It cannot, she thinks, designate some one, peculiar sorrow, like the sorrow of the Wotan, as distinct from some other noble sorrow. In fact music may designate emotions "ambiguously," as is evident from this quotation:

It is a peculiar fact that some musical forms seem to bear a sad and a happy interpretation equally well. At first sight that looks paradoxical; but it really has perfectly good reasons, which do not invalidate the notion of emotive significance, but do bear out the right-mindedness of thinkers who recoil from the admission of specific meanings. For *what music can actually reflect is only the morphology of feeling;* and it is quite plausible that some sad and some happy conditions may have a very similar morphology.[29]

But in spite of recognizing this ambiguity, she holds that the isomorphism between music and the emotions is what gives music its importance; it enables music to act as a sign that gives us "insight" into the emotions.

It should be noted that Mrs. Langer often calls music a "presentational" symbol of the emotions. The essential part of what she means by this is evident from her remark that the parts of such a symbol can be understood "only through the meaning of the whole, through their relations within the total structure." [30] This bears out the present interpretation, which compares her conception of music to a map of the emotions. A circle on a map is not destined by its shape to be a sign, say, of Ann Arbor, but becomes a sign of it mainly because of its relations to other parts of the map; and similarly, a chord in music is not destined to have tension, and to designate an intense phase of an emotion merely because of its own nature, but acquires this function because of its relation to the whole context of notes in which it occurs. It is on this ground that Mrs. Langer finds it misleading to call music the "language" of the emotions. Language, whose symbolic function is "discursive," as opposed to "presentational," has a fixed vocabulary, the significance of its words depending only a little on their context; but music has no analogue of a word, almost everything depending on the longer message of which a note, chord, or short phrase forms a part.[31]

A criticism of Mrs. Langer's theory will be developed in the next section; but it may be well to indicate in advance some points that she has left incomplete:

Her view about the "morphological similarity" between music and the emotions, which we have taken to refer to an isomorphism, needs to be formulated much more specifically. If music can be isomorphic with something so remote from it as chess (and we have seen that it can), we do not learn much on being told that it is isomorphic with the emotions as well. We must be told *just how* it is isomorphic with the emotions, and why this particular isomorphism is so important to music. But to whatever extent Mrs. Langer goes beyond the "tensions and resolutions" mentioned here, she becomes altogether general and indefinite.

She also needs more evidence for saying that music is really a sign of the emotions. For a morphological similarity need not involve any sign function at all. Thus if a child, drawing lines on a piece of paper, should happen by accident to map a remote region in Siberia, its drawing would not be a sign of that region unless someone interpreted it as such, as perhaps nobody would. The same is true of a musical map of an emotion; it cannot be a sign unless it is connected with its designatum by some interpretant. Yet Mrs. Langer gives us no evidence for believing that her "conceptual" interpretant is present in music; she simply takes it for granted. In Morris' work, as we have seen, the interpretant of a sign is conceived so broadly that it tends to trivialize his conclusions; and although Mrs. Langer is clearly striving for something that isn't trivial, it is interesting to see that for her, too, the interpretant presents a difficult issue.

IV.

A profitable way of criticizing any theory—and a particularly profitable way when the theory is incompletely developed—is to present an alternative theory that is equally tenable. And that, it will now be argued, can easily be done for Mrs. Langer's view. The alternative theory to be developed is not new. It can take several different forms, one of which was suggested by Hanslick [32] some one hundred years ago; and perhaps Hanslick's form of it differs less sharply from the others than it initially seems to—as has been argued, and most plausibly, by John Hospers.[33] But it will be of interest to expound the theory once more, with the emphasis that the present chapter requires. It may or may not be a correct theory, regardless of the form that it takes; but it will at least show that Mrs. Langer's view, with its emphasis on the symbolic function of music, has no special theoretical advantage. And perhaps it will show, more generally, that the importance of the theory of signs to all the arts, rather than merely to those commonly classified as representational, is seriously open to question.

Let us begin by noting that our efforts to describe a work of art are frequently attended by the realization that we haven't a vocabulary to say just what we want to say. We must accordingly *borrow* words, extending their normal senses. Thus, many of the melodies of Handel are "square," whereas there is rarely anything "square" in the music of Debussy. Or there is a certain "heaviness" in Browning that is not found in Tennyson. Or there is a certain "soaring" quality in Tintoretto that is not found in Cézanne. And so on. This borrowing of terms is likely to be the first thing one notices in examining the terminology of criticism (which is the first of the four studies as mentioned at the beginning of this chapter, that relates symbolism to aesthetics); and although it may at first seem remote from our present topic, perhaps it will later prove to be very close to it.

It is more than an accident that we choose just these terms rather than others—that we say "square" rather than "jagged," for instance, in describing Handel's music. Psychological tests have been made that help to confirm this. In an experiment conducted by Willman,[34] various composers were shown four figures, one of them square and the others of irregular shapes, and were asked to write music to go with each of them. The music they wrote for the square was then examined by trained critics, who agreed that it was of much the same character in each case, in spite of the different personalities of the composers, and that it differed markedly from the music that the composers wrote for the other figures.

We extend the word 'square' from a shape to a melody because we feel that the two resemble one another. But the resemblance is not an ordinary one. Note that it is generically the same sort of resemblance that we have dealt with earlier, in connection with Pratt's view that music sounds the way moods feel. And it is the same sort of resemblance that Professor Heinz Werner [35] has discussed in his chapter on "Physiognomic Perception," where, in a manner reminiscent of Hornbostel and other Gestalt writers, he emphasizes similarities that cut across the familiar sense fields. Among other examples, he mentions an experiment (which for convenience can here be simplified) in which various observers are shown the following diagrams:

and are then required to name one of them 'iron' and the other 'gold' without being permitted to use any other name. There is a great deal of agreement in naming the left one 'iron' and the right one 'gold'; and Werner finds reason to suppose that this is not due to association of ideas—as if the left figure were called "iron" because it reminded the observers of a crosspiece in an ironwork gate—but that it comes as a much more immediate reaction to the figures.

Let us now see how this bears on the relation of music to the emotions, and in particular, how it helps to suggest that Mrs. Langer's evidence can be explained in an alternative way. It will be obvious that a part of Mrs. Langer's evidence (though only a part, of course) is concerned with the appropriateness of describing music as 'sad,' 'gay,' and so on. She accounts for this by saying that music is a symbol of an emotion—implying, in effect, that an *emotion* is in music only in the sense that a man is in a picture. So she herself tacitly acknowledges that the emotional terms have extended senses when they apply to music. But we have now to ask, in view of the fact that such a word as 'square' can also be applied to music, whether the principle exemplified by the latter term will not apply to the emotional terms as well. When we say that music is sad, are we not, perhaps, extending the sense of 'sad' *only* in the way that we extend the sense of 'square'—and thus extending it quite differently from the way that she emphasizes? And if so, will it not be possible to dispense altogether with the notion that music *symbolizes* the emotions?

More specifically: We are not tempted to say that a square melody, heard in any usual way, leads us to take account of the geometrical square; for we there realize that we are calling the melody 'square' in the lack of any other appropriate adjective. And perhaps we should not be tempted, with Mrs. Langer, to say that a sad melody leads us to take account of sadness. Instead of supposing that the melody symbolizes an emotion, we have the alternative of saying that it merely resembles an emotion—and resembles it, perhaps, in a rather imperfect way. In that case there will be only one symbolic relation that requires attention: that between the *word* 'sad' and the music, where the word is used in an extended sense. And this symbolic relation will not be an unusual one. It will be just another of the many instances in which the poverty of our language forces us to borrow a term.

Perhaps this further analogy will be of interest. Suppose that pastel colors occur only in paintings, the colors of nature being always darker or more highly saturated. And suppose that in a certain community the vocabulary for colors has grown up entirely in connection with the colors in nature. If the members of this community are asked to name a certain color in a painting—one that *we* should unhesitatingly call 'lavender'—they will probably call it 'purple.' But that will not require us, in theorizing about their aesthetic sensibilities, to say that they take lavender to be a symbol of purple, or to say that they have a conceptual insight into purple every time they enjoy the lavender of the painting. It permits us to say that they normally have an experience of lavender that is nonsymbolic, and that they become concerned with symbolism only when their efforts to keep from being inarticulate lead them to borrow 'purple' as a name for this experience. We have only to compare lavender to the properties of music, and the term 'purple' to the term 'sad,' to obtain a model for the view that is now in question— one that accounts for our calling music 'sad' without having to acknowledge that music is a symbol of sadness.

v.

Let us now see whether this alternative to Mrs. Langer's view can be developed in ways that will make it seem less arbitrary. There are four ways of developing it, differing with regard to the degree of complexity that they recognize in our experience of music. Each of them has its place in traditional aesthetic theory, the last three being variants of the expression theory.

In the first place, there is a view that emphasizes very much the same similarities between music and the emotions that Mrs. Langer wishes to emphasize. (The preceding section deliberately made more of this view than of the others that will be mentioned, but only in the interest of simplifying exposition.)

The view is normally limited to the recognition of intersense field or "physiognomic" similarities, as Pratt's version of it is: but there is nothing that prevents it from taking into account isomorphic similarities as well, to whatever extent these can be found. Indeed, Hanslick's view anticipates Mrs. Langer's in this respect. The theoretical use that it makes of these similarities, however, has nothing to do with a symbolic function of music. It has entirely to do with an explanation of our habit of describing music by borrowing such terms as 'sad' and 'gay.'

In the second place, there is a view which holds that the sounds of music are actually accompanied by (and *not* merely signified by) a certain feeling or mood—one that is *something* like an everyday-life emotion but not *exactly* like it. For instance, the feeling or mood that attends sad music may have a generic resemblance to that attending a bereavement, but need not resemble it in provoking tears, or in being uncontrollable, etc. Our application of the term 'sad' to music is then explained, as before, by our tendency to extend the term to this otherwise unnamed feeling or mood; and here the meaning is taken to be extended much less severely than it was by the previous view.

In the third place, there is a view that combines the two just mentioned—one that accounts for our calling music sad by saying that we extend the term in a way that makes it apply *both* to a musical pattern *and* to a mood or feeling. To make a somewhat eccentric but helpful comparison, 'sad' in its extended sense is then taken to behave rather like the term 'feeling of dizziness.' If we are asked what the latter term designates, we may be inclined to mention a feeling vaguely located in the stomach (say), and then go on to mention a certain swimming in the visual field as well. So we take 'feeling of dizziness' to designate both a feeling and a variety of five-sensory experiences that accompany it; and in the same way, 'sad' is taken by the present view to designate both a feeling and a sound-pattern.

The view just mentioned, like the preceding two, makes no provision for saying that *music designates* an emotion. It could do so, however, provided that only unusual cases were in question. Thus when a piece is performed with exaggerated sentimentality a sophisticated hearer is likely to inhibit any mood that first tends to arise and proceed to laugh *at* the music rather than to feel *with* it. But the pattern of sounds permits him to know, on the basis of past experience, what sort of mood the performer is indulging in; so in an appropriate sense we can say that he takes the music as a sign of the sentimentality. Or again, a listener may be so fatigued that he can't, as he says, "properly react" to a certain composition; but he may take the notes as a sign of the mood that he would have if he were not so fatigued. But these symbolic situations, for the view now in question (and, more indirectly, for the preceding view), hold only in atypical cases. In the typical cases there is no musical signification of the emotions at all—no "taking account" of them (as distinct from *feeling* counterparts of them) by those who are appreciating the music. According to Mrs. Langer, on the other hand, the symbolic situations hold in the typical cases, any suspension of them being atypical.

In the fourth place, there is a view to the effect that certain moods or feelings "fuse" with musical patterns. (The main contemporary writer who emphasizes fusion is Stephen Pepper.[36]) There is a sense of 'fusion' that is appropriate to the mental chemistry of John Stuart Mill—a view holding that two elements can be so related in an experience that neither is introspectable, each being disguised, so to speak, by the relationship. This view is now abandoned by most psychologists as empirically useless. But the term lends itself to other definitions, one of which would take 'is a fusion of Y and Z' as a way of saying, merely, that X resembles Y in a certain way, and resembles X too in this way, but does not have either of them as a component. In this sense the color orange is a fusion of red and yellow. In the same sense our experience of expressive music is said to involve a unique experience which is a fusion of a sound pattern and a feeling. We need not here be concerned with what *kind* of resemblance is involved in fusion (though that is otherwise a pertinent question) because *any* sort of resemblance between sound patterns and emotions will be sufficient to establish the point we are making. The resemblance need not be taken to show that music has a symbolic function; it can equally well be taken to show that music is sad or gay only in extended senses of the terms.

Let us now, somewhat arbitrarily, take the second of these views (which is a kind of expression theory) and see what else, beyond our habits of applying terms like 'sad' and 'gay' to music, it permits us to explain.

It freely allows us to say, with Mrs. Langer, that a member of a lynching party howling round the gallows tree is not, in spite of his emotion, in a fit mood for composing. For if the mood of music *imperfectly resembles* its everyday-life counterpart, it will *differ* from it as well; and nothing obliges us to hold that the mood attending the lynching party is ever expressed in music.

There is, again, no difficulty in accounting for the way a virtuoso adapts himself successively to the varying moods of a sonata. It would indeed be odd if the emotions of everyday life changed in this "mercurial" way; but if the moods attending music differ from those of ordinary life (though not completely, of course) then the change is not so odd. The dependence of the moods on the musical sounds is scarcely a psychological accident, however difficult it is for psychology to explain the relationship; so the very fact that the performer is playing different notes will help to bring about his change from sadness to gaiety (in the extended senses of those terms).

Finally, the view here presented can take account of the importance we attach to music. If music simply reduplicated the feelings of everyday life, it could have only a modest importance, just as Mrs. Langer implies. It would be a substitute for living, much as a travel book is a substitute for traveling; and although there is nothing wrong about such a substitute, there is also nothing very exciting about it. But if music gives us new moods—moods partly the same and partly different—and if this is simply concealed by the way in which our limited vocabulary forces us to call them by the old names, then the moods can become important for enriching our experience. Perhaps they will be new sources of intrinsic value. It is not so evident that they will be new sources of extrinsic value, since that will depend on the consequences of the moods. But any uncertainty on that point arises for Mrs. Langer's theory no less than for the present one. No matter whether music symbolizes moods or produces them, its extrinsic value must (by definition) be estimated in the light of its consequences, which still await a careful study.

What has here been said of the second of the four views can presumably be said, *mutatis mutandis,* of the other three; so it will be convenient to think of them as the several forms of *one* view that provides an alternative to the view held by Mrs. Langer. It is an alternative that can accept any analogies between our reaction to music and the emotions of everyday life that she wishes to emphasize, though it is not committed to precisely those; it can take into account all the evidence that she presents for her view; and finally, it can do this without granting to music *any* symbolic function. It locates the problem not in a study of the symbolic function of music but only in a study of the vocabulary of criticism.

VI.

Our considerations have shown that Mrs. Langer's view is *no more* tenable than its alternative, but have not shown that it is *less* tenable. And indeed, the difficulties of the issue are too great to permit us to decide, categorically, which of the two views is correct. It may be useful, however, to consider just what the difficulties are, and to see what sort of study could hope to surmount them.

Some of the difficulties are of a psychological character. They attend the general question, "What happens when we listen to music, and how are our reactions related to the emotions of everyday life?" Here the evidence, though in some respects abundant, is not decisive. One must normally use questionnaires, etc., and it is not easy to make them at once intelligible, reliable, and relevant to the sort of information that is wanted.[37]

Perhaps some further light on the topic will eventually come from the work being done in psychology on the felt similarities that extend beyond any one sensory field—work like that previously mentioned with reference to Werner and others. Within a given sense field, such as vision, the various qualities and their similarities are well studied, as the color-solid manner of representing them will indicate. But much more work will be needed before we have a precise "dimensional" study of the physiognomic, intersense-field similarities; and this work will be particularly difficult when it concerns similarities between sounds and emotions, which are emphasized both by Mrs. Langer's view and by some forms of the alternative here presented to it.

It would be interesting, for instance, to see whether there is any intervening mood between people's reaction to music and their reaction to the emotional situations of daily life—an intervening mood in the sense that blue is an intervening hue between violet and green. If that could be shown it would do something to support the view advanced here, or rather, the second form of this view; and if it were shown impossible it would take us a step, perhaps, in the direction of Mrs. Langer's view. That there are such intervening states is suggested by the fact that handkerchiefs are often visible at plays, though more psychic distance is preserved there than in real-life situations, and by the fact that handkerchiefs are rarely visible at concerts. But such offhand observations are by no means an adequate substitute for a detailed study.

But although it is difficult to get psychological evidence that will help to decide between Mrs. Langer's view and its alternative, the main problem actually lies elsewhere. It lies not in psychology but in analytical philosophy. In essentials it is a problem of making clear just what we are asking when we ask about the symbolic character of music. And it is difficult because it requires us to deal with such terms as 'thought,' 'concept,' and 'cognition,' which have long been troublesome in philosophy.

More specifically, the problem lies in clarifying what is meant by the 'interpretant' of a sign. If we try to do this without making use of the traditional terms, 'thought,' 'concept,' and 'cognition,' we shall probably be led to use terms that are even more untrustworthy than these. We have seen at the beginning of this chapter that Morris has difficulties in this connection; and we have seen subsequently that Mrs. Langer does. In fairness to them both we must remember that the difficulties are not peculiar to their views; similar difficulties arise in *any* theory of signs, and it would be rash to expect any immediate success in surmounting them. For the moment, however, we need not discuss the difficulties in their full generality, but can be content to see how they are involved in an attempt to decide between Mrs. Langer's view and the present one.

Suppose, entirely for the sake of argument, that there is such a thing as a pure thought-experience—an experience that reveals its full nature to introspection, and in the same way reveals what the thought is *about*. And suppose that this pure thought-experience is always the interpretant in any sign process, being uniquely caused by the sign. In that case we could readily test Mrs. Langer's view by getting people to listen to music and by asking them whether the music caused them to have a pure thought-experience that was about emotions. If the people answered affirmatively, music would presumably be a genuine sign of the emotions, its resemblance to the emotions being attended by an interpretant. If they answered negatively, some form of the alternative view, developed here, would be required. It will be evident, however, that we find no pure thought-experience that reveals its nature to introspection in anything like so obliging a way; nor is it certain, even, that the phrase 'pure thought-experience' makes sense. And so long as we are still seeking a more adequate conception of the interpretant in a sign-process (for a *promise* of a behavioral definition, or of a definition in terms of this or that disposition, is not the same as an actual definition) the adequacy of Mrs. Langer's view, *or of the present one,* is scarcely clear enough to be tested.

So it seems advisable to reserve judgment, adopting one or

the other of the views tentatively, to be sure, but without considering it the only possible view.

VII.

Our discussion of symbolism in the arts commonly classified as nonrepresentational will not be complete unless it mentions theories of program music—and in particular, theories maintaining that programs are present even in music for which the composer himself has provided no program in words. In Mrs. Langer we have emotions as the designata, but in these views we have other events as the designata—a sunrise, for example, or the death of a hero. The view is not, to be sure, necessarily confined to music. Just as an orchestral composition may be alleged to represent the death of a hero, so too a nonobjective painting (i.e., one that doesn't resemble the *shapes* of objects that are familiar in real life) may be alleged to represent the death of a hero. But critics of painting are less likely to recognize such "programs" than are critics of music; and critics of architecture, ceramics, etc., are likely to defend "programs" still more rarely. So it will be convenient, as before, to draw our examples from music.

In discussing this topic we shall encounter the same difficulties that were mentioned in the preceding section—difficulties about the nature of the resemblance between an iconic sign and its designatum, and difficulties about the nature of the interpretant.

The central questions have been partly anticipated in section III, but can be made clearer by developing this quotation from Sapir:

Aside from the emotional substratum which we feel to be inseparable from a truly great and sincere work of musical art, are there not in the earlier supposedly absolutistic art plenty of instances of direct realistic suggestion, sometimes intentional, no doubt, at other times a spontaneous product of association on the part of the listener? . . . I do not think it would be going too far to say that all musical art worthy of the name has implicitly, if not avowedly, some of the fundamental qualities of so-called "programme" music; from a musical standpoint it should make little difference whether the emotional appeal is left to declare itself [of its realistic suggestions] in the mind of the sympathetic listener or is trumpeted at him by means of a formidable printed analysis.[38]

It will be noted here that Sapir emphasizes the "emotional substratum" or "emotional appeal" of music, though it is not evident whether he takes the emotions as being closely like those of ordinary life or, as in the view suggested in section IV, only a little like them. In any case, these emotions "declare themselves." So Sapir recognizes a *similarity* between our immediate reaction to music and our reaction to the sort of thing that he takes it to represent: the music "declares itself" to be about the death of a hero, for instance, because the emotion it presents is like the emotion we would feel at the death of an actual hero. To that extent he makes a comparison between music and an *iconic* sign.

In an important respect the comparison is not a close one. No one would ever take a representational picture of a hero's death to be a picture of the fall of an empire; yet in the musical case the emotional similarity to a hero's death is not any more striking, perhaps, than is its similarity to the fall of an empire, and some listeners might feel that the composition in question "really" represented the latter. It is possible, however, to take this into account by saying that music is an ambiguous sign of its program; or alternating we may say that it is merely a very general sign—a sign that represents neither the death of a hero, specifically, nor the fall of an empire, but rather the termination of *anything* that is of great human interest.

If we were to pursue this matter, we should have to consider essentially the same question that we mentioned in the preceding sections. Just *what is* our emotional reaction to music, and just how much does it resemble our emotional reaction to real-life situations? And even if that were settled we should still have our old question about the interpretant; for the interpretant must be present before the similarity becomes a sign-situation.

It will be useful to show that the question about the interpretant has here no simple, straight-forward solution. One can argue (as Morris [39] and others actually have) that the presence of an interpretant, in music that at first seems to have no program, is evidenced by the strong preference we have for one verbally formulated program over another—this being evident when, for purposes of experiment, we are *forced* to choose between programs. If we were asked, for instance, whether Schubert's "Moment Musical" in F minor is better suited to depicting a little girl dancing than it is to depicting a wounded elephant, we should almost all (including some tone-deaf people, even) answer in the affirmative. And this preference between the alternatives, even though we may never before have formulated them to ourselves in words, might be taken to show that we are "unconsciously" in the habit of using Schubert's composition as a sign—if not a sign of a little girl dancing, then of something generically like that. A moment's thought, however, will show that this proves nothing at all about a sign or an interpretant, so long as we let 'interpretant' mean anything that will really interest us. For consider this counterexample:

Suppose that Mr. A is admiring the new Ford sedan that he has bought; and suppose he has previously noted that Mr. B has one just like it, and that Mr. C has an aged Chevrolet coupe. Now if we interrupt Mr. A, in his aesthetic admiration, and ask him whether he thinks his car better suited to be a sign of Mr. B's car than it is of Mr. C's, requesting him, for purposes of our experiment, not to reject both alternatives, he will answer in favor of Mr. B's car, pretty certainly. But in this case we shall scarcely wish to argue that Mr. A, in the course of admiring his car under any ordinary set of conditions, actually takes his car as a sign of Mr. B's, or as a sign of anyone else's car. In spite of the great similarity between A's car and B's, we shall be inclined to recognize no sign situation at all, feeling that there is nothing here that we want to call an interpretant—nothing that is sufficient to make the similarity into an iconic sign-situation. And if in this case Mr. A's strong preference, given a forced choice, does not establish the presence of such an interpretant under normal circumstances, there is no reason to suppose that it does in the case mentioned above about Schubert's "Moment Musical." One can insist that the musical case is "different"; but the point is that an appeal to forced choices does not in itself show this. And our perplexity in showing it by some other means testifies to our uncertainty about what we want 'interpretant' to mean. (Note that we should like, as before, to have some pure thought-experience that we could appeal to in deciding whether an interpretant is present.)

We must not forget that program music can depend on other sorts of similarity than those that involve the emotions. Music may be taken to have a program because its sounds are similar to sounds that occur elsewhere. Crude and humorous examples of this may take the form, say, of a musical imitation of the cackling of a hen (as in Rameau); and more subtle examples may take the form of musical imitations of *verbal* inflections (as in Schumann's *Warum?* or Ravel's *Beauty and the Beast.*) But more interesting examples are found when music resembles the *visual* appearance of certain objects. Here we find once more a similarity that cuts across the sensory modalities. Thus Debussy's *Reflections on the Water* has little to do with the sound or the mood of water; but it has a certain similarity to the way quietly shimmering water *looks*. Often this resemblance between sound and sight is attended by a resemblance of mood as well. Thus Schumann's *Prophet Bird* and Mac-Dowell's *The Eagle* both imitate the visually perceivable flight of a bird, but the mood of Schumann's music is appropriately mysterious, while that of MacDowell's is one of dignity. Some may feel, in such cases, that there are other sorts of similarity involved, depending, say, on a kind of empathy, yielding something similar to a kinaesthetic sense of flying.

These points of resemblance are worth further study; but they do not show that music is always of a symbolical character, or even that it typically is. In the above examples a title to the music provides a key to the program; and if we take the title as a part of the whole work, as seems appropriate, we have the effect of music reinforced by the obviously symbolic function of language. In works without a title the music sometimes invites us, as it were, to supply a program; but it does so only because of similarities that are highly generic—similarities that are variously perceived, and may suggest a program to one listener that is sharply different from the one that it suggests to another. So before saying that music is an iconic sign of something else we must pause to ask ourselves whether 'iconic' can profitably refer to a situation in which the similarities are quite so generic, and whether 'sign' can profitably refer to a situation in which the interpretant, or alleged interpretant, is quite so inconstant. We are left, in short, with our recurrent questions.

Nothing has been said here that helps to answer these questions; but in the present current of opinion in aesthetics it is of the utmost importance to realize that they demand an answer, and an answer that can be given only after many difficult issues have been carefully examined. Meanwhile, it is necessary to protect aesthetics from an understandable but misguided enthusiasm—an enthusiasm that induces people to hope that the theory of signs will soon disclose the "true nature" of the arts. The theory of signs is not a well-developed discipline that can be applied to the arts in the way that mathematics can be applied to physics. On the contrary, a study of the (allegedly) symbolic aspects of the arts is largely of interest for disclosing the problems that lie in the theory of signs itself—problems that must be solved before the theory can be of much use in contributing to the solution of other problems.

VIII.

In this chapter, which is concerned with the aesthetically relevant signification, or alleged signification, of the arts commonly classified as nonrepresentational, these points have been stressed:

In a highly generic sense of 'sign,' as used by Morris, there can be no doubt that sign situations arise in all the arts; but it remains to be seen whether anything illuminating to aesthetics will come of this observation.

In a more specific sense, such an art as music can be taken to signify emotions, in the manner suggested by Mrs. Langer. But such a view is no more plausible than an alternative one, which takes music to resemble emotions without signifying them, or which takes it to be attended by something rather like the emotions. The fact that we use 'sad,' 'gay,' etc., to describe the music can then be accounted for by recognizing extended senses of those terms.

Music (or, *mutatis mutandis,* any other art commonly classified as nonrepresentational) can also be taken to signify something other than emotion. We then have the traditional issue about program music. And there, although people will often acknowledge that a composition is better fitted to represent one thing than it is to represent another, it may be doubted whether the composition is *in fact used* to represent anything.

In each case there is a problem of establishing the nature of the *interpretant* in a sign situation; and since the alleged sign is usually taken to be iconic, and iconic in some extremely subtle way, there is the further problem of indicating the precise respects in which it resembles what it signifies. Until these difficult problems are settled, the theory of signs is likely to make only a modest contribution to aesthetics.

Chapter 9

SYMBOLISM

IN THE REPRESENTATIONAL ARTS

I.

We have found reason to doubt that the theory of signs has important applications to the nonrepresentational arts; but perhaps our results will be more encouraging when we turn to the representational arts, such as literature, sculpture, and much of painting. The relevance of signs is there obvious; and although a study of the interpretant of the signs may again present difficulties, it is likely to present them less insistently. The examples of symbolism that demand attention will no longer be borderline cases. The present chapter will accordingly discuss symbolic situations in the representational arts: it will deal with the third, rather than the fourth, of the topics that were mentioned at the beginning of the previous chapter.

In literature, in particular, the aesthetic importance of meaning or significance is beyond serious question. As Hospers has remarked:

Spoken words, apart from all meaning and association from life, simply for the pleasure of their esthetic surfaces and rhythms alone, would very soon fail of any effect. Words have far fewer esthetic (in the thin sense) elements than colors or [musical] sounds do, so there must be more thickening, more life-values "held in solution." [1]

And if Hospers is to be criticized here, it must be on the ground that he understates his case. Even the *rhythms* of words, though they seem to be aesthetic in the "thin sense" only, often depend on a "thickening" that comes from our knowledge of what the words mean. That is to say, when we hear poetry read in a language we do not understand, the "musical" rhythm that we experience is not the same, presumably, as that experienced by those who understand the language.

In order to see this we need only compare Heyse's line:

Und willst du deinen Liebsten sterben sehen,

with N. H. Dole's English translation of it:

Wouldst thou behold thy lover sadly dying.

It is possible to read the English with a marked stress on the first syllable of 'sadly,' corresponding to the stress one would normally put on the first syllable of *'sterben'* in the German, and a person who understood German but not English would presumably find that way of reading the English at least half-faithful, in rhythm, to the German original. But those of us who understand English find that our rhythmic sense is disturbed by such a reading. We want the strong accent on a word whose designative function is relatively important, so when it is put on "sadly," which in this context has no such importance, the word becomes all too prominent in our protesting attention, and we find it not even half-faithful to the German rhythm.

This becomes particularly evident when the words are sung to Hugo Wolf's musical setting, for which the English translation was made.[2] Wolf emphasizes *'sterben'* by the drop of a major sixth amid a context of notes in which there is little variation in pitch, and with the accent that normally attends the beginning of a new measure; and the effect in preserving the speech-rhythms of the German is excellent, even when judged by the high standards that Wolf set for himself in this respect. But when sung in English, where the music imposes the same stress on "sadly," the effect is one of excessive emphasis, little short of being ludicrous. One feels that the rhythm, and not just the total effect, is wrong.

This dependence of rhythm on significance has sometimes been strongly emphasized in the theory of literature. William Wimsatt, for instance, goes so far as to say that rhythm is a matter of "putting the right *idea* in the right place."[3] Nor is rhythm the only "formal" factor (in some sense of that vague term[4]) that depends on significance—as will be evident from the fact that we cannot point out such formal features as the climax or denouement of a play without understanding the meaning of the actors' words.

It is doubtless because of the aesthetic poverty of the sounds of words, together with the dependence of these, even, on their signification that explains why we have no recognized schools of "nonobjective" literature, corresponding to schools of non-objective painting. Such a literary form was contemplated by Gertrude Stein, who, according to Edmund Wilson, at one period of her life

. . . made a practice of shutting herself up at night and trying utterly to banish from her mind all the words ordinarily associated with the ideas she had fixed upon. She had come to believe that words had other values than those inherent in their actual meanings, and she was attempting to produce a kind of literature which should work with these values exclusively.[5]

Yet it is by no means clear that Miss Stein wanted to divorce words from their symbolic function altogether, the term "actual meanings," in the quotation from Wilson, perhaps having a sense opposed merely to "potential meanings, which are realized only in unusual contexts." For in such a line as

Chicken. Alas a dirty word, alas a dirty third, alas a dirty bird.[6]

which Miss Stein wrote during the period in question, there is a certain symbolic use of terms, though it is similar (and intentionally so, Wilson says) to the assemblages of half-guitars, bits of newspaper, etc., that are depicted in cubist still-lifes—assemblages that still retain *some* use of representation in the paintings. In fact, Miss Stein writes in a vocabulary, though not always in a syntax, that is closer to English than Carroll's "Jabberwocky." And even in "Jabberwocky," by the way, we have more than "nonobjective" literature; for in "a vorpal blade" for instance, "blade" is functioning as usual, and "vorpal," whatever else, is an adjective.

Among critics of literature the only issue is concerned with *the way* in which the sign-function of words is relevant to literature. Thus, I. A. Richards, who is accustomed to emphasize the emotive function of poetic language—a function in which emotions and attitudes are aroused, rather than designated—takes pains to recognize the role of beliefs in our reaction to poetry.[7] And since some, at least, of these beliefs arise in the course of our "understanding" the words, and thus in realizing what they designate, the sign-function of the words is not dismissed by him as irrelevant—as in sanity it could not be. Where Richards differs from some others, then, is in maintaining that the beliefs are not of aesthetic interest in their own right, or as means to the sort of ends that an engineer, say, might have, but are of interest because they are essential in *causing* us, when believing, to have certain emotions and attitudes. To say that, of course, is only to suggest the way in which beliefs, and the symbolic function of words that help to make the beliefs possible, enter into literature; it is in no way to question that they *do* so enter.

In painting, the situation is somewhat different: there is nonobjective painting as well as representational painting. But if we look only to the latter (the former raising questions like those mentioned in the preceding chapter) there is again very little inclination among critics to dismiss the representational or symbolic elements as aesthetically irrelevant. When Roger Fry, for instance, emphasized the formal or "plastic" aspects of painting, he did not maintain that people usually do, or usually should, look at *all* paintings without attending to what they represent. Thus he writes of Pieter Brueghel's "Carrying the Cross":

> We recognize at once that this is a great psychological invention, setting up profound vibrations or feeling within us by its poignant condensation of expression . . . But is . . . almost pure illustration, . . . and we must regard illustration as more closely akin in its essence to literature than it is to plastic art, although in its merely external and material aspect it belongs to the latter.[8]

Here the term, "merely external and material aspects," though it shows Fry's partiality for the "plastic" means of expression as distinct from that "closely akin in its essence to literature," can scarcely be taken as *dismissing* representation as irrelevant to the painting; the "illustrational" function is not only recognized by him as being relevant to it, but elicits his reluctant admiration.

Let us now, taking it for granted that symbolism has an important function in such arts as literature and painting, proceed to raise some questions about the way in which it functions. The remainder of the chapter will divide into two main parts. There will first, in sections II, III, and IV, be a discussion of how symbolism in literature and painting can be given an intelligible place in a general theory of the arts—a general theory that many writers are accustomed to defend. And thereafter, in sections V and VI, there will be a discussion of the aspects of symbolism that, for purposes of art criticism, and in particular, of literary criticism, seem most to repay attention.

II.

It will be pertinent to begin by explaining why the first of the two topics just mentioned—the place of symbolism in a general theory of the arts—is likely to be of interest. Most writers on aesthetics, as well as many critics and artists, have had an intuitive conviction that literature, painting, architecture, music, etc., have a great deal in common. Although each may have its own special effects, and even its own special sort of excellence, there is presumably some good reason for our grouping them together under the generic term, "arts," and in comparing them with respect to their beauty or their expressiveness. The question arises, then, as to just what fundamental and essential characteristic they have in common. One way of answering this, as we have implicitly seen in considering the views of Susanne Langer and Charles Morris, is to maintain that all the arts involve *symbols* of this or that special sort. But this is not, of course, the only possible answer; nor is it the most usual one. And since we have reason to doubt that symbolism is found in all the arts, it will be well to consider the most familiar of the alternative views—one that points to something quite different from symbolism as being common to the arts. This alternative must allow a place for the representational (and hence symbolic) arts, of course; but it must also allow a place for those that are not, or at least, may not be, representational. And it will be of interest to consider how this can be done without implying a "bifurcation" of the arts, so to speak—without implying that their points of similarity are negligible.

The theory to be discussed is one that takes the arts to have, as their essential, common characteristic, a suitability for being observed in the "aesthetic attitude," and thus a suitability for yielding "aesthetic experience." Aesthetic experience is often taken as the main subject matter of the whole of aesthetics, the problems being concerned with describing it in all its varieties, of explaining it, and in showing how it is related to an interpretation and evaluation of the arts. Not all writers, to be sure, subscribe to this view. In addition to those who reject it in favor of an "art of symbol" type of view, as above noted, there are others who, like I. A. Richards, hold it suspect on the ground that it seems to make an artificial divorce between our experience of the arts and our experience in everyday life.[9] But it remains the case that either "The Aesthetic Attitude" or "The Aesthetic Experience" is normally the title of the first chapter of a book on aesthetics, and that psychologists, critics, and artists often begin their discussions of the arts with the same point of emphasis.

A definition of "the aesthetic attitude" that is at once clear, useful, and reasonably faithful to what most writers have wished to mean, could not be developed without prolonged discussion. But for present purposes it will be sufficient to say that this attitude might more happily be called a "set," in the sense of the latter term that has now become current in psychophysics; or it might be called, more simply, a "way of paying attention," or "a way of observing." More particularly, it is a way of observing in which we are absorbed and engrossed in whatever is before us, our experience of the latter being taken not for its cue-value to some practical action or theoretical speculation, but dwelt upon for its own sake. For example: we normally "see" our coffee spoon just enough to permit us to stir our coffee—our way of observing it then being the opposite of the aesthetic attitude, usually called the "practical" attitude. And note that if, under these circumstances, we are later asked what kind of spoon it was—whether graceful or clumsy, ornamented or plain, polished or dull—we shall normally be unable to answer. If these qualities are to register in our consciousness we must look at the spoon with greater *absorption, dwelling* on its appearances, and inhibiting our tendency to take the sight of it merely as a *cue* to using it. That is to say, we must observe it in the aesthetic attitude.

The aesthetic attitude is of interest not in its own right, but (as the preceding example will suggest) because of the qualitative difference that it is held to make to our experience. And it is this qualitative difference that makes the experience "aesthetic," distinguishing it from other kinds of experience. Note that there is nothing about a physical work of art that is sufficient, even when the physical and overtly physiological conditions attending our observation are favorable, to make it present us with aesthetic experience. A painting will not do so, for instance, when we look at it in order to guess its shipping weight, or to decide what chemicals were used in its pigments. The aesthetic attitude or aesthetic "way of paying attention" is necessary before the ordinary appearances of the work give place to those that have the special qualities of aesthetic experience. As remarked above, aesthetic experience is often taken as the central topic of all aesthetics; and it must be emphasized that many consider it essential to any observation in which a work of art is being appreciated, or being judged with regard to its peculiarly artistic value.

Before leaving this topic it may be well to guard against certain misapprehensions. In the first place, aesthetic experience is not necessarily confined to the experience of the five senses. The aesthetic attitude may make a difference to our imagery, for instance, giving it a greater definiteness or vividness. And it may affect our experience of emotions. In fact Roger Fry makes a special point of this, remarking that the "artistic vision" (that being his near-synonym for "aesthetic attitude") frees us from the "numbing" effect of practical life on our emotions, which he compares to "the paralyzing influence of fear in some animals." [10] Thus the term 'aesthetic experience' is broader than the term 'aesthetic surface,' at least for most uses of the latter term; for 'surface' is often a metaphorical way of referring exclusively to the five-sensory experiences.

In the second place, aesthetic experience, whenever it *is* of the five-sensory sort, need not lose what the Gestalt psychologists call its "structure" (or, roughly, the prominence of certain parts of it over others); that is to say, when we look at a portrait while maintaining the aesthetic attitude, the visual appearance of the represented human figure is normally more prominent than the appearance of the background. It may be that this relative prominence is *due to* our practical attitude, which *in the past* has made us particularly sensitive to the human form. But we must remember that this practical attitude, operating since childhood, leaves a relatively permanent effect on our perceptual habits, and that these habits continue to influence our experience when the practical attitude gives place to the aesthetic attitude. Thus, aesthetic experience is still *rather* like ordinary experience. Though it has its own peculiar qualities it does not (whatever I. A. Richards may care to say about it [11]) require us to make an impassable barrier between art and non-art, as if our aesthetic experience were never influenced by our manner of living.

Let us now turn to our central question, namely: "Just how may theories that emphasize the aesthetic attitude and aesthetic experience account for the relevance of symbols like those used in literature and representational painting?" The question is not so simple as it may at first appear. In fact, Lucius Garvin, in attempting to answer it, calls his paper "The Paradox of Aesthetic Meaning." [12] And the paradox, or difficulty, is essentially one of explaining how signs can contribute to experience that is genuinely *aesthetic*. Since signification involves a reference to something *else*, will not any experience that attends it be secretly tainted with a cue-value, as aesthetic experience must not be? Or, if it is not so "tainted," then how can this be explained? Those who wish to emphasize aesthetic experience, and who wish (as they virtually must) to do justice to the meaning of literature and of much of painting, must find an answer to this question.

Let us examine the possibilities. Aesthetic experience may arise from the appearances of the sign vehicle itself, or from what the sign signifies, or from the interpretant that relates the two. Now there is no serious problem, of course, about the sign vehicle itself, considered as an object or event in its own right. It manifestly presents us with appearances, no matter whether a word, a picture, or something else; and in certain cases it presents us with very complicated appearances, which can be "dwelt upon" as usual. But that seems altogether insufficient to constitute the whole of what is aesthetically relevant in the representational arts; and even when we remember that the appearance of the sign vehicle may be altered by our manner of interpreting it as a sign (as remarked in section I with reference to the rhythm of words), it continues to seem insufficient. We are likely to feel that it leaves out the sorts of experience that are most typical of its sign-function. Nor can we identify these typical experiences, of course, with the appearances of what the sign signifies. For what it signifies, save in rare cases, presents us with no immediate experiences at all (as when, in America, we read a poem about England). We are left, then, with the possibility of finding the aesthetic experience in question as something involved in the *interpretant* of the sign process. So once again, we encounter a problem of characterizing the interpretant; and we are likely to meet some of our former difficulties.

In the current literature, efforts to reconcile aesthetic experience with symbols are normally concerned with the interpretant; but of course this concern is often implicit, and sometimes attended by qualifications. To see that this is so, let us examine some recent work of Stephen Pepper and of Arnold Isenberg.

In a supplementary essay in his *The Basis of Criticism in the Arts*,[13] Pepper remarks that in literature, particularly for works that are normally read silently, rather than aloud, the five-sensory aspects of our experience—which are simply our visual experiences of the printed words—are virtually negligible. And so, in locating the sort of experience that he considers relevant and important to our appreciation of literature, he says that

it is not strictly imagining or thinking since these experiences are supposed to go on without external control. And the term perception is usually regarded as involving sensory material, which, as we have shown, is very nearly lacking from this sort of experience. This sort of experience is that of externally controlled imagery and thought. I propose to call it "unsensory perception." [14]

It seems evident, in this passage, that the "externally controlled imagery and thought" is controlled by symbols, and hence that it is (or at least, includes) the interpretant in a sign-process. But Pepper, having called it "unsensory perception," proceeds as though no further analysis were necessary, whereas it is not at all clear what sort of experience he has in mind. To the extent that he refers to "imagery" there is no great obscurity; but many will doubt that images have a central role in our understanding of poetry. So the burden of Pepper's view is born by the word "thought," which he seems to take as naming a special kind of experience. Perhaps he has in mind the pure thought-experience that was mentioned in the preceding chapter. But until such an experience is indicated more carefully—and thus kept from seeming suspiciously like an entity postulated purely for theoretical convenience, and not introspectively discernible at all—any view that rests content with it is rather less than satisfactory.

Arnold Isenberg, in two somewhat recent papers, addresses himself to the same question.[15] Since his writing is itself so condensed, it is virtually impossible to do justice to it in a brief summary; but perhaps these passing remarks will be a rough clue to what he says: When we read a literary work, the meaning of the words, in the only sense of 'meaning' that is aesthetically revelant, is immediately *felt* in our experience. It is not, however, possessed of some one, unique quality, as would be held by a pure thought-experience view, but rather manifests itself in extremely complicated ways, through alterations in our feelings, "plus the admittedly fragmentary and eccentric flow of imagery." [16] In fact its complexities are such that a full description of it is scarcely to be hoped for, since that would presuppose "an elaborate psychological theory that we do not possess," or else would require us "to say something which has exactly the same meaning, that is, the same influence on feeling, as the work of art—and this, for various reasons, may well be impossible." [17] In this respect, then, Isenberg hopes only to warn us against an overly simple conception of the aesthetic experience in question—a conception which, when discovered to be inadequate, might lead us to suppose without warrant that there is no such experience at all.

He then goes on to say that this literary meaning, which functions "so as to expand the field on which attention rests," [18] is nonreferential; that is to say, the aesthetic attitude in some way conceals the reference that the words would have if they were read in a practical attitude. So the reference—i.e., the semantical or designative function of the words—is only as a factor in the *genetic explanation* of the aesthetically relevant experiences. The fact that the component words in the poem have *previously* been used referentially is what makes them, in the literary context, acquire their influence on our varied feelings and images; but when the literary work is read as literature the reference is no longer present. His main reason for saying this, apparently, is that he thinks that any reference involves a practical, rather than an aesthetic, attitude, and thus "turns away from a given content to obtain or avoid what it does not yet possess," [19] whereas in aesthetics the content (that is, the experience) must be dwelt upon for its own sake.

The first part of Isenberg's view, emphasizing the complexity of aesthetic experience in literature (and also in painting) seems altogether sound, and will be embodied in the account that will be suggested in the following sections. But the second part, which looks askance at the referential aspects of the arts, seems rather strange. He is not correlating the relevant aesthetic experience with the interpretant of a sign, since without reference there is no sign, but is correlating it with what *would* be the interpretant of a sign *if* the sign-situation had not terminated—if the previous function of the words as signs, having built up the aesthetically relevant feelings and images, had not ceased (leaving only its effects) when the context became literary. Now this makes a sharp distinction between our reading of literature and our reading of history, say, or of psychology. There is a difference, no doubt, but it may be questioned whether the difference is quite so great as to remove reference altogether. So let us now see whether the difference can be indicated in a somewhat different way, retaining much that Isenberg says, but doing better justice to our intuitive convictions. The remarks that follow will not attempt to defend the general importance of the aesthetic attitude and aesthetic experience, for that would be too large an undertaking. But they will attempt to show that *if* anyone accepts these theoretical concepts as important he can easily account for the relevance of signs in the arts and can do so without being committed to any special view about the interpretant of the signs and without taking the signs as functioning in any unusual way.

III.

The first point to establish is this: No matter what view we may have about the nature of the interpretant of a sign, among all the views that would commonly be taken seriously, we can hold that the statement, "Mr. X interpreted the sign while maintaining the aesthetic attitude," is a consistent one. It may *seem* inconsistent because (as suggested on page 232) when we understand the sign, taking it to stand for something else, we seem to add that very "cue-value" to the sign that the aesthetic attitude, by definition, must suspend. But a moment's thought will show that that is not the case. (In establishing this point we shall not, of course, have an answer to our question about the sort of aesthetic *experience* that sign-interpretation brings with it; but we shall at least prepare the way for that question, which will be discussed in section IV.)

For some views about the nature of the interpretant the point to be established is very nearly self-evident. So long as the interpretant is taken as itself some kind of *experience* that *immediately* attends one's perception of the sign—such as an image, say, or a pure thought-experience—its role in connecting sign and symbolized presupposes no cue-value at all. For in the image theory, the relation of the image to the designatum is conceived as simply a relation of similarity; and in the pure thought-experience view, the relation is conceived as some unique sort of self-transcendence; so in neither case do we have anything that requires a practical orientation to the object signified, or anything that prevents the image or pure thought-experience from being "dwelt upon for its own sake." It has been remarked previously that such views are not easily maintained; but if anyone should maintain them, as Pepper was suspected, above, of doing, he would have no problem in reconciling his views with the aesthetic attitude.

Theories of a pragmatic type, however, which are the only alternatives to the above that are customarily held, will require a little more attention. Such theories do *not* identify the interpretant of a sign with an experience that attends it. The metaphorical phrase, "an idea is a plan of action," which is typical of pragmatic theories, in no way implies that the "plan" is a kind of image of the action which pictures it in advance. It is rather a "readiness" to respond in action. Or, in one form of pragmatism that James presents, an idea is a "possibility" of experiencing, *subsequently,* various feelings of "transition" and "termination." [20] Now if we take an idea as being of this nature, and consider it as the interpretant in a sign process, we may at first be tempted to suppose that it introduces a cue-value that is the mark of the practical attitude, and hence makes the aesthetic attitude impossible.

In point of fact, however, no pragmatic theory has ever been so emphatic on "practice" as to suppose that an idea or thought, whether arising as an interpretant of a sign or in some other way, must always lead to immediate, overt action, or any other *immediate* practical concern with an object. This is evident when we consider what happens when we understand, under normal circumstances, such a statement as "There are tigers in India" (to take one of James' examples [21]). Clearly, in understanding, and even in believing, this sentence, we do not immediately rush to buy tickets for a trip, either to India or in the opposite direction; nor do we go out to buy a rifle. We simply note the fact and do nothing about it. Now pragmatic theories are not, of course, accustomed to ignore this. Such words as "readiness" to respond, or "possible" reactions, adequately take it into account; for one may be "ready" to respond without responding, and reactions may be "possible" without being actual. In short, pragmatic theories identify an idea or a thought not with an actual practical reaction, whether in behavior or subsequent experience, but rather with a *disposition* to such a practical reaction. Since the notion of a disposition has been introduced elsewhere in this volume, it will be sufficient here to emphasize merely this: Any reference to a "disposition" to certain actions (or to certain "felt transitions" and "felt terminations" in subsequent experience) is a reference to actions (etc.) that *would* occur *if* certain supplementary causes were present. In many cases, of course, the "if" will be contrary to fact; hence in many cases a person may think about, or have beliefs about, so and so, and in particular, take something as a sign of so and so, without doing anything that overtly affects so and so.

The point to be established can now be presented in this way: If such a sentence as "There are tigers in India," which we would not be very likely to read in any special poetic or literary way, can be *understood* without any action on our part —if, that is to say, the interpretant of that complex sign, which makes it refer to a situation that is remote from us, requires only a *disposition* to certain practical reactions, rather than any actual practical reactions—it is clear that the reference of the sentence is not dependent on its having for us any *actual* 'cue-value.' Its *actual* cue-value (as distinct from its disposition to have it) can be blocked by all manner of things, such as our lack of interest in doing anything about tigers in India, or our inability to do anything about them. And if it can be blocked by such factors as these, without making the sentence lose its reference to there being tigers in India, there is no reason to suppose that it cannot, in the same way, be blocked by another factor which either supplements or replaces them—namely the aesthetic attitude. Thus it is possible to understand a sentence, and understand it in a way that makes it refer to something else, without abandoning the aesthetic attitude in the slightest degree.

Perhaps these remarks will be clearer if restated more briefly. The aesthetic attitude, as commonly conceived (if one may judge from the contexts in which writers use the term) suspends only the *actual* cue-value of any experience. It does not, necessarily, put an end to a *disposition* to take the experience as a cue, but only makes the disposition unrealized (like the inflammability of a match which is not struck). And since the interpretant of a sign, by the pragmatic type of view, requires not an actual cue-value but only one that is dispositionally present, it becomes possible for a person to react to a sign—to interpret it as standing for something else—even though he inhibits the actual cue-value in the special way that the aesthetic attitude requires.

These remarks apply to *any* dispositional view of the interpretant of a sign that is at all likely to be held; and since we have previously seen that no problem arises, in this particular connection, for views of the interpretant that take it as non-dispositional, the compatibility of symbolism and the aesthetic attitude is readily established. But we still, of course, have our central question: "What sort of aesthetic experience does symbolism contribute to our appreciation of the arts?" We have found only that there *can* be such experience, since the symbol can be interpreted in the aesthetic attitude; but we have not found whether there is any experience that in fact serves (as Isenberg put it) to "expand the field on which attention rests," nor have we any good idea of what sort of experience this would be. So to that question we must immediately turn.

IV.

In discussing aesthetic experience it will be sufficient to limit attention to the way it can be dealt with by a dispositional view of the nature of the interpretant. That is feasible, not because nondispositional views are entirely beyond hope of being tenable, and not because the dispositional views have been worked out in a wholly adequate fashion (for in point of fact, they have not); it is feasible simply because the dispositional views present the most interesting test case to those who emphasize aesthetic experience. If aesthetic experience can be taken as central to aesthetics even by those who hold a dispositional view of the interpretant, it can be taken as central by any other view of the interpretant as well.

Clearly, if the interpretant of a sign is a disposition, and in particular, if it is a disposition to responses which, through the operation of the aesthetic attitude, are prevented from being actual, there will be no sense in supposing that the interpretant of the sign, per se, is an experience that can be "dwelt upon." A disposition is a sort of if-then relationship, and of a nature that cannot significantly be said to *be* an experience, or to attend sign in the same felt way that an image, say, might be thought to attend it. Yet the formation of a disposition, when a person interprets a sign, might nevertheless have "conscious accompaniments"—these being experiences of *various* sorts. And to the extent that the disposition is responsible for these conscious accompaniments, its presence may serve to enrich our aesthetic experience. That, in its essentials, is the view to be developed.

The term, "conscious accompaniments," which will be particularly useful in what follows, can be introduced by this analogy. Suppose that a runner gets ready for a race in a way that makes possible a quick start—that, accordingly, he has a tendency, potentiality, or *disposition* to start quickly. If we ask, "What sort of experience is this disposition?" it will be obvious that the question is inappropriate. But suppose we alter the question, asking, "What sort of experiences does the runner have that are likely, if not in all cases, then in many, to attend the tendency or disposition to make a quick start?" The question now becomes an appropriate one, and may lead us to find, for instance, that the runner has certain feelings of tension, certain emotional tinglings, and even certain structurings in his visual field, etc., which arise in a way correlated (at least roughly) with his disposition to start quickly. Now when we answer this second question we shall be specifying the "conscious accompaniments" of the runner's disposition or readiness to respond. And it will be evident that the term will apply, *mutatis mutandis,* to the sort of disposition that (by the theory here under discussion) is the interpretant of a sign.

We must accordingly ask what the conscious accompaniments of the interpretant of a sign are likely to be when the sign occurs in a work of art. Here the evidence, partly introspective and partly based on the various remarks of critics, who in turn are introspecting, is less decisive than one could wish. Perhaps the answer here to be given will be incorrect on certain points of detail. But it seems sufficiently trustworthy to show that the conscious accompaniments of an artistic sign are of great variety.

In the first place, one of the conscious accompaniments may take the form of making subtle differences to our experience of the sign-vehicle itself. We have seen this previously, in the example of rhythmic effects that was given in section I. But it is well to note that a similar situation holds with various other 'musical' aspects of literature. Thus, our understanding of a sentence may affect the way we hear its phrasing, so to speak. In the case of the sentence, "Some men are born great, others achieve greatness, and others have greatness thrust upon them," we can deliberately read without any pause, and even with a certain hurrying up, at the places corresponding to the commas; but in spite of that we will still *hear* a certain sound phrasing that corresponds to these places, these being marked in our auditory attention by the changes in sense. This has often a marked effect in poetry, since it varies phrasing that would otherwise be monotonous. In any fixed verse form, for instance, like that of iambic tetrameter in rhyming couplets, the line lengths and rhymes often set up a phrasing different from that set up by the meaning of the words. Thus in this familiar passage from Marvell's "To His Coy Mistress,"

> Thy Beauty shall no more be found;
> Nor, in thy marble Vault, shall sound
> My echoing Song; then Worms shall try
> That long preserv'd virginity:

it will be noted that the word 'song,' closing, as it does, a phrase established by the meaning of the words, stands in agreeable opposition to the phrases set up by the rhymes—an opposition that, as we hear the words, will continue even if we make no pause after 'song' in reading aloud.

We have further conscious correlates of symbolic interpretation, in its effect on the sign vehicle, in onomatopoeia. Note that we are attentive to the z-sound of 'buzz' in a way that we are not likely to be for certain words that rhyme with it, such as 'does.' Here the reason, presumably, is that the auditory similarity between 'buzz' and what it signifies makes us find a similarity, in attention, that otherwise would attract attention only slightly. And onomatopoeia has many near parallels, in the music of verse, where the point of similarity is not between sound and sound, but rather takes the form of subtle physiognomic similarities, which again come to sharp attention in the sign vehicle only when the sign vehicle signifies something that accentuates them. Thus if we think that *papillon* is a happier name for a butterfly than *schmetterling*, this has obviously nothing to do with sounds that butterflies make, but only to do with a certain delicacy in the sound of *papillon* that we feel in the flight of butterflies—a delicacy that we would not be likely to notice so much if the word signified something else. Such differences in our experience are unquestionably subtle, but so, too, are the sources of poetical effects.

Not dissimilar effects are found in painting. Suppose, for instance, that a picture is painted in so abstract a manner that we at first take it to be nonobjective, but that with a change in attention we suddenly "see" that it represents a man. So far this change in the appearance of the sign vehicle (which involves a restructuring of our experience, with figure becoming ground, let us say, or with certain lines seeming to have a greater continuity) need not be taken as a conscious accompaniment of sign interpretation, but rather as something that must take place *before* the (iconic) sign interpretation is possible. But note that the change in the appearance of the sign does not stop at that point. Once we recognize that a man is represented, our attention turns to parts of it we are accustomed to notice in the men of ordinary life; we look at the painted eyes, for instance, and the painted curve of the mouth, since these forms interest us in real men. And the result is that aspects of the very *pattern* we experience, varying with our attention, are among the conscious accompaniments of our taking the picture as being of a man—the pattern being one that we can "dwell upon," of course, rather than take as a cue to some practical orientation to men.

It remains the case, however, that these conscious accompaniments of interpretation which affect appearances of the sign vehicle are not (as previously said in section II) sufficient to constitute the whole aesthetic experience that attends signs. And it is easy to think of further examples that do not involve changed appearances of the sign vehicle:

In literature, for instance, there is often a subtle "awareness" of sensuous effects that are different from the sounds of words. Thus when Keats writes in "The Eve of St. Agnes" of

> . . . jellies smoother than the creamy curd,
> And lucent syrups, tinct with cinnamon

there is such an awareness, which seems to depend as much on reference as on the music of the lines. In painting, this is paralleled by the way in which a picture, though it mainly gives us the qualities of visual experience, can somehow make us half feel qualities normally assigned to the other senses. Thus, there is a "sense of motion" in our reaction to certain pictures that borders on a kinaesthetic sense, and a "sense of texture" that borders on a tactile sense. The exact "feel" in question is not easily described, but whether one wants to speak of nonvisual "images" in these cases (as I. A. Richards does) or of "physiognomic qualities," or of actual sensations arising from unusual stimuli, it may fairly be presumed that those who are particularly sensitive to the arts have subtleties in their experience that such terms (perhaps imperfectly) serve to suggest. (We are often procrustean in our classification of experiences, tending to mention only those that the older psychologists managed to call attention to.) Now it may well be—and it will be sufficient to say this for the case of painting only, though parallel remarks could be made about verse—that these subtleties can be conveyed by nonobjective paintings; but representational paintings seem to present them much more forcibly. Thus "moving" lines best give a sense of motion when they depict something moving, such as a man running, and a sense of tactile softness is heightened when "soft" lines depict velvet. We realize that a moving man is represented, or a velvet cloth; and although this "realizing," taken as a dispositional property, is not itself an experience, its conscious accompaniments make a difference to these aspects of our experience. Nor can it be said of these aspects of experience, as can sometimes be said of this or that visual image, that they have little connection with our artistic appreciation.

We have still to consider the conscious accompaniments of sign interpretation that take the form of moods or emotions. And in certain cases these are quite marked. It must be understood, of course, that these emotions or moods need not be the exact counterparts that we experience in daily life—the general principle here being the same as that suggested, in the previous chapter, for the case of music. But all the same, the horror that attends our reading of certain of Poe's tales is obviously a conscious accompaniment of our understanding what the tales are about. And the same is true of our suspense in following the development of the plot in many novels—not necessarily those that are "thrillers," but even such sedate novels as *Pride and Prejudice*. And there are counterparts of these moods or emotions in our reaction to paintings. We are likely to find any of El Greco's versions of "St. Francis in Prayer," for instance, to be sharply different in mood from Manet's "Bar of the Folies-Bergères"; and although this is in great measure due to differences in predominating color, etc., it is in part due, so it would certainly seem, to our realization that one represents a saint in prayer, and the other represents a barmaid. And when we turn to obviously story-telling pictures such as Hogarth's "The Rake's Progress," or to satirical pictures, such as Goya's drawing of a priest walking a tight-rope, the fact that various subtleties of mood, in our reaction, depend on what the pictures symbolize is scarcely open to question.

In these various ways, then, sometimes involving appearances of the sign vehicle itself, and sometimes involving other experiences, either in subtle near-sensory awareness or in mood, the process of interpreting a sign has conscious accompaniments that can be dwelt upon and can thus serve to enrich our aesthetic experience. These experiences have been exemplified only in a rough way; but perhaps enough has been said to show the full compatibility of symbolism (even when conceived as involving an interpretant that is dispositional in nature) and the general theory of the arts that emphasizes aesthetic experience and the aesthetic attitude.

Perhaps the net import of these remarks can best be emphasized by comparing them to the view of Isenberg that was previously mentioned. In many respects the present account agrees with Isenberg's: in particular, it emphasizes, in his fashion, the variety of aesthetic experience that is contributed by words, or by the forms in painting that resemble those of everyday life. And these experiences, per se, are nonreferential. They have here been called "conscious accompaniments" of an interpretant of a sign process, but there would be no particular objection to calling them "nonreferential meanings," since the term "meaning" lends itself to many senses. The only difference between the present account (which is certainly indebted to his careful reflections) and his own is that he seems to take the relevant aesthetic experiences as somehow hindering cognitive reference, and thus as making what *used to be* symbols into something less than symbols; whereas by the present account the relevant aesthetic experiences are *dependent* upon the reference. There is nothing about reference that entails a practical, rather than an aesthetic, attitude; for the aesthetic attitude requires no more than a suspension of actual steps in acting in accord with one's thoughts or beliefs, and this happens time and again, for other reasons, in the course of interpreting symbols in daily life. Our reaction to symbols in art, then, though it focuses attention more strongly on the conscious accompaniments of our cognitive reaction, does not make the symbols less than symbols, or in any way require us to hold that symbolism is a kind of stepchild of aesthetic theory.

v.

As has previously been remarked, this chapter is divided into two broad parts, the first being concerned with the place of symbolism in a general theory of art, and the second with a discussion of the aspects of symbolism that, for purposes of criticism (and in particular, literary criticism) seem most to repay attention. Since the first of these topics has now been dealt with, let us turn to the second.

Stated in other terms, this second topic is concerned with the way in which critics have emphasized this or that aspect of the meaning of symbols in their efforts to interpret literature. It will be obvious that this topic is much more specific than the one previously discussed. It could, perhaps, be discussed in its own right, without any effort to make explicit how it connects, in this or that respect, with the conclusions that have been drawn above. But it will be of interest to refer back, now and then, to our previous discussion, showing that views about aesthetic experience and the interpretant in a sign process, though rarely given explicit mention in the discussions of critics, may nevertheless continue to be a part of the theoretical background that guides them in their work.

Perhaps the most arresting aspect of contemporary criticism is its exploration of nuances of meaning. Typical examples can be found in what has elsewhere in this volume been called "secondary conceptual content"; but examples can be found, more generally, in all aspects of sign-situations that are *not* limited to *literal*, primary conceptual content. Sometimes the emphasis on nuances is of a sort that most readers will find extreme. Thus F. W. Bateson, in commenting on Shakespeare's line,

The expense of spirit in a waste of shame,

maintains that the word "expense" suggests "expanse," and thus prepares the way for "waste" (in the sense of wasteland); and he adds that the word "waste" suggests "waist," which thereby "reinforces the sexual implications of the sonnet." [22] Whatever may be thought of this post-Joycean criticism, it must be acknowledged that the conceptual content alleged to be present is very secondary indeed, depending on word sounds and on ambiguities. And a further example, again of a sort that many will find extreme, is assigned to F. C. Prescott by Cleanth Brooks:

[Prescott] shows that the verb "to die" was used in the seventeenth century with the meaning "to experience the consummation of the sexual act," and suggests that there is a shade of this meaning latent in

Juliet. Yea, noise?—then I'll be brief. —Oh happy dagger! [*Snatching Romeo's dagger*]
  This is thy sheath; [*Stabs herself*] there rust, and let me die. [*Falls on Romeo's body and dies.*]

Prescott points out that the mature and thoughtful reader "will remember Shakespeare's constant word-play—sometimes coarse, sometimes poetical—in this tragedy and throughout." [23]

But of course there are many instances less extreme than this, some of them common to criticism both of this age and previous ones. Thus one way of revealing secondary conceptual content is found in paraphrases of metaphors, which are as old as pedagogy. And there are straightforward efforts to point out innuendoes, as when Brooks himself, in the volume previously mentioned, appends to Auden's line "It is later than you think," the parenthetical comment, "An English gentleman is never late to appointments—even the ruling classes will listen to an indictment couched in these terms, the poet implies." [24]

This tendency to stress nuances of meaning has presumably both influenced, and been influenced by, the tendency to revolt from a too "logical" conception of language, as mentioned at the beginning of Chapter 5. Note that a scientist is usually anxious to avoid such nuances, feeling that he can obtain exactness only by restricting himself to the aspects of primary conceptual content that are strictly literal; and note that the same is true of a lawyer. In common life we sometimes make use of the nuances, as in hinting; but note that this is a *risk* in communication that politeness requires, since a hint may not be "taken." In literature, however, the nuances are commonly recognized to be as important as are the obvious and literal aspects of primary conceptual content.

Now there are three things that require attention in this connection, all of them closely related. The first and most important of them is too complicated to be developed here, but can at least receive passing mention. It can be explained by emphasizing this contrast between the literal aspects of primary conceptual content and the nuances of meaning.

When we ask about the literal, primary conceptual content of a sentence, our question is normally a dictionary question or a grammatical one; the answer depends on the *conventions* that govern our language. But when we ask about nuances of meaning, a reference to the dictionary or the grammar book, though it may help, does not fully answer the question. We cannot in that way learn the appropriate force of certain metaphors—until, that is, the metaphors have lost all their originality and become conventionalized in their turn. And the same is true of other nuances. One may acknowledge that Prescott was right in pointing out his Elizabethan sense of "to die," for instance, and still feel that this sense is "read into" the passage from Romeo and Juliet, rather than "in" it. The question arises, then, as to how we determine whether a given nuance of meaning is really "in" a sentence. And in the present state of our analysis of sign-situations, no answer has as yet gained general acceptance.

It may be argued, of course, that nothing is a sign save when *taken* as a sign, and hence, whenever there are individual differences between readers, some assigning a particular nuance to a sentence, and others not, all we can say is, "It has this meaning for some readers and not for others." But many feel that this, though true so far as it goes, does not go far enough. They feel that there is, somewhere within our language or the culture that molds our language, some less relativistic criterion for determining whether a certain nuance of meaning assigned to a poetic line by reader X and not by reader Y, is "correctly" or "appropriately," or "properly" so assigned to it. Yet it is not easy to say what this criterion is. It is decidedly "unfashionable," and perhaps that puts it too mildly, to decide the issue by reference to the poet's intention—any such insistence having been sharply criticized by Wimsatt and Beardsley, in their paper "The Intentional Fallacy," [25] which remarks that, in the first place, the poet's intention must normally be inferred from the meaning we can find in his poem, rather than *vice versa*, and, in the second place, that a poet may intend to say a great deal more (and sometimes, a great deal less) than the words he puts down actually make articulate. Stevenson,[26] in a recent article, acknowledges the propriety of arguing about the "proper" nuance of meaning that can be assigned to a poem, but claims that the argument cannot always be settled impersonally, since any conclusion reflects the "sensibilities" of those who are arguing. He takes "proper" to behave like a value-term. I. A. Richards, in personal conversation, said that he was confident that there were impersonal criteria, but that he was not at all confident of any list he was prepared to suggest. No view, to repeat, has gained general acceptance. The question lies a little to one side, perhaps, of the theory of signs; so no further effort will be made here to suggest an answer to it.

The second point to notice, with regard to nuances of meaning, arises from a reflection on the first point. It is somewhat surprising that the work of critics—based as it is on no specified criterion for distinguishing between what nuances of meaning are "in" rather than "read into" literature—should be so helpful, as many readers will acknowledge it to be. And this is the more surprising when we consider that even such a distinction as that between primary and secondary conceptual content (which is often made, though not by means of these particular terms) is itself vague, being usually introduced (as indeed it is in this volume, Chapter 5) by examples, rather than by exact definitions. How can such a yet-growing theory yield such interesting applications? But perhaps this question can be answered very simply: One of the important steps in coming to understand poetry, though admittedly only one of many steps, lies in developing an awareness of what Richards has called the "flexibility" of language—the variety of interpretations that, whether appropriate or inappropriate, a verbal context admits of. And this can be learned even when somewhat fantastic nuances of meaning are suggested, nor does it require one to give notice whether the conceptual content is actually secondary, say, rather than primary. One of the achievements of contemporary criticism, then, is to limber up our habits in this direction, getting us at least to consider possible meanings or "implications" that we might otherwise overlook. That is perhaps all one can expect, so long as critical theory, and in particular, the theory of signs, is in a controversial and not altogether precise state of development; but it is at least an important beginning, which promises eventually to lead to results that are still more important. It is something to be sensitive to the various things that literature *might* mean, even if we are puzzled, still, in deciding how to select from them in determining what it does mean.

The third point to be noticed takes us back to our previous discussion of the aesthetic attitude. It arises from the question, "Why is it that in literature the nuances of meaning are recognized as being important, whereas in science, etc., they are so often dismissed as inessential or even misleading?" Now this question can be answered from the point of view considered in the earlier sections of this chapter. For *if* the interpretant in a symbolic situation is of interest only for its *conscious accompaniments,* and not for preparing us for practical situations as it is in science, then it will not so much matter whether these conscious accompaniments attend the sort of interpretant that we find in literal, primary conceptual content, or whether they attend the sort of interpretant that gives us the nuances. To be sure, the latter will be less intimately and less certainly connected with the symbol, and may be "missed" by some readers, and "improperly read in" by others. But just as a painting, when its representational aspects are conventionalized to a degree that makes them ambiguous may be the more interesting for that reason—allowing us a certain freedom in our reaction, and varying a little with our varying moods—so the uncertainties of the nuances of meaning in a poem may be interesting. The conscious accompaniments of the interpretant, when they come, have a variety that keeps the poem with its nuances always fresh. This observation is only a very partial confirmation of the view that aesthetic experience is essential to aesthetics; but it shows us, once more, by relating the view to currently accepted critical practice, how readily the view can take account of situations that involve symbolism.

We have only to extend the above considerations, and very slightly, to reach Empson's conception of the importance of "ambiguity" in poetry; [27] for as he uses the term, "ambiguity" refers not to an uncertainty as to which primary conceptual content belongs to a word, phrase, or sentence, but rather to the simultaneous presence of several conceptual contents, most of which are likely to be secondary. And a "complex word," as discussed more recently by Empson, simply extends his study of ambiguity.

For the moment, only a little of Empson's work—which promises to be the most influential of all recent work done on the theoretical basis of literary criticism in the present century, along with the work of Richards which partly inspired it—can adequately be developed. One can best compare his analysis with the sort of analysis of verse rhythms, for instance, which makes us too attentive to the rhythms, causing us to hear more than any sensitive listener wants to hear. Such an analysis is of use only as a temporary exercise, which leaves its desired effect only when it is half-forgotten; that is to say, one must first hear too much in order, later, to hear just enough. Now with Empson a similar situation arises simply because, in pointing out his ambiguities, he *uses* words whose literal, primary conceptual content is taken as identical with meanings in the poem which are only nuances, and hence not really evoked by the poem so strongly as his analysis suggests. So he overemphasizes the nuances, sometimes to a point that makes us suspect he is finding too much in a poem. But this is inescapable, given his method; and it seems not to need a remedy. For we tend to forget much of his analysis, remembering only enough to enable us, when we read the poem unselfconsciously, to enrich our reaction to it. Or so it is, rather, in the fortunate cases; but the point is, fortunate cases are possible. Meanwhile, it is helpful to have an explicit dismissal of the "either-or-but-not-both" approach to the meanings of poetry, which by its too great dependence on the view of language developed in connection with logic and science, would make us insensitive to the richness of poetry. It does not greatly matter, incidentally, that metaphors and various figures of speech cannot *in practice* be given wholly accurate paraphrases, and hence that Empson's manner of drawing out poetic meanings must in this respect always be inexact. For it is not the function of such criticism to preserve in plain language what the poem has conveyed in figurative language. Rather, the plain language is a sort of preliminary exercise, having its function in leading us back to the poem with more flexible habits of reacting, and with a certain preparation for this or that nuance. Thus, the poem, finally, and not the words of the critic, must be the artistic symbol—nor will anyone be likely to wish it otherwise.

Put in terms of those who emphasize the aesthetic attitude and with attention to a dispositional view of cognition, the above remarks amount to this: When we read a poem we dwell on the sound or sight of the words, and on the various experiences that are conscious accompaniments of the interpretant of their sign function. But *what* these experiences are will be determined, not merely by the words, but by the training, sensibility, etc., that we *bring to* them. And criticism such as Empson's, which is read at a time normally prior to our full aesthetic enjoyment of the poem, provides some of this training, and a certain exercise of our sensibilities. Only when the criticism has had its effect do we have, in reading the poem, the varied experiences to dwell upon; and only then (by any view emphasizing the aesthetic attitude that is likely to be advanced) do we need to sustain the aesthetic attitude in appreciating the poem.

VI.

In concluding this chapter it may be well to say something about the role of emotive meaning, or of the emotive function of words, in literature. Since the topic has been treated, though more generally, elsewhere in this volume, it can here be treated very briefly.

We are at present concerned with the practical applications of the theory of signs to problems of literary criticism, so we can be content to assume (simply on the authority of certain critics) that emotive meaning has enough connection with literature to warrant discussing it in that connection; hence the question will be simply this: *If* the emotive aspects of literature are to be pointed out, as a means of enhancing our appreciation of literature, *how* can a critic proceed to do this?

One procedure is this: By using words of his own the critic tries to evoke an emotion *like* the one that a poem is alleged to express, and in this way he "shows" his readers the sort of emotion he thinks they should get when they read the poem. There will be no gain unless the critic's words evoke the emotion in some simpler, more trustworthy way than the words in the poem do. It may be doubted whether this is ever possible; and even if it were possible, it would thereby give ground for the suspicion that the poem, by expressing the emotion in a needlessly complicated or untrustworthy way, was not worth the labor that the critic saw fit to expend upon it. To be sure, the method is not altogether hopeless. The critic might be content to convey to us an emotion that is only a *little* like that of the poem, the latter being much more subtle; and in that way he might hope, in an imperfect way, to take us a step or two toward a sensitiveness to the more subtle mood, which could come only from the poem itself. Something like the same device is used in certain types of notes for symphonies, where the critic's prose is apparently aimed at evoking in us some of the feelings, in less subtle form, that we are expected to get in subtle form from the music itself. But this device is not generally felt to be very helpful by musicians, and is often felt to be positively harmful in directing attention away from the composer's good music to the critic's indifferent prose. The same is likely to be the result, *mutatis mutandis,* when the device is used in an effort to enhance our appreciation of poetry.

A second procedure is to *name,* rather than evoke, the emotion that the poem is alleged to express. Thus, a critic may say that such and such a poem expresses a somber, morose mood, whereas another a mood of gaiety, etc. But note that this helps the reader (assuming that the reader trusts what the critic says) only for the most elementary steps of learning to appreciate the poem. Whenever subtleties of mood are in question, the critic will find it virtually impossible to use this method. And the reason is a very simple one: The emotion-designating terms in our language are highly generic, and it is not easy to introduce terms that are more specific. Many poems are of a sort that might be called "morose," for instance, and if we want to indicate *this* kind of moroseness rather than *that,* we are normally at a loss for words. So although this method is again not a hopeless one, it is definitely *limited* in its utility.

The third, and apparently most important, method is one that does not, like the first, try to evoke the emotion by other words; and does not, like the second, try to name the emotion by use of other words; but rather tries to help the words in the poem themselves better to evoke the emotion. This can be done either by remarking that such and such a word in the poem is the key word, that its rhythmic effect on the line should be particularly noted, and so on. And it can also be done, of course, by pointing out nuances of meaning in the way discussed in the preceding section; for so far as the cognitive field theory (as mentioned in Chapter 6) holds true—and to *some extent*, at least, it obviously does—these nuances of meaning, even though descriptive in themselves, will bring with them whatever emotions are dependent upon them. Note that this latter method, so far as it bears on the emotions, is simply the well-known device of calling attention to the "objective correlative" of the emotions.

Now it will be obvious that this third method is one that does not make us self-conscious about the emotional expressiveness of the poem. The critic doesn't talk about emotions, or about emotive meaning, at all. He talks about key words, rhythms, nuances of descriptive meaning, and the like, in such a way that the reader, in successful cases, is *caused* to get a different emotional reaction to the poem; but, meanwhile, the emotion itself is not an object of explicit attention. Perhaps this is an important advantage of the method, since emotions of a subtle sort arise most easily when they are not "forced," but are allowed to arise spontaneously; our attention being directed, not to them, but to whatever occasions them.

These observations have this bearing, it would appear, on the prevalent types of theory which emphasize the importance of emotive meaning in poetry. It may be that these theories have much to be said in their favor; for although an *exclusive* emphasis on our emotional reaction to poetry would seem rather extreme (since aesthetic experience need not be emotional experience, but can involve sounds, images, and indeed, any sort of conscious accompaniment of the interpretant in a sign-process) it remains the case that a *partial* emphasis, and even a strong emphasis, on emotions is a not indefensible view. But even so, one cannot properly infer from this that references to emotive effects ought to be more familiar than they are in work of critics. For since the third of the above methods seems the most practicable one, emotive meaning should remain a conception which, at most, guides the critic's procedure without having to be expressly mentioned by him. From the point of view of the practical critic (though perhaps not, if you will, from the point of view of aesthetics more generally) the concept of emotive meaning is of interest as a reminder that poetic language, in this and in certain other ways, has a function that is not always comparable to the function of scientific language. Once this important but rather obvious point is clear, however, the critic's efforts seem best directed not to a discussion of the emotions, but rather to a discussion of the aspects of a literary work which are likely, when attended to, to *evoke* emotions.

NOTES

Chapter 1

[1] Edward Sapir, "Conceptual Categories of Primitive Languages," *Science*, 74 (1931): 578.

[2] Notably in "Science and Linguistics," *Technology Review*, 42 (1939–40): 229 ff.; "Linguistics as an Exact Science," *ibid.*, 43 (1940–41): 61 ff.; "Languages and Logic," *ibid.*, 43 (1940–41): 250 ff.; "The Relation of Habitual Thought and Behavior to Language," in *Language, Culture and Personality: Essays in Memory of Edward Sapir*, ed. by Leslie Spier, A. Irving Hallowell, and Stanley S. Newman (Menasha, Wis., 1941), pp. 75 ff. These four articles have been reprinted under the title *Four Articles on Metalinguistics* (Washington, D.C.: Foreign Service Institute, Department of State, 1949), and in *Language, Thought, and Reality, Selected Writings of Benjamin Lee Whorf*, ed. by John B. Carroll (Cambridge, Mass.: Mass. Institute of Technology, 1956). This work is referred to hereinafter as Carroll.

[3] "Gestalt Techniques of Stem Composition in Shawnee," appendix to "Shawnee Stems and the Jacob P. Dunn Miami Dictionary," in *Prehistoric Research Series* (Indianapolis: Indiana Historical Society, 1940), 1, no. 9: 395. Carroll, p. 169.

[4] Clyde Kluckhohn and William H. Kelly, "The Concept of Culture," *The Science of Man in the World Crises*, ed. by Ralph Linton (New York, 1945), p. 97.

[5] M. E. Opler, "An Application of the Theory of Themes in Culture," *Journal of the Washington Academy of Sciences*, 36 (1946): 137 ff.

[6] Benjamin L. Whorf, "Science and Linguistics," *Technology Review*, 42 (1939–40): 6. Carroll, p. 216.

[7] Edward Sapir, "Language and Environment," *American Anthropologist*, n.s., 14 (1912): 228. Reprinted in *Selected Writings of Edward Sapir*, ed. by D. Mandelbaum (Berkeley, Calif., 1949), pp. 90–91.

[8] Jerome S. Bruner and Cecile C. Goodman, "Value and Need as Organizing Factors in Perception," *Journal of Abnormal and Social Psychology*, 42 (1947): 34.

[9] Clyde Kluckhohn and Dorothea Leighton, *The Navaho* (Cambridge, Mass., 1948), p. 204.

[10] Dorothy D. Lee, "Conceptual Implications of an Indian Language," *Philosophy of Science*, 5 (1936): 90.

[11] Bertrand Russell, *History of Western Philosophy* (New York, 1945), p. 202.

[12] Benjamin L. Whorf, "The Relation of Habitual Thought and Behavior to

Language," pp. 75–93. Carroll, pp. 134–59. Unless otherwise noted subsequent references to Whorf are to this paper in Carroll's edition.

[13] Lee, *op. cit.*

[14] *Ibid.*, pp. 94–95.

[15] *Ibid.*, p. 102.

[16] Harry Hoijer, "Cultural Implications of Some Navaho Linguistic Categories," *Language*, 27 (1951): 111–20.

[17] *Ibid.*, p. 115.

[18] *Ibid.*, p. 117.

[19] Kluckhohn and Leighton, *op. cit.*, pp. 227–28.

Chapter 2

[1] Gottlob Frege, "On Concept and Object," trans. by P. T. Geach revised by Max Black, *Mind*, n.s., LX (1951): 168–80.

[2] Rudolf Carnap, *Introduction to Semantics* (Cambridge, Mass., 1946), p. 230.

[3] Nelson Goodman and W. V. Quine, "Steps Toward a Constructive Nominalism," *Journal of Symbolic Logic*, 12, no. 4 (1947): 105.

[4] *Ibid.*

[5] Morton White, "Ontological Clarity and Semantic Obscurity," *Journal of Philosophy*, 48 (1951): 373.

[6] W. V. Quine, "Semantics and Abstract Objects," *Proceedings of The American Academy of Arts and Sciences*, LXXX (1951): 91.

[7] Goodman and Quine, *op. cit.*

[8] Alonzo Church, "Abstract Entities in Semantic Analysis," *Proceedings of The American Academy of Arts and Sciences*, 80, no. 1 (1951): 104.

[9] Robert Leeper, "Cognitive Processes," in *Handbook of Experimental Psychology*, ed. by S. S. Stevens (New York and London, 1951), p. 755.

[10] Leeper, *op. cit.*, p. 736.

[11] Grace DeLaguna, "Perception and Language," *Human Biology*, I (1929): 555–58.

[12] Ernest Cassirer, *An Essay on Man* (New Haven, 1944), p. 132.

[13] Leeper, *op. cit.*, pp. 754–55.

[14] Jean Piaget, *The Psychology of Intelligence* (London, 1950), p. 4.

[15] Hans Walloch, "Some Considerations Concerning the Relation Between Perception and Cognition," *Journal of Personality*, XVIII (1949): 6–7.

[16] *Ibid.*, p. 6.

[17] *Ibid.*, p. 7.

[18] I. A. Richards, *Interpretation in Teaching* (London, 1938), pp. 48–49.

[19] Karl Schuessler and Anselm Strauss, "A Study of Concept Learning by Scale Analysis," *American Sociological Review*, XV (1950): 752–62. Cf. also their "Socialization, Logical Reasoning, and Concept Formation in the Child," *ibid.*, XVI (1951): 514–23, and A. L. Strauss, "The Development and Transformation of Monetary Meaning in the Child," *ibid.*, XVII (1952): 275–86.

[20] *Op. cit.*, p. 4.

[21] Kurt Goldstein, "Methodological Approach to the Study of Schizophrenic Thought Disorder," in J. S. Kasanin, *Language and Thought in Schizophrenia* (Berkeley and Los Angeles, 1946), pp. 17–39.

[20] *Op. cit.*, p. 20.

[23] Jurt Goldstein and Martin Scheerer, "Abstract and Concrete Behavior," *Psychological Monographs*, LIII (1941), no. 2: 3.

[24] John Dewey, *How We Think* (New York, 1910), p. 137.

[25] *Ibid.*

[26] *Judgment and Reasoning in the Child* (New York, 1928), p. 149.

[27] "Methodological Approach," p. 19.

[28] Goldstein and Sheerer, *op. cit.*, p. 4.

[29] *Supra*, p. 36.

[30] See, for example, Dorothea McCarthy's "Language Development in Children" in L. Carmichael's *Manual of Child Psychology* (New York, 1946).

[31] In a lecture to the Michigan Language and Symbolism Group, February 11, 1952.

[32] *Linguistic Aspects of Science* (International Encyclopedia of Unified Science; Chicago, 1939), I, no. 4: 19–20.

[33] Edward Sapir, "Conceptual Categories in Primitive Language," *Science*, V (1931): 578.

[34] *Language* (New York, 1933), p. 426.

[35] *Op. cit.*, p. 428.

[36] *Op. cit.*, pp. 429–30.

[37] *Op. cit.*, pp. 435–36.

[38] *Op. cit.*, pp. 439–40.

[39] In a series of lectures and discussions with the Michigan group on January 7, 8, 10, and 14, 1952.

Chapter 3

[1] B. F. Skinner has, in lectures delivered at Columbia and Harvard, applied some of the general principles of animal behavior to human linguistic functioning. These lectures are not published, but Professor Skinner has kindly loaned us the detailed notes taken by a student in the Columbia course. We have been pleased to discover some points of agreement with these notes. Since our treatment was independently developed, none of the errors that it contains can be traced to Professor Skinner, although some of its virtues are anticipated in his lectures.

[2] Leonard Bloomfield, *Language* (New York: 1933), p. 26.

[3] E. R. Hilgard and D. G. Marquis, *Conditioning and Learning* (New York, 1940), p. 51.

[4] B. F. Skinner made the same distinction earlier in his book *The Behavior of Organisms* (New York, 1938). He further suggested that "Respondent" learning (classical conditioning) operates on the basis of contiguity while "Operant" learning (instrumental) follows the law of effect. Skinner added that a rough topographical distinction could be made between them: Operants are largely skeletal, whereas Respondents involve primarily those effectors, smooth muscles and glands, that are controlled by the autonomic nervous system. O. H. Mowrer in his article "On the Dual Nature of Learning—A Re-Interpretation of 'Conditioning' and 'Problem Solving,'" *Harvard Educational Review*, 17 (1947): 102–48, supported a slight variant of this position. He

agreed that skeletal learning operates on the law of effect and that "emotional" learning, involving the autonomic nervous system, follows the principle of contiguity. He differed, however, in holding that skeletal responses could be acquired either by classical conditioning or instrumental learning.

⁵ It should be remembered that the "trial and error" learning with which Edward Lee Thorndike's name is identified is essentially the same as instrumental learning. The formulations to which we have referred are obviously indebted to Thorndike's earlier work.

⁶ *Op. cit.* W. J. Brogden has suggested reducing these four varieties to two in his chapter, "Animal Studies of Learning," *Handbook of Experimental Psychology,* ed. by S. S. Stevens (New York: John Wiley and Sons, 1951).

⁷ J. B. Wolfe, "Effectiveness of Token-rewards for Chimpanzees," *Comparative Psychological Monographs,* 12, no. 5.

⁸ There is some dispute as to the proper conceptualization of the facts of generalization and discrimination. The following presentation is intended to follow the theory of Lashley and Wade as it appears in K. S. Lashley and M. Wade, "The Pavlovian Theory of Generalization," *Psychological Review,* 53 (1946): 72–88, rather than the Pavlovian-Hullian position which is described in Clark Hull's *Principles of Behavior* (New York: D. Appleton-Century Co., 1943). For the use that we make of generalization and discrimination, this difference in point of view seems not to be important.

⁹ C. L. Hull, "Quantitative Aspects of the Evolution of Concepts: An Experimental Study," *Psychological Monographs,* 28 (1920), whole no. 123: 1–85.

¹⁰ Dorothea McCarthy, "Language Development in Children," *Manual of Child Psychology,* ed. by Leonard Carmichael (New York: John Wiley and Sons, 1946).

¹¹ This formulation resembles Professor B. J. Skinner's description of speech as an Operant that is socially reinforced.

¹² Kenneth Burke, *A Rhetoric of Motives* (New York: Prentice-Hall, 1950).

¹³ Bronisilaw K. Malinowski, "The Problem of Meaning in Primitive Languages," in C. K. Ogden and I. A. Richards, *The Meaning of Meaning* (London, 1923), p. 312. Italics ours.

¹⁴ D. O. Hebb, *The Organization of Behavior: A Neuro-psychological Theory* (New York: John Wiley and Sons, 1949), p. 17.

¹⁵ O. H. Mowrer, *Learning Theory and Personality Dynamics* (New York: Ronald, 1950), Chap. 24. Mowrer found that he could teach birds to "talk" when his loving care caused them to "identify" with him. This identification he explains in terms of secondary reinforcement. It is notable that the "talk" of these birds did not extend to the production of novel meaningful utterances.

¹⁶ Neal E. Miller and John Dollard, *Social Learning and Imitation* (New Haven, Conn.: 1941), p. 81.

¹⁷ *Ibid.,* p. 122 ff. In this book Miller and Dollard also develop the theory of acquired drives which further broadens the scope of behavior theory.

¹⁸ *Ibid.,* Chap. 7, 8 *passim.*

¹⁹ M. M. Lewis, *Infant Speech* (London: 1936), Chap. 6 *passim.*

²⁰ Charles C. Fries, *The Structure of English* (New York: Harcourt, Brace and Co., 1952), pp. 49 ff.

²¹ Joel Greenspoon, "The Effect of a Verbal Stimulus as a Reinforcement,"

Proceedings of the Indiana Academy of Science, 59 (1950): 287.

[22] George A. Miller, *Language and Communication* (New York: McGraw-Hill, 1951), p. 252.

[23] G. A. Heise and G. A. Miller, "Problem Solving by Small Groups Using Various Communication Nets," *Journal of Abnormal and Social Psychology,* 1951, p. 335.

[24] Leon Festinger, "Informal Social Communication," in L. Festinger *et al., Theory and Experiment in Social Communication* (Ann Arbor: Institute for Social Research, 1950), pp. 15–16.

[25] Jean Piaget, *The Language and Thought of the Child,* trans. by Marjorie Gabain (2d ed.; London, 1932), p. 9.

[26] B. Bloch and G. L. Trager, *Outline of Linguistic Analysis* (Baltimore, 1942), p. 23.

[27] *Op. cit.,* p. 79.

[28] *Ibid.,* p. 80.

[29] B. F. Skinner, "The Operational Analysis of Psychological Terms," in "Symposium on Operationism," *Psychological Review,* 52 (1945): 270–78. Skinner recognizes more possibilities in this article.

[30] I. A. Richards, *Practical Criticism* (London, 1929), Chap. I.

[31] *Op. cit.,* p. 56.

[32] *Op. cit.,* p. 49.

[33] E. Meumann, "Die Entstehung der ersten Wortbedeutungen beim Kinde," Wundt's *Philosophische Studien* (Leipzig, 1902), XX.

[34] Kenneth L. Pike, *The Intonation of American English* (Ann Arbor: University of Michigan Press, 1945), pp. 25 ff.

[35] John B. Watson, *Behaviorism* (New York, 1925), pp. 21–24.

[36] Susanne K. Langer, *Philosophy in a New Key* (Cambridge, Mass., 1942; New York: Mentor Books, 1948), p. 48.

[37] K. Zener, "The Significance of Behavior Accompanying Conditioned Salivary Secretion for Theories of the Conditioned Response," *American Journal of Psychology,* 50 (1937): 384–403.

[38] Charles Morris, *Signs, Language, and Behavior* (New York: Prentice-Hall, 1946), p. 12.

[39] Charles Morris, *Foundations of the Theory of Signs* (International Encyclopedia of Unified Science; Chicago, 1938), 1, no. 2: 3–4.

[40] Clark L. Hull, "The Concept of the Habit-Family Hierarchy and Maze Learning," *Psychological Review,* 41 (1934): 35–54, 134–52.

[41] The contested assumptions, that reinforcement of one response sequence spreads throughout the hierarchy, and that all the sequences are mediated by a fractional anticipatory reaction, are not critical issues here.

[42] Neal Miller, "Studies of Fear as an Acquirable Drive: I. Fear as Motivation and Fear-reduction as Reinforcement in the Learning of New Responses," *Journal of Experimental Psychology,* 38 (1948): 89–101.

[43] *Op. cit.*

[44] Cf. Max Black, *Language and Philosophy* (Ithaca, N.Y.: Cornell University Press, 1949), Chap. 7 *passim.*

[45] Charles L. Stevenson, *Ethics and Language* (New Haven: Yale University Press, 1944), pp. 53 ff.

[46] Max, L. W. "An Experimental Study of the Motor Theory of Consciousness III. Action-current Responses in Deaf-Mutes During Sleep, Sensory Stimulation and Dreams," *Journal of Comparative Psychology*, 19 (1935): 469–86.

[47] Charles E. Osgood, "The Nature and Measurement of Meaning," *Psychological Bulletin*, 49 (1952): 207.

[48] *Op. cit.*, p. 203.

[49] Clark L. Hull, "Knowledge and Purpose as Habit Mechanisms," *Psychological Review*, 37 (1930): 511–25.

[50] M. F. Bassett and C. J. Warne, "On the Lapse of Verbal Meaning with Repetition," *American Journal of Psychology*, 30 (1919): 415–18.

[51] When a patient tells his troubles to a clinician or psychiatrist the words he uses may, at first, be given their usual lexical and structural values. If the patient says that his wife intends to murder him this statement may, at first, be taken very seriously. Without actually checking the facts, the clinician sometimes extinguishes on these lexical meanings because of a lack of corroborative evidence, internal inconsistency, or the simple improbability of what is said. In the interpretation of dreams and projective protocols there is always the danger that statements will be given depth meanings without any evidence that the usual lexical meanings do not apply. It is important in projective interpretation and in diagnosis that the clinician have life-history data which make it possible to "break the code" of the patient's verbalizations.

[52] It is difficult to think of cases in which the meaning of a name undergoes a more complete extinction as a result of its no longer being applied to the same man. Some fictional cases exist in the Gilbert and Sullivan operas, as when the captain of H.M.S. "Pinafore" proves to be Ralph Rackstraw—a common seaman.

[53] John Dollard and Neal E. Miller, *Personality and Psycho-therapy* (New York: McGraw-Hill, 1950), pp. 116 ff.

[54] H. Cason, "Sensory Conditioning," *Journal of Experimental Psychology*, 19 (1936): 572–91.

[55] *Op. cit.*, pp. 35–36.

[56] *Op. cit.*, p. 56.

[57] G. H. S. Razran, "Studies in Configural Conditioning. I Historical and Preliminary Experimentation," *Journal of General Psychology*, 21 (1939): 307–30.

[58] In two important respects the mechanisms demonstrated in these experiments differ from sign processes:

1) There is no indication of an enduring lexical element which is simply modified by context. The response to the pattern is quite unlike the response to the component.

2) The responses here are overt rather than implicit. However, we have suggested that meanings have the properties of overt responses, and it is the purpose of this discussion to bring out that overt responses show the contextual modification which must be attributed to the implicit "meaning" responses.

[59] *Op. cit.*, p. 47.

[60] *Journal of Psychology*, 6 (1938): 311–24.

[61] In this experiment, like those from the Russian laboratories, the response is overt rather than implicit but, again, we are here interested in demonstrating

that overt responses manifest the contextual modification and sensitivity to syntactical requirements that must be attributed to the implicit "meaning" responses.

[62] Harry F. Harlow, "The Formation of Learning Sets," *Psychological Review*, 56 (1949): 51–65.

[63] Keith and Cathy Hayes, who reared a young ape much as one would rear a child, have reported that the ape is capable of "understanding," in the sense of responding appropriately to, perhaps fifty different word groupings in the form of expressions and commands. The passage quoted below reveals the ape's inability (in the absence of special training) to respond appropriately to familiar forms when presented in novel combinations: "She performs perfectly on 'Kiss me' and 'Bring me the dog.' When we first said, 'Kiss the dog,' Vicki did nothing at all." From Cathy Hayes, *The Ape in Our House* (New York: Harper and Bros., 1951), p. 231.

Chapter 4

[1] Following Alonzo Church in "The Need for Abstract Entities in Semantic Analysis," *Proceedings of the American Academy of Arts and Sciences*, 80, no. 1 (1951): 100–112.

[2] As they are called by Leonard Bloomfield in *Language* (New York, 1933), p. 506.

[3] *Analytica Priora*. 24ᵃ–10, trans. by Jenkinson.

[4] "Logic," by C. S. Peirce and C. Ladd-Franklin, in Baldwin's *Dictionary of Philosophy and Psychology* (New York), II: 21.

[5] "Logic, Formal," by Alonzo Church, in D. D. Runes, *Dictionary of Philosophy* (New York, 1942), p. 170.

[6] Aristotle, *op. cit.*, 25ᵃ–30 and *passim*.

[7] Alfred N. Whitehead, *An Introduction to Mathematics* (London, 1911), p. 61.

[8] Euclid's proof and a brief discussion of the mistake in question can be found on pages 241–43, Volume I, of *The Thirteen Books of Euclid's Elements*, by Sir Thomas L. Heath (Cambridge, 1926). An example of how the same type of mistake in reasoning can lead to conclusions which are false or even self-contradictory, can be found on pages 77–78 of *Mathematical Recreations and Essays*, by W. W. Rouse Ball (London, 1892).

[9] A distinction has been drawn between a *logistic system* and a *formalized language* on the basis that "the former is an abstractly formulated calculus for which no interpretation is fixed, and thus has a syntax but no semantics; but the latter is a logistic system together with an assignment of meanings to its expressions." Church, "The Need for Abstract Entities," p. 100. Cf. also the preface of *Introduction to Semantics*, by Rudolf Carnap (Cambridge, Mass., 1946). In what follows, we shall use the terms 'artificial symbolic language' and 'formalized language,' following Church, in the sense of *interpreted* logistic system.

[10] *Treatise Concerning the Principles of Human Knowledge*, in *Works*, ed. by A. C. Fraser (Oxford, 1901), Introduction, I: 21.

[11] Max Black, *Language and Philosophy* (Ithaca, N.Y., 1949), p. 113.

[12] *Ibid.*, p. 126.

[13] One instance is the Russell paradox, which can be given an intuitively plausible formulation as follows. Some classes of objects obviously do not contain themselves as members. For example, the class of all men is not itself a man, the class of all chairs is not a chair, the class of all trees is not a tree, and so on. These may be called "non-self-membered" classes. If we now ask whether the class of all such classes, that is, the class of all non-self-membered classes contains or does not contain itself as a member, we arrive at a contradiction. If the class of all non-self-membered classes *does* contain itself as a member, then (by its class-defining characteristic) it must be a non-self-membered class, and so it does *not* contain itself as a member. On the other hand, if it does *not* contain itself as a member, then it is a non-self-membered class and therefore (by its class-defining characteristic) it *does* contain itself as a member. Since it either does or does not, it both does and does not, which is explicitly self-contradictory.

[14] Bertrand Russell, "Vagueness," *Australasian Journal of Psychology and Philosophy*, I (1923): 85.

[15] F. P. Ramsey, *The Foundations of Mathematics* (London, 1931), p. 113.

[16] Bertrand Russell, "Vagueness," *op. cit.*, p. 84.

[17] A. H. Sayce, *Introduction to the Science of Language* (London, 1880), col. 2, p. 329.

[18] *Collected Papers of Charles Sanders Peirce*, ed. by Charles Hartshorne and Paul Weiss (Cambridge, Mass., 1932), II: 37.

[19] *Principles of Mathematics* (Cambridge, 1903. 2d ed.; New York, 1938), p. 42.

[20] Bertrand Russell, *An Inquiry into Meaning and Truth* (New York, 1940), p. 438.

[21] Ludwig Wittgenstein, *Tractatus Logico-Philosophicus*, Introduction by Bertrand Russell (London, 1922), p. 8 of Russell's Introduction; cf. 2.18 of the text.

[22] Russell, *An Inquiry into Meaning and Truth*, p. 415.

[23] Wittgenstein, *op. cit.*, 3.325.

[24] *Ibid.*, Introduction, p. 7.

[25] *Ibid.*, p. 8.

[26] *Ibid.*, 5.4731.

[27] *Ibid.*, 3.325.

[28] Russell, "Vagueness," p. 90.

[29] *Ibid.*

[30] Wittgenstein, *op. cit.*, 3.1432 (italics in text).

[31] "Vagueness," p. 90.

[32] This is one aspect of the Whorf thesis, which was discussed at length in Chapter 1.

[33] Church, "The Need for Abstract Entities," pp. 100–101.

[34] *Language*, 2 (1926): 153–64.

[35] *Language*, 24, no. 1 (1948): 3–46.

[36] Clark Hull *et al.*, *Mathematico-Deductive Theory of Rote Learning* (New Haven, 1940).

[37] J. H. Woodger, *The Axiomatic Method in Biology* (Cambridge, 1937).

[38] Cf. Bloomfield, *Language*, p. 413.

[39] *Ibid.*, p. 423.

[40] *Ibid.*, p. 425.

[41] *Ibid.*, p. 419.

[42] *Ibid.*, p. 409.

[43] *Ibid.*, p. 44.

[44] *Ibid.*, p. 48.

[45] *De Poetica* 1457[b]–1458[a]. Here Aristotle explains that "metaphor consists in giving the thing a name that belongs to something else" and observes that "the transference" may have alternative bases, one of which is "on grounds of analogy." He prescribes that "that from analogy is possible whenever there are four terms so related that the second (B) is to the first (A), as the fourth (D) to the third (C); for one may then metaphorically put D in lieu of B, and B in lieu of D." For a further discussion of metaphor, see Chapter 7 of the present volume.

Chapter 5

[1] See Chapter 1.

[2] Grace A. DeLaguna, *Speech: Its Function and Development* (New Haven, 1927), Chap. I *passim*.

[3] *Language* (New York: 1921), pp. 39–42, 237 ff.

[4] Cf. especially his "Language as a Form of Human Behavior," *English Journal*, 1927, pp. 421–33; *Selected Writings of Edward Sapir*, ed. by D. G. Mandelbaum (Berkeley and Los Angeles: University of California Press, 1951), pp. 61–62, 565–66.

[5] Toulmin and Baier have lately referred to it as the theory of the Great Divide; see "On Describing," *Mind*, LXI (1952): 13–38. It should be noted that this theory does not entail or presuppose metaphysical or psychophysical dualism.

[6] See p. 140.

[7] The hearer may, of course, misunderstand the speaker, and then the primary conceptual content evoked in the hearer is not that which was intended by the speaker. This fact must not be forgotten, but it is unimportant for the purposes of this essay.

[8] Cf. Max Black, "Some Questions about Emotive Meaning," *Philosophical Review*, 57 (1948): 114.

[9] When we speak of the primary conceptual content of an utterance, we do not mean, of course, to deny that an utterance may be vague or ambiguous with respect to its primary conceptual content, at least so far as the hearer is concerned. Nor do we mean to deny that it may be hard to distinguish primary from secondary conceptual content on occasion.

[10] *The Philosophy of Rhetoric* (New York: 1936), p. 49.

[11] See "Imperative Sentences," *Mind*, LVIII (1949), 27–30. For other expressions of the view here stated, see C. H. Langford, "Moore's Notion of Analysis," *The Philosophy of G. E. Moore*, ed. by P. A. Schilpp (New York, 1942), pp. 332–34; V. Aldrich, "Do Commands Express Propositions?" *Journal of Philosophy*, XL (1943): 654–57.

[12] C. C. Fries, *The Structure of English* (New York: Harcourt Brace, 1952), Chap. 6.

[13] See R. Carnap, *Philosophy and Logical Syntax* (London, 1935), p. 23; B. Russell, *Religion and Science* (New York: 1935), p. 247; A. J. Ayer, *Language, Truth, and Logic* (London: 1936), pp. 158–59.

[14] W. Empson, *The Structure of Complex Words* (London: Chatto & Windus, 1951), p. 15.

[15] *Ibid.*

[16] *Ibid.*, Chap. II, esp. pp. 39, 40, 44.

[17] *Ethics* (London, 1911), p. 125; cf. Ayer, *op. cit.*, pp. 162 f; B. Russell, *Inquiry into Meaning and Truth* (London, 1940), p. 206.

[18] Empson, *op. cit.*, p. 17.

[19] *Practical Criticism* (London, 1929), p. 182.

[20] Cf. Carnap, *op. cit.*, pp. 27–28; Sapir, *op. cit.*, p. 425.

[21] Empson, *op. cit.*, p. 34.

[22] For the distinction here used, see, e.g., S. Langer, *Philosophy in a New Key* (Cambridge, Mass., 1942), Chap. III; C. W. Morris, *Signs, Language and Behavior* (New York: 1946), p. 24.

[23] S. C. Pepper, *A Digest of Purposive Values* (Berkeley and Los Angeles: University of California Press, 1947), p. 14.

[24] The quotations are from DeLaguna, *op. cit.*, Chap. I.

[25] A. Sinclair, *The Conditions of Knowing* (London: Routledge and Kegan Paul, 1951), p. 110; Cf. J. Holloway, *Language and Intelligence* (London: Macmillan, 1951), pp. 124–26.

[26] *Op. cit.*, p. 96.

[27] Bloomfield, "A Set of Postulates for the Science of Language," *Language*, 2 (1926): 159.

[28] *The Meaning of Meaning* (London: 1923), *passim*, e.g., pp. 10, 149.

[29] H. F. Pommer and W. M. Sale, Jr., *The Use of Language* (New York: Appleton-Century-Crofts, 1947), p. 134.

[30] Cf. Langer, *op. cit.*, esp. Chap. 8.

[31] See Chap. 8.

[32] E.g., Sapir, *op. cit.*; R. A. Hall, *Leave Your Language Alone* (Ithaca, N.Y.: Linguistica, 1950), p. 123.

[33] Here see Russell, *op. cit.*, pp. 55, 166; Fries, *op. cit.*, pp. 54 ff.; T. Segerstedt, *Die Macht des Wortes* (Zurich: 1947), pp. 77, 79.

[34] *Op. cit.*, p. 90.

[35] See Chap. 7. Remarks similar to those made here apply to Russell's claim, *Inquiry*, p. 28, that most sentences can fulfill their function of causing action only in virtue of the indicative character of the object words involved.

[36] *Die Bedeutung des Wortes* (4th ed.; Leipzig, 1925), esp. Chap. IV.

[37] For A. Marty see *Untersuchungen zur Grundlegung der allgemeinen Grammatik und Sprachphilosophie*, Erster B., 1908, Zweites Stuck, Teil II; for the others see notes 17 and 20.

[38] *A System of Logic* (8th ed.; London, 1881), Bk. I, Chap. III, sec. 13.

[39] See Fries, *op. cit.*, p. 295.

[40] Empson, *op. cit.*, Appendix II.

[41] *Op. cit.*, a good brief analysis is in A. Sinclair, *op. cit.*, Appendix A. A. Kaplan has very useful unpublished work on our subject.

Chapter 6

[1] Morris, Charles, *Signs, Language and Behavior* (New York: 1946), p. 264.

[2] M. Black, "Some Questions About Emotive Meaning," *Philosophical Review*, 57 (1948): 115.

[3] H. Wodehouse, "Language and Moral Philosophy," *Mind*, XLVII (1938): 202. For Carnap's claim cf. *Philosophy and Logical Syntax* (London: 1935), p. 29.

[4] *Ibid.*, p. 200.

[5] W. Empson, *The Structure of Complex Words* (London: Chatto & Windus, 1951), p. 33. For further discussion of the point at issue here, see below.

[6] *The Meaning of Meaning* (London: 1923), p. 150.

[7] "Axiology as the Science of Preferential Behavior," *Value: A Cooperative Inquiry*, ed. by R. Lepley (New York: Columbia University Press, 1949), pp. 218–19.

[8] It may be thought that when I say "Be careful!" I am asserting that there is danger (cf. L. Ruby, *Logic* [New York, 1950], Chap. IV) and that my utterance is cognitive in our third sense, and not merely cognitively grounded. But all that can be shown is that my utterance pragmatically presupposes that there is danger, i.e., it has no point or serves no purpose unless there is danger. It may also be said to express my concern or fear. It does not follow, however, that I am asserting that there is danger or that I am afraid. Similar remarks apply to "Hurrah!" and many other utterances.

[9] Especially C. L. Stevenson, *Ethics and Language* (New Haven, 1944), Chap. III; K. Britton, *Communication* (New York, 1939), Chap. I.

[10] E.g., Black, *op. cit.*, p. 125; H. D. Aiken, in a review of Stevenson's *Ethics and Language* in the *Journal of Philosophy*, XLVII (1945): 465; J. Ladd, "Value Judgments, Emotive Meaning, and Attitudes," *Journal of Philosophy*, XLVI (1949): 124.

[11] E.g., Wodehouse, *op. cit.*, p. 200.

[12] E.g., Empson, *op. cit.*, pp. 19–33 *passim*.

[13] R. B. Brandt, "The Emotive Theory of Ethics," *Philosophical Review*, LIX (1950): 307.

[14] *Die Bedeutung des Wortes* (4th ed.; Leipzig, 1925), p. 109.

[15] Stevenson, *op. cit.*, pp. 72–73, 78–79, 88, 212; R. Robinson, "The Emotive Theory of Ethics," *Proceedings of the Aristotelian Society*, Suppl. Vol., 22 (1948).

[16] Brandt, *op. cit.*; Aiken, *op. cit.* and "Emotive 'Meanings' and Ethical Terms," *Journal of Philosophy*, XLI (1944): 456–70; R. C. Cross, "The Emotive Theory of Ethics," *Proceedings of the Aristotelian Society*, Suppl. Vol., 22 (1948): 127–40.

[17] Erdmann, *op. cit.*, p. 109.

[18] J. Hospers, *Meaning and Truth in the Arts* (Chapel Hill, N.C., 1946), p. 131; cf. Britton, *op. cit.*, Chap. X.

[19] Stevenson, *op. cit.*, p. 78.

[20] Brandt, *op. cit.*, p. 307.

[21] See *Straight and Crooked Thinking* (London: 1932), pp. 17–18.

[22] Stevenson, *op. cit.*, p. 73.

[23] See Brandt, *op. cit.*, p. 307; Aiken, "Review of Stevenson's *Ethics and Language*," p. 462 n.

[24] Erdmann, *op. cit.*, Chap. IV, sec. A.

[25] Brandt, *op. cit.*, p. 308.

[26] Erdmann, *op. cit.*, Chap. IV, sec. 1.

[27] C. L. Stevenson, "Brandt's Questions About Emotive Ethics," *Philosophical Review*, LIX (1950): 532.

[28] *Ibid.*

[29] Erdmann, *op. cit.*, p. 114.

[30] These arguments are largely drawn from Brandt, "Stevenson's Defense of the Emotive Theory," *Philosophical Review*, LIX (1950): 537–38.

[31] "Brandt's Questions About Emotive Ethics," p. 532.

[32] *Ethics and Language*, pp. 72–73.

[33] Empson's discussion of the word 'lust' is interesting here, *op. cit.*, pp. 28–29.

[34] *Language* (New York: 1921), p. 40 n.

[35] See *Grondbeginselen der Psychologische* (Leipzig, 1904), pp. 126–27.

[36] See E. McGinnies, "Emotionality and Perceptual Defense," *Psychological Review*, 56 (1949): 244–51; D. H. Howes and R. L. Solomon, "A Note on McGinnies 'Emotionality and Perceptual Defense,'" *Psychological Review*, 57 (1950): 229–34; E. McGinnies, "Discussion of Howes' and Solomon's Note," *ibid.*, pp. 235–40.

[37] "Brandt's Questions About Emotive Ethics," p. 531.

[38] *Ibid.*, p. 531. It must be admitted, in view of the above discussion, that it is difficult to see how conclusive experiments could be designed; they would in any case require better definitions of emotional tone and conceptual content than we have given.

[39] Sapir, *Language*, pp. 39–41; Empson, *op. cit.*, p. 35.

[40] Brandt, "Stevenson's Defense of the Emotive Theory," p. 539; his original statement on "The Emotive Theory of Ethics," p. 306, does not make this clear.

[41] See Stevenson, "Brandt's Questions About Emotive Ethics," p. 533.

[42] This example is from Morris, *Signs, Language and Behavior*, p. 98.

[43] For the point here made see D. H. Parker, "Discussion of John Dewey's 'Some Questions about Value,'" *Value: A Cooperative Inquiry*, p. 236.

[44] The phrase "revelatory significance" is due to J. E. Ledden, "On the Logical Status of Value," *Philosophical Review*, LIX (1950): 354–69.

[45] See Grace A. Delaguna, *Speech: Its Function and Development* (New Haven, 1927), T. Segerstedt, *Die Macht des Wortes* (Zurich, 1947), and M. M. Lewis, *Infant Speech* (New York, 1936); *Language in Society* (New York, 1948), Chap. I.

[46] Susanne K. Langer, *Philosophy in a New Key* (Cambridge, Mass., 1947), Chap. II, V.

[47] B. Malinowski, "The Problem of Meaning in Primitive Languages," Ogden and Richards, *The Meaning of Meaning*, Suppl. I, pp. 297, 316; cf. also Malinowski's *Coral Gardens and Their Magic* (New York, 1935), II, Pts. 4 and 6.

[48] In a review of Holloway's book in *Mind*, LXI (1952): 282.

[49] Malinowski, *op. cit.*, pp. 313, 315.

[50] E.g., John Holloway, *Language and Intelligence*. We do, however, wish to recognize the force of Mrs. Langer's polemics against the utilitarian theory of language, *op. cit.*, Chap. II, V.

[51] *Op. cit.*, pp. 41–42.

[52] *Op. cit.*, pp. 125–68.

[53] *Op. cit.*, pp. 235–36.

[54] Toulmin and Baier, "On Describing," *Mind*, LXI (1952): 13–38; Morris, *op. cit.*, p. 98.

[55] See B. Russell, *Enquiry into Meaning and Truth* (London: 1940), pp. 21, 65.

[56] Aiken, "Review of Stevenson's *Ethics and Language*," p. 461.

[57] E.g., by H. D. Aiken, "Evaluation and Obligation," *Journal of Philosophy*, 47 (1950): 16–22; J. A. Tomas, "Ethical Disagreements and the Emotive Theory of Values," *Mind*, LX (1951): 205–22.

[58] *Op. cit.*, pp. 33 ff.

[59] *Op. cit.*, p. 72.

Chapter 7

[1] *Poetics* Chap. 21, 1457b, trans. by Bywater.

[2] *Paradise Lost*, II, 112.

[3] Thus in 'The Oxford Movement may be a spent wave' Richards says that the vehicle is the spent wave—which agrees with our use of literal sense—but the tenor is the Oxford Movement whereas we would say that the figurative sense, approximately, is no longer having influence. Cf. *Interpretation in Teaching* (London, 1938), p. 121.

[4] *The Structure of Complex Words* (London: Chatto & Windus, 1951), p. 38.

[5] "To Hope," in *Poems*, 1817.

[6] It makes some difference to the imagery which is chosen. A person huddled in a blanket suggests someone cold and forlorn, but not the active malevolence of the other possibilities. This affects what will be called the induced content of the metaphor later in this chapter.

[7] Virginia Woolf, *Between the Acts* (New York, 1941), p. 9.

[8] Cf. *Collected Papers* (Cambridge, Mass., 1932), II, Bk. II, Chap. 3. It is not always clear whether Peirce treats icon and symbol as distinct kinds of signs or as distinct ways of symbolizing, both of which might be embodied in the same sign. We have taken the latter view. Peirce also distinguishes a third mode of signifying, the indexical, but this is irrelevant to the present discussion.

[9] *Countries of the Mind*, 2d series (Oxford, 1931), p. 3.

[10] *Odyssey* XI, trans. by T. E. Shaw.

[11] *Anthony and Cleopatra*, II, 2.

[12] Opening line from John Hall's "The Call."

[13] New York, 1859. Pp. 304–5.

[14] See Chap. 1.

[15] In discussions, unfortunately unpublished, presented to this group studying language and symbolism.

[16] *A Preface to Logic* (London, 1946), p. 83.

[17] *Poetics* Chap. 21, 1457b.

[18] *A Grammar of Motives,* by Kenneth Burke, (c) 1945, by Prentice-Hall, Inc., published by Prentice-Hall, Inc., Englewood Cliffs, New Jersey, pp. 503–4.

[19] Murry, *op. cit.,* p. 2.

[20] R. Herschberger, "The Structure of Metaphor," *Kenyon Review,* 5 (1943): 433.

[21] *The Well-wrought Urn* (New York, 1947), p. 181.

[22] *Op. cit.,* p. 84.

[23] *Interpretation in Teaching,* p. 135.

Chapter 8

[1] New Haven, 1943.

[2] Sigmund Freud, *Leonardo Da Vinci,* trans. by A. A. Brill (New York, 1916).

[3] *Wife to Mr. Milton* (London, 1943).

[4] W. Empson, *The Structure of Complex Words* (London: Chatto & Windus, 1951). I. A. Richards, *Philosophy of Rhetoric* (London, 1936). J. M. Murry, *Countries of the Mind* (London, 1931). K. Burke, *A Grammar of Motives* (New York, 1945). C. Brooks, *The Well-wrought Urn* (New York: Harcourt Brace and Co., 1947).

[5] *World as Will and Idea,* trans. by R. B. Haldane and J. Kemp (London, 1883–86), I, 336.

[6] See Croce's *Aesthetic as Science of Expression and General Linguistic,* trans. by D. Ainslie (2d ed.; London, 1922).

[7] *Foundations of the Theory of Signs* (International Encyclopedia of Unified Science; Chicago, 1938), Vol. I, no. 2.

[8] C. W. Morris, "Aesthetics and the Theory of Signs," *Journal of Unified Science,* VIII (1939): 131–50.

[9] *Ibid.,* pp. 136, 141.

[10] *Ibid.,* p. 141.

[11] *An Essay in Criticism,* Pt. II, 1. 347.

[12] *Op. cit.,* p. 145.

[13] *Ibid.,* p. 149.

[14] *Signs, Language and Behavior* (New York, 1946).

[15] Cambridge, Mass.: Harvard University Press, 1942; New York: Mentor Books, 1948. References are to the Mentor edition.

[16] Susanne K. Langer, *Feeling and Form* (New York, 1953).

[17] *Philosophy in a New Key,* p. 197.

[18] *Ibid.,* p. 181.

[19] *Ibid.,* p. 175.

[20] *Ibid.,* p. 176.

[21] *Ibid.,* p. 177.

[22] *Ibid.,* p. 176.

[23] *Ibid.,* p. 198. The quotation is from Carroll Pratt, *The Meaning of Music* (New York, 1931), pp. 191, 203.

[24] *Ibid.,* p. 180.

[25] *Ibid.,* p. 193.

[26] *Ibid.*, p. 184.

[27] Paul Hindemith, *Craft of Musical Composition*, trans. by Arthur Mendel (New York, 1942), Bk I., p. 117 and *passim*.

[28] *Philosophy in a New Key*, p. 183.

[29] *Ibid.*, p. 193. Italics in text.

[30] *Ibid.*, p. 78.

[31] *Ibid.*, p. 76 ff., 185.

[32] Eduard Hanslick, *The Beautiful in Music*, trans. by Gustav Cohen (New York, 1891), pp. 37, 38, 75. (The German edition first appeared in 1854.)

[33] *Meaning and Truth in the Arts* (Chapel Hill, N.C., 1946), Chap. IV, sec. 3.

[34] Rudolph R. Willman, "An Experimental Investigation of the Creative Process in Music," *Psychological Monographs*, ed. by John F. Dashiell (Evanston, Ill., 1944), 57, no. 1.

[35] *Comparative Psychology of Mental Development* (New York, 1946), pp. 70–71. This is a translation of *Einfünrung in Die Entwicklungs-Psychologie* (Leipzig, 1933).

[36] *Esthetic Quality* (New York, 1938).

[37] See *Music and its Lovers* by Vernon Lee (London, 1932), and *The Psychology of Music* by Max Schoen (New York, 1940).

[38] "Representative Music," *Selected Writings of Edward Sapir*, ed. by David G. Mandelbaum (Berkeley and Los Angeles: University of California Press, 1951), p. 492.

[39] *Signs, Language and Behavior*, p. 193.

Chapter 9

[1] John Hospers, *Meaning and Truth in the Arts* (Chapel Hill, N.C., 1946), p. 118.

[2] See No. 17 of Wolf's *Italian Songs*. The translation previously quoted is included in *Fifty Songs of Hugo Wolf*, ed. by Ernest Newman (Chicago, 1909), p. 148.

[3] *The Prose Style of Samuel Johnson* (New Haven, Conn., 1941), p. 8. Italics ours.

[4] The various senses of 'form' have been discussed by Morris Weitz in *Philosophy of the Arts* (Cambridge, Mass., 1950), Chap. III.

[5] Edmund Wilson, *Axel's Castle* (New York, 1932), p. 242 f.

[6] *Ibid.*, p. 242.

[7] I. A. Richards, *Principles of Literary Criticism* (New York, 1928), Chap. XVI.

[8] Roger Fry, *Transformations* (London, 1926), p. 15.

[9] Richards, *op. cit.*, Chap. II.

[10] Roger Fry, *Vision and Design* (New York: Penguin Books, 1937), p. 31. (Article quoted was first published in 1909.)

[11] Richards, *op. cit.*, particularly p. 17 f.

[12] *Philosophy and Phenomenological Research*, VIII (1947): 99–106.

[13] Cambridge, Mass.: Harvard University Press, 1945.

[14] *Ibid.*, p. 162.

[15] "Perception, Meaning and Subject-matter of Art," *Journal of Philosophy*,

XLI (1944): 561–75; and "The Aesthetic Function of Language," *Journal of Philosophy*, XLVI (1949): 5–20. Hereafter referred to as I and II.

[16] Isenberg, II, p. 12.

[17] Isenberg, II, p. 12.

[18] Isenberg, I, p. 575.

[19] *Ibid.*

[20] William James, *Essays in Radical Empiricism* (New York, 1912), particularly pp. 54 ff., and 62 ff.

[21] William James, *The Meaning of Truth* (New York, 1909), Chap. 2.

[22] F. W. Bateson, *English Poetry and the English Language* (Oxford, 1934), p. 21.

[23] Cleanth Brooks, *Modern Poetry and the Tradition* (Chapel Hill, N.C., 1939), p. 27.

[24] *Ibid.*, p. 127.

[25] *Sewanee Review*, LIV (1946): 468–88.

[26] "Interpretation and Evaluation in Aesthetics," in *Philosophical Analysis*, ed. by Max Black (Ithaca, N.Y.: Cornell 1950).

[27] See William Empson's *Seven Types of Ambiguity* (London, 1930) and *The Structure of Complex Words* (London: Chatto & Windus, 1951).

SELECTED ANN ARBOR PAPERBACKS

works of enduring merit

For a complete list of Ann Arbor Paperback titles write:

THE UNIVERSITY OF MICHIGAN PRESS / ANN ARBOR